HANDO'S GWENT

VOLUME TWO

EDITED
BY
CHRIS BARBER

To the memory of Fred Hando
the artist/historian who was
a true 'Man of Gwent'
and his son, Robert, who accompanied
him on many of his journeys.

First Published 1989

ISBN Hardback 0 9510444 8 6
ISBN Softback 0 9510444 9 4

3, Holywell Road, Abergavenny, Gwent NP7 5LP.
Tel: Abergavenny 3909.

Typeset by Able TypeSetters, Unit 27, Enterprise Way
Newport, Gwent NP9 2AQ. Tel: (0633) 244534.

Printed by South Western Printers Ltd.
Caerphilly, Mid-Glamorgan, South Wales.

Front cover photograph: The Monnow Bridge. Chris Barber

Back cover photograph: Llanfoist Church. Chris Barber

Artwork by Derek Lawton.

Tyn-yn-y-Cae (The geographical centre of the county).

    Most of our visitors see Gwent in late spring or summer. They must be tired of hearing us say, "Ah! but you should see it in Autumn!" Yet many of our secret haunts reach supreme grandeur only at the end of the growing time. When the amber and russet, the purple and gold of Autumn descend on the wooded hills, and all its magic is reflected in the great pools, when the only sound is the flutter of a falling leaf as it drifts, a flake of rose pink, on to the still waters, while its reflection floats up to meet it, then you may capture some of the unearthly beauty of Gwent.

CONTENTS

INTRODUCTION

It is with considerable pleasure that I have compiled and edited this second volume of *Hando's Gwent*. The first volume was published in November 1987 to celebrate the centenary of Fred Hando's birth in 1888. It was an immediate success and warmly received by the many readers who used to follow the Hando articles which were published as a weekly series in the South Wales Argus during the decades of the fifties and sixties.

Fred J. Hando

Fred Hando was a Gwent author, artist, historian and headmaster who died on Tuesday, February 17, 1970, ending a lifetime devoted to the county that he loved and whose treasures he brought to countless numbers of readers all over the world.

In his long association with the *South Wales Argus* he wrote the amazing total of 795 articles about the county. Many of them have been republished in the numerous books which bear his name. His final article was on February 13, 1970, and he had produced the series entitled 'Monmouthshire Sketchbook' with very few breaks for 17 years.

Fred Hando was appointed the first headmaster of Hatherleigh Central School, Newport. He worked there from 1925 to 1953 — the year that he was awarded the MBE for his services to education and to Monmouthshire.

He wrote seven books on the county. He was president of Newport Headteachers' Guild, Newport Debating Society and Monmouthshire Local History Council. In addition he was very interested in church affairs and was organist and choirmaster at Summerhill Baptist Church, Newport, for many years.

Following his death, a fund was opened to receive donations from people who had derived pleasure from his work with a view to erecting a number of memorial seats at vantage points in the county which Fred, himself, had always thought to be among the most beautiful. In this way he was honoured with several memorials, which was a practical way to perpetuate his memory and to serve the beautiful county that he loved so much.

Few counties can have been researched and described in such detail as Gwent, by one man whose lifetime was enthusiastically devoted to such a task. Fred Hando was an artist historian with a personal mission to explore and record the history, legends, architecture and scenery of a land that he loved passionately. His object was to persuade his readers *to see the little places of a shy county* — barely known corners of this ancient land such as Alteryn, Cwmyoy, Llangwm, Mounton or Penallt.

Gwent is a county of amazing contrasts with a rich and varied landscape. It is an ancient kingdom where Celtic camps, Roman walls and Norman castles have stood witness to battles and dramatic events of long ago. From its ridgeways such as Mynydd Maen and Cobblers' Plain there are sweeping views and its many green valleys are blessed with fine rivers fed by rippling streams.

Historic towns such as Abergavenny, Chepstow, Usk and Monmouth are beautifully situated and contain many fascinating and graceful buildings. Other settlements such as Caerleon and Caerwent still proudly display relics reminding us of the glory of Rome.

Leafy lanes lead to secluded hamlets picturesquely situated in hidden valleys or on rising ground where ancient churches, historic inns and other fine buildings reflect the story of our unique county.

Today, past and present still mingle together and we should be grateful to Fred Hando who sought to preserve the memory of so many ancient buildings threatened by the march of progress and also the memory of the people of Gwent — country characters with tales to tell and legends to relate. Good farming folk who cared for our heritage and they helped him to record the history and folklore of our land.

Personally, I feel strongly that the re-publication of Fred Hando's work is most desirable and by taking advantage of modern technology it is possible to produce his material to a high standard and this volume contains a great deal of his writings and drawings that have not been previously published in book form.

As a youngster I was very much influenced and enthused by Fred Hando and was fortunate to have the opportunity, with my father Bill Barber (who Fred referred to as Will o' the Hills) to accompany Fred on many of his journeys.

In this volume I have concentrated on the historic towns of Gwent, bringing together all the material that Fred Hando wrote about each location and including interesting journeys that can be undertaken between the towns. As a result the book provides an excursion which starts and finishes in Monmouth and the reader may follow it either by car or from the armchair. I am sure that it will bring considerable pleasure to all who love our County and wish to know more of its history through the fascinating record compiled by Fred J. Hando.

Chris Barber
June 1989.

Gwent

Black Mountains

Llanthony

Cwmyoy

Grosmont

Skirrid Fawr

Skenfrith

Monmouth

Sugar Loaf

Abergavenny

White Castle

Blorenge

Ebbw Vale Blaina

Blaenafon

Trellech

Tredegar

Llanover

Llandogo

Raglan

Tintern

WYE VALLEY

Pontllanfraith

Pontypool

Usk

Devauden

Aberbeeg

Llantrisant

Newbridge

Crumlin

-on-Usk

St Arvans

Abercarn

Caerleon

Wentwood

Chepstow

Cwmfelinfach

Risca

Newport

Ponthir

Catsash

Sudbrook

Caldicot Level

Caldicot

Rogiet

Bassaleg

Llanwern

St Mellons Marshfield

Nash

Redwick

St Brides

Peterstone

Mouth of the Severn

Wentllwg Level

Chapter One

THE ANCIENT KINGDOM OF GWENT

Gwent has never sought the limelight and her sons, with few exceptions, have not brought its rays to bear upon her. Visitors travelling through by train get glimpses of a flat land, small villages and one industrial town. Motorists wind through the Wye Valley, call at Monmouth and Raglan and feel that they have *done* the county justice. To the outer world, Llandegveth and Llanfair, Mounton and Mathern, are as little known as the Skirrid and Twyn Barllwm, the Soar Brook and the Honddu.

We have four rivers — the Wye, Usk, Ebbw and Rhymney. The Wye, from Bicknor to Beachley, is too well-known to be missed. I have travelled along it from Plynlimmon to the Severn, and know no lovelier stream, but its fame has caused its humbler neighbours to remain undiscovered. A journey from Llanwenarth along the Usk through Abergavenny and Usk to Caerleon; a day spent exploring the Soar Brook; a swim in the Monnow at Skenfrith; a rest on the banks of the Honddu, or

Ebbw's voice in such a wild delight
As on he dashed with pebbles in his throat
Gurgling towards the sea with all his might

— these are the joys of Gwent waters. The names are very ancient. *Usk* and *Wye* are among our oldest names for water; *Ebbw* is *talking Water; Candwr* is *singing-water;* and the *Rhymney,* now a black stream, was originally the *Swans' River.*

The levels near the coast are drained by 'reens'. This word, like *Rhone* and *Rhine,* is and old water-word. (*Rhondda* is *good water*). There are 500 miles of ditches on the moors, and this ample supply of water produces such good pasture-land that some of the fields yield three tons of hay to the acre and have not been fertilised within living memory. In the olden days the labourers used a long pole called a *powt* to help them in leaping over the reens. Severn salmon, caught at Goldcliff, are taken in 'putchers' — long tapering baskets made from the pollard *withies* of the Llanwern district. 'Putchers' were in use in the reign of Henry IV.

Much of the modern prosperity of Gwent has been due to its 200 square miles of coal-beds in the north-west. Yet over a half of the county is covered with Old Red Sandstone, which provided excellent building material for the post-war reconstruction following 1485. The Tudor houses and many of the castles which I describe, owe some of their charm to the beauty of the stone, quarried in the hills and will survive when the post-war houses of the last generation are forgotten. The rich colour of our soil is due also to the *old red,* and I recommend you to see a ploughman at work at Llanfair in autumn, turning over the red-brown earth, while a flock of sea-gulls follows the plough.

The people of Gwent lived first in the uplands, as we may see by the remains of their camps, roads, tumps and stones. Relics found within the tumuli indicate that these races, 1,500 years before Christ, believed in a further life after death. My study of pre-Roman Gwent has convinced me that even if there was no actual sunworship here, the points of midsummer and midwinter sunrise and sunset and the North-South line, held significance in the minds of the people. Probably the alignment of roads, etc. on these points enabled the knowing ones to indicate a change of season, all-important to a race dependent on crops.

Many of the hilltop settlements overlooked the villages or towns which superseded them, as at Caerleon and Caerwent. The Romans had difficulty in conquering the Silures under Caractacus, the tribe which occupied this land, but in A.D. 75 set up their military capital at Caerleon (Isca Silurum), the headquarters of the 2nd Augustan Legion — a rectangular camp of fifty acres — in which buildings of varying function have been excavated. Outside the walls were the great amphitheatre (designed to seat 6,000 spectators), temples, married quarters of the legionaries, baths and cemeteries. The amphitheatre is now held by the National Trust.

The Romans built excellent roads, frequently over the ancient tracks and established important military stations at Burrium (Usk), Blestium (Monmouth), and Gobannium (Abergavenny). Here and there, in my journeys through the county, I have come across rectangular embankments, sometimes in an open field, sometimes in a wood. These were the wayside strong points, fortified to guard a road junction, a strategic height, or, as at Penrhos, the home of an officer.

Caerwent — Venta Silurum — was the seat of civil government and is now a fascinating relic. Inside the walls lived sophisticated people, who used a town hall, market place, club, casino, baths, shops, library and temple and whose houses were fitted with central heating. A stone of 220 A.D. shows that the Silures had by that time won a measure of autonomy. The Romans left in 449 A.D.

The application of the name Gwent to what is now *Monmouthshire dates from the 6th Century. Before that time, Gwent appears to have extended from Gloucester to Carmarthen. The Saxons had met with fierce resistance from Arthur, Prince of the Silures, whose capital city was at Caerleon (and whose *Round Table* at Caerleon has been exposed as a Roman amphitheatre), but after his death the invaders caused such devastation that Morgan, King of Gwent, moved his court westwards, giving his name to Morganwg, the origin of Glamorgan. Gradually, then, the name Gwent came to imply the land between the Wye and the Rhymney.

For the triumphs of King Arthur, who was, according to Geoffrey of Monmouth, conqueror of Iceland, Ireland, Gothland, the Orkneys, Norway, Aquitaine and Gaul, the reader is referred to Tennyson's *Idylls of the King*, some of which was written in the *Magistrates' Room at the Hanbury Arms at Caerleon*.

The Norman Conquest was followed by a period of peace, but William soon evolved a plan for subduing the Welsh. He appointed three chief Barons at Chester, Shrewsbury and Hereford, where strong fortresses were built, and later, when the Welsh raiders again grew troublesome, he encouraged other Normans to invade Wales and take possession of any lands which they conquered. Such conquerors were created Lords Baron, and in later times their lands were known as the Lordship Marches, extending from Chester to the Bristol Channel.

The new Barons built castles on the conquered lands; there are twenty-five in Gwent. They divided their land amongst their knights who paid them in peace and war the same kind of service which they in turn rendered to the King. Thus arose the manorial system, with all its picturesque duties, laws, customs, privileges and ceremonial.

In the Domesday Survey, while reference is made to the villages between the Wye and the Usk, such as Llanfair, Caldicot and Caerwent, the land west of the Usk, except Caerleon, is not included, showing that up to 1085 William's authority was not there acknowledged.

The unsubdued Welsh broke out in frequent revolt. Their insurrections became so serious in the reign of William Rufus that the King erected castles throughout Gwent. To protect the Royal Chase of Wentwood, six agrarian castles were built at Penhow, Pencoed, Llanfair, Dinham, Castroggy and Llanfaches. Picturesque ruins of four of these survive.

At Grosmont, in northern Gwent, there was the influence of the House of Lancaster. Henry of Lancaster deposed Richard II and as King Henry IV created his son Henry (born at Monmouth) Prince of Wales. This new appointment, together with the harsh laws imposed upon the Welsh, and the inhuman mis-government practised by the Lords Marchers, resulted in the enthusiastic support given by the Welsh to their new champion, Owain Glyndwr, a Welshman of royal blood.

Entering Wales in 1402, Glyndwr, now styled *Prince of Wales*, stormed through Gwent, sacking and burning castles and towns, and attacked Cardiff. Overcoming stern resistance, he destroyed castle and town proceeding then to ravage Llandaff, Caerphilly and the other castles of Glamorgan.

In 1405 Henry gave orders to his son, aged 17, to attack. Glyndwr's armies were defeated at Grosmont and near Usk. The rebellion, supported by 10,000 Frenchmen, dragged on for many years and there was no real collapse until Owain's death in 1415.

Harry of Monmouth, as Henry V, relaxed in some measure the harsh laws against the Welsh and, when his life was endangered at Agincourt, he was saved by a man of Gwent, David Gam, of Oldcourt.

The Wars of the Roses split Gwent in twain. The north of the county favoured, of course, the Lancastrians, but Richard, Duke of York, was the son of Anne Mortimer (heiress of Caerleon and Usk) and therefore the southern half lay under Yorkist influence. During the wars Owen Tudor, a great Welshman and a warm supporter of the Lancastrian cause, was captured and confined in Newport Castle, but a hundred gentlemen from Anglesey liberated him by a trick. Owen Tudor married Catherine, the widow of Henry V. Their son was Jasper Tudor, the great builder of church towers (including those at Newport and Llandaff); their grandson became Henry VII.

Through all these years the evils of the Lords Marches system had grown until, when the Tudors came to the throne, each of the Marches was a refuge for the criminals from the next march. Henry VII did nothing to suppress this lawlessness, but under Henry VIII the problem of the Marches was second only in his mind to the Reformation. He put down the brigandage practised by the Lords Marches and in 1534 established the Council of the Marches. The next year saw Henry effect radical treatment of the trouble by his creation of counties and abolition of the Lords Marches.

In various chapters of this book references are made to the growth of religion in Gwent. It is probable that Christian martyrs suffered near Caerleon in the Diocletian persecution; that Christian churches were built here as early as the 6th century; and that, in spite of the lawlessness under the Norman barons and the Lords Marches, Christian communities kept the lamp of faith burning. Under Bishop Urban, who was promoted to the See of Llandaff in 1108, the Church imposed upon the rich the duty of erecting and maintaining places of worship. The first churches were built partly for defence, partly for worship, but soon each little settlement owned its sanctuary and these ancient shrines form part of the Monmouthshire scene.

At the Reformation there were still eighteen houses of religion in Gwent, although Llanthony had fallen into decay long before. The Dissolution of the Monasteries was accompanied here, as elsewhere, by gifts of land to the wealthy.

The religious terrors of Tudor and Stuart days have their place in the records of Gwent, hovering like dark clouds over their fair fame of Mathern and Usk.

The Civil War, the advance of industry and commerce, the gallant struggle of the Chartists, are dealt with in books of easy reference. Their impact on Gwent comes but slightly within the scope of this volume.

Here, then, is an attempt to interpret the magic of the sequestered places of Gwent. Such enchantment is not for all, but I hope that some of my readers will be tempted to take the advice of W. H. Davies, to *stand and stare*. The results of such contemplation will justify this book.

F. J. Hando

* Monmouthshire was the name of the county when Fred Hando was writing. The name was changed back to Gwent in 1974 following the reorganisation of local government. This would have pleased Fred for he always preferred the historical name of Gwent.

11

The Monnow Bridge, Monmouth. *Chris Barber*

Monnow Street, Monmouth.

Chapter Two

MONMOUTH — THE OLD COUNTY TOWN

Monmouth, Abermynwy, Trefynwy, Blestium — call it what you will — was for centuries the county town of a shire uniquely its own. Geographically Monmouth is not in Monmouthshire (geographically Monmouthshire is in Wales) for that snaky river and county boundary, the Monnow, performs a semi-circular meander west, south-west and south-east of the town before it decides to join the Wye.

Like its old county town, Monmouthshire has been for four centuries in two minds about itself. Before the coming of the Normans and for a century later, Monmouth was part of the diocese of Llandaff; thence, until 1843, it was subject to the authority of the Bishops of Hereford.

And the county? Legally within the Oxford Circuit, with some of its schools taking Welsh, others the Oxford GCE; with Welsh Rugby and English Association Football; with a gloriously bacchanalian tale of confusion in its licensing laws, and countless other joyous anomalies, our county has a richly schizophrenic personality.

There are people who wish us to sign up for England! And others for Wales! I plead that as we have the virtues of both nations and the vices of neither we should at all costs preserve our uniqueness.

Open out your *Wye Valley* O.S. sheet, you lovers of maps, and study the great road which comes down from Ledbury, through Ross to Monmouth and on through Wonastow, *Jingle Street*, Dingestow to Raglan. Monmouth was a one-street town — *Monnow Street* — on the triangle edged by the Monnow and Wye. *Cinderhill Street, Chippenham Meadow, Inch Lane, Nailers' Lane, Monk Street, Whitecross Street, Grinder Street!* How these names evoke images of the old Monmouth!

With the probability of pre-history at Overmonnow, with evidence of Roman occupation at Blestium on the site of the present town and with relics surviving of the 1071 Norman Castle, the foundations of Monmouth's story are deep and strong.

OVERMONNOW, MONMOUTH AND THE CAPPERS

Five-and-a-half centuries ago an invading army from this island led by Harry of Monmouth and including some quite articulate Welshmen descended on France.

Do you remember, from your schooldays?

Flu.   *Your grandfather of famous memory and your great-uncle Edward the Plack Prince of Wales, as I have read in the chronicles, fought a most Prave Pattle here in France.*

K. Hen.   *They did, Fluellen.*

Flu.   *Your majesty says very true: if your majesties is remembered of it, the Welshmen did good service in a garden where leeks did grow, wearing leeks in their Monmouth caps . . . and I do believe your majesty takes no scorn to wear the leek upon Saint Tavy's day.*

Fluellen had previously told his fellow-officer Gower, *There is good men Porn at Monmouth* — that Welsh town which he compared with Macedon, birthplace of Alexander: *There is a river in Macedon; and there is also moreover a river at Monmouth . . . and there is salmons in both.*

King Henry's claim to be Welsh, being born at Monmouth, was warmly applauded by Fluellen: *All the water in Wye cannot wash your majesty's Welsh Plood out of your Pody.*

These references to Monmouth, its river and its cap, as well as the inclusion of our *Pwcca* as Puck in *A Midsummer Night's Dream* strengthen the tradition that Shakespeare had visited these parts when his *Henry V* was published, c.1599.

Agincourt was as great a source of pride and glory as Waterloo is to us, and I can imagine our great dramatist sitting in a Monmouth tavern — say the *Robin Hood* —soaking in with his ale the town's talk of caps, of leeks, of the bowmen of Gwent.

My purpose in this chapter is to tell you of the Monmouth caps, and the *Ultra pontem* suburb of Monmouth where they were manufactured.

" LEEKS
in their Monmouth Caps "

Overmonnow, as it is called, is probably the site of the oldest settlement in Monmouth. The black dyke — *clawdd du* in Welsh — remains as a semi-elliptical boundary; its counterpart may have completed the ellipse but of that there is no trace across the Monnow.

Cinderhill Street stands on a layer, several feet thick, of slag from the ancient furnaces — like the slag that Mr. Sockett and his boys have found deep in the soil of Monmouth school grounds.

Overmonnow is sometimes *Cappers' Town;* its church of St. Thomas is the Cappers' Church. In addition to their own church, the Cappers, it seems, had their own Cappers' Chapel in the Church of St. Mary, Monmouth, described by Fuller as *better carved and gilded than any other part of the church.*

The Monmouth cap held in the mid-16th century an important place in the national economy. For centuries previously the industry of cap making throughout the land had engaged, according to Fuller, *so many thousands of people, especially before the invention of fulling-mills, all caps before that time being wrought and thickened by the hands and feet of men.*

Fuller lists fifteen distinct types of workers in the cappers' industry and instances laws passed in the reigns of Edward IV, Henry VIII and Elizabeth to encourage the wearing of caps. In 1571 it was enacted that caps should be worn by all persons (some of worship and quality excepted) *on sabboth and holydays,* on the pain of forfeiting ten groats for omission thereof.

He continues, *The best caps were formerly made at Monmouth . . . but, on the occasion of a great plague happening in this town, the trade was removed to Beaudly in Worcestershire. These 'best caps' were made of wool in different colours with expensive linings, and that lively and enterprising group the Monmouth Local History Society discovered in their borough records how, in 1548, 'one Christofern Here sued Jahannem Matthew at Monmouth for a breach of an agreement for teaching her the art of knitting Monmouth caps'* — the earliest reference to knitting in Britain!

When I came across the sign of the *Monmouth Cap* inn at Llangua I noted that I had always wished to own a Monmouth cap. In a charming letter a well-known lady of Gwent advised me that *in the early 1920's a lady died leaving instructions that her body should be buried in a leaden casket on which should be placed her Monmouth cap and that the members of Pandy church choir should sing 'Rule Britannia' over her grave for which they should each receive five shillings.*

My correspondent named the churchyard of burial. I am still without a Monmouth cap.

FRED HANDO. 1963.
OVERMONNOW.

The Norman Chancel-arch, Overmonnow Church.

The Norman church of St. Thomas, Overmonnow, is worthy of a visit. While the nave was restored and the west doorway rebuilt in 1880, the splendid chancel arch and north doorways, the *squint* for the worshippers in the north pew of the nave, and the rectangular piscina in the south wall of the chancel are original work.

The church was not mentioned in the taxation list of the 13th century and this may imply, according to Canon E. T. Davies, that it was worth less than the six marks which was the minimum value to justify inclusion in the lists.

In the western bell turret hangs the bell of 1701 inscribed with the names of James Mercer and Jos Devis. Mercer beame mayor of Monmouth in 1709, but I should mention that *Little Monmouth,* i.e. Overmonnow, had its own mayor and corporation up to 1832.

Among the church plate are a 17th-century chalice and an 18th-century paten.

The Monnow Gatehouse, Monmouth.

THE MONNOW GATEHOUSE

Close to Overmonnow church is the almost unique gatehouse on the Monnow bridge. I beg my transatlantic readers, who have *done* Monmouthshire when they have flitted through Raglan and Tintern, to come again and spend a whole day in Monmouth and a whole hour on and around the Monnow bridge.

Biding a cessation of the traffic through the arch, I unlocked the ancient door and threaded myself — there is no better phrase — up the spiral stone stairs and the steep wooden steps to the upper floor of the tower. Here were the slits and the bigger windows giving views of Overmonnow and Monnow Street. There at the far end, guarded by a bar, was a forbidden hole, circular in section, which obviously led once to the waters beneath. My readers, with memories of Plas Machen and many other houses and castles, will know this to be a garde-robe.

On the table, amid stone carved fragments, lay a most fascinating framed document. It was a copy, beautifully executed, of patent-rolls of Edward I, A.D. 1296-7, and of Edward II, 1315, and began thus:

The King to the baliffs and honest people of Monmouth, greeting. *Know that at the instance of Henry of Lancaster, our well-beloved nephew and your lord, we have granted to you in aid of enclosing the aforesaid town and for the greater security of these parts, that from the day of the completion of this present for five years ye may levy in the said town . . .* — and then follows a list of commodities and tolls which give a picture of Monmouth trading in the 13th and 14th centuries.

Instance a quarter of corn, 1 obol (about a halfpenny), every fresh salmon, 1 farthing, ten small pigs, 1 obol, 100 skins of wooled sheep, goats, stags and fallow deer, 1 penny, a cartload of salt, 1 penny, 100 of cloth (Irish, Welsh, or Worsted), 1 obol, every piece of silk-with-gold of Samite Diaper et Baudekyn, 1 obol. (Samite Diaper was patterned material on a ground of another, Baudekyn a costly stuff of gold shot with colour). All the coins named were silver.

Every ship paid threepence, every cask of wine and ashes three obols. (These ashes may have been put on the heads of penitents and were made from dried leaves). A cart load of Viron (iron) paid one penny, of lead, twopence, 100 Spanish steel, one obol, 100 Aberdeen fish, one obol, a cash of honey, one penny and many more.

This document dates the Monnow gatehouse and the walls, some distance away, of Monmouth. It shows that, like the West-gate with its tollhouse at Newport, the Monnow tower exacted tolls; it shows also that we should not refer to the *Norman* gatehouse, spite of semi-circular arches.

The Monnow Gatehouse before the passages were cut, showing the pedestrians' by-pass.
(From a drawing in the Gatehouse).

Occupied alternately by Royalists and Roundheads during the Civil War, the old tower was prepared in 1839 for an attack by the Chartists which did not take place. At about that time passages were made through the masonry to replace the pedestrian by-passes of timber shown in my smaller sketch — copied from one of the interesting pictures in the tower.

17

THE ROBIN HOOD INN

Of the Monmouth inns the Robin Hood is the first on the right from the Monnow bridge, and probably the most venerable. The roof, now of good slates, contains a pretty dormer window and a separate light of one pane; the bedroom windows, with their sixty panes, and the stone-framed windows below, with moulded mullions and transoms, give character to the street facade.

Robin Hood Inn, Monnow Street, Monmouth.

But it is the doorway which is the great attraction. Stout masonry supports an arch with decorated spandrels which was there in Shakespeare's days, and I repeat that it may have been in this tavern that the great Will heard of the Monmouth caps, of our pwcca (his Puck) and of Davy Gam. Scorn my conjecture if you will, but in my mind the light relief in his *Henry V* savours of the Robin Hood taproom.

This Elizabethan ale-house has not been chromium-plated out of recognition. It is still pleasantly redolent of the days when the Briton's last stronghold had not been invaded by the ladies, who would be ill-advised to attempt its capture.

After closing time on the afternoon I was invited, if I wished, to visit the upper rooms. Here I found great beams, some unhewn, and in one room a decorated plaster ceiling and a pleasant old fire-place.

It was in this upper room that the Catholics of Monmouth held their services before their own church was built. My fancy was captured, however, by the attic, where the principals, massive enough for a mansion, were held by imposing collar-beams, and one purlin, less than five feet above the floor, almost decapitated me. One of the partitioned walls displayed the old plaster amid the laths and hazel uprights.

MONNOW STREET

The main streets of most country towns and villages combined function with beauty. Nowhere is this better seen than when the street, wide at the base, narrows as it climbs to a castle, an inn, a church, or a great house. I think of Ludlow, of Bishop's Castle, of Ross, of Monmouth. While the approach to Monmouth from Hereford or Coleford (via Fiddler's Elbow) shows the little town nestling so sweetly at its river confluence, I like best the Monnow bridge entrance.

I drove from Troy station along Cinderhill Street to the church and crossed, threading carefully the narrow archway of the bridge-tower, and there, as if with its arms thrown wide to welcome me, was the bright old street of Monmouth, curving gracefully, narrowing delightfully, with all its lines leading to the delicate spire of St. Mary's.

"Monnow Street," I mused, "is on the line of a track which was worn long before the Romans came. The legions used it marching to and from their settlement of Blestium at the top of the street.

"Over the Monnow bridge the Normans built a gatehouse; they threw an arch across the street near the entrance to their castle. Cavaliers and Roundheads — yes, the old cobbles rang as the pages of history were turned." Did I say *cobbles?* We have vivid pictures of the condition of the old street in the writings of R. Waugh of Monmouth. It was, of old, *a barbarous hollow way as deep as a horse's back, almost impassable from mud and ruts.* In the narrower part and in the side streets overhanging houses almost met at the top, intercepting the free circulation of air. Hence the fires and plagues. There were wells on each side of the footpaths, and these, contaminated by filth, contributed to the frequent epidemics.

We read that before 1755 there were no waggons, only pack-horses. On one Saturday 500 horses each carrying five bushels of corn entered by way of the Monnow gate. The farmers would erect posts on which rafters were laid, or sell their produce in the little pent-houses at the fronts of the cottages, paying the house-holders with handfuls of corn. In Butcher's Row and other meat-markets beef only was sold by weight, measured by steel-yards; other meat by *supposed weight.*

Two centuries and more ago, Mr. Mountain kept five pack-horses at his place in Monnow Street. These horses, driven by John Niblett, formed the principal goods transport, travelling nose to tail, the leading horse wearing a leather collar on which belts were affixed. This was the *octuple tintinnabulator,* a fine example of which is still at Trellech.

After 1755, Mr. Mountain, that forward-looking transport director, established a *stage-waggon* service. The waggon left Monmouth at 2a.m. on the Monday, reached London on the Saturday evening and took the following week to return.

Among the public entertainments Mr. Waugh cites the whipping at the cart's tail of convicted delinquents. Preceded by a mob of people beating basins, etc., the central figure of the drama, roped to the cart and stripped to the waist, was beaten, sometimes all round the town. In 1731, for instance, Hanna Young and Joanna Winnot, for theft, were taken to the market-place, *stripped naked from the waysts upward, and publickly whipt till their bodyes were bloody.*

How impossible all this seemed as I strolled up Monnow Street! Houses, shops and inns gleamed in their *new look,* the car-traffic was well organised, business was brisk, everybody smiled.

Here and there, however, I came across memories, relics, survivals. Before the houses were stuccoed, many of them bore tablets inscribed with initials and dates. I used to imagine that these were the signatures of the builders — just as an artist signs his pictures — and I suggested that the practice should be resumed, heaven help us all! All the dates were of the 18th century. How many of our houses will survive after two centuries?

GEOFFREY OF MONMOUTH

Previously I have suggested that if, as I suspect, Shakespeare visited Monmouth, he found there material which he used in his *Henry V*. That he made use of the work of Geoffrey of Monmouth when planning *King Lear* and *Cymbeline* is more certain, but if I were to ask my readers for information about the said Geoffrey my quiz would be greeted with small response.

Geoffrey of Monmouth, otherwise Galfridus Artur or Galfridus Monemutensis, came of a Breton family. Born c.1090, possibly in Monmouth, he appears to have had his schooling in the priory there, these family and childhood influences colouring all his later life at Oxford.

The quality of Geoffrey's scholarship induced Walter, Archdeacon of Oxford, to offer him a very ancient manuscript for translation. Walter had brought it from Armorica and Geoffrey was obviously well suited for the task of translating it from the "ancient British language" into Latin. No trace has since been found of this original document.

Drawing also from the works of Gildas, Bede and Nennius (7th century Abbot of Chester), Geoffrey completed his *History of the British Kings* some say in 1136, others in 1147.

That it was accepted as a work of integrity and authority is proved by the appointment of Geoffrey, in 1151, as Bishop of St. Asaph and I should add that in several documents dated between 1129 and 1151 he is referred to as *magister* at Oxford. His work was published in Paris in 1517 and in Heidelberg in 1587.

The Miller.

In 1718 *The British History,* translated into English from the Latin of Geoffrey by Aaron Thompson, late of Queen's College, Oxon., was printed in London. Our copies, in the Newport Borough Library, include a preface of 116 pages which constitutes a shrewd and weighty plea for the acceptance of Geoffrey's work in the spirit in which it was written. Briefly stated, this plea invites the reader to accept the book as a translation of writings which cover a period of history otherwise unillumined.

Many of the chapters in the book are heavy going. We learn that Britain was named after Brutus, grandson or great-grandson of Aeneas. So it was that when Julius Caesar attacked Albion he was met by the comment of the islanders, *We, too, are Trojans.*

We read of the founding of Caerosc (Caerleon), the metropolis of Demetia by Belinus, and remind ourselves that the magnificent Iron Age camp above Caerleon is still called the stockaded camp of Bellin — Bellinstock. *Billingsgate in London* is here named *Belinsgate* and in a golden urn on top of the tower above Belinsgate the ashes of Belin were deposited.

Cymbeline and Lear, the coming of Christianity, the martyrdoms of Julius and Aaron at Caerleon, the transfer of the great stones from Ireland to Stonehenge by Merlin, the departure of the Romans — they are all related in these pages. Vortigern, Hengist, Horsa flash across the screen, leaving trails of blood.

A star of wonderful magnitude and brightness darting forth a ray, at the end whereof was a dragon, appears above Winchester. Merlin proclaims to Uther Pendragon, *The star and the dragon signify yourself, the ray portends that you will have a most potent son to whose kingdom's power all those shall be subject over which the ray reaches.*

Enter Arthur, in Book Nine. Dubricius, Archbishop of Caerleon, places the crown on the 15-year-old boy's head. In turn, Arthur subdues England, Scotland, Ireland, Iceland, the Orkneys, Norway and all that land which is now France and then, at the approach of the Feast of Pentecost, resolves to hold a magnificent court such as the world had never seen — at Caerleon!

Think of Caerleon today. Now read Geoffrey's description: *Besides the great Wealth of it above the other Cities its situation upon the River Uske near the Severn Sea was most pleasant and fit for so great a Solemnity . . . Kings from Countries beyond the Seas could sail up to it. On the other side the Meadows and Groves and Magnificence of the Royal Palaces made it rival the Grandeur of Rome.* There were the church of St. Julius, the church of St. Aaron and a college of over 200 Philosophers.

To this noble city came five Kings of Britain, three Archbishops, innumerable Consuls from Britain and abroad, seven foreign Kings, peers and dukes innumerable, each with mules, horses, retainers and furniture.

When the King was invested with his royal habiliment he was crowned in St. Aaron's Church, while his queen, preceded by four queens bearing white doves, was crowned in the Temple of Virgins in the church of St. Julius.

Then, *observing the ancient custom of Troy,* the men held their banquet in one place, the women in another. The dishes were served by 1,000 young noblemen clothed with ermine, while 1,000 attendants served the wine. Jousting, archery, tossing the pike and endless other sports followed in the fields without the City and these revelries continued for three days.

Here is Geoffrey's portrait of King Arthur.

Also Arthur, having put on a Coat of Mail suitable to the Grandeur of so potent a King, fits his golden Helmet upon his head, on which was engraven the figure of a dragon; and on his shoulder his shield called Priwen, upon which the picture of the blessed Mary Mother of God being drawn, put him frequently in Mind of her. Then girdling on his sword Caliburn made in the Isle of Avallon, he graced his right Hand with his Lance called Ron . . . "

The Knight.

Of all his personal combats, I like best Arthur's duel with the giant Ritho upon Mount Aravius. This giant had made a fur coat from the beards of kings he had killed and sent word to Arthur to remove his own beard and send it to him. Ignoring this request Arthur engaged him in conflict, proved victorious and took the beard and fur coat of the giant as spoils.

The sequel, with its wars against the Romans and the traitor Modred, is anti-climax.

The Angel.

And when we expect a Tennysonian death-scene we are a little mortified to read, *And even the renowned King Arthur was mortally wounded, who, being carried thence to the Isle of Avallon, gave up the crown of Constantine.*

No Excalibur (*Caliburn* in Geoffrey's story), no white samite, no queens, no funeral barge disappearing into the sunset. Just a bare under-statement, unadorned. If nothing else proved for me Geoffrey's integrity, this refusal to dramatise would.

21

There is, of course, much more, but I shall be happy if my few extracts persuade you to dip into this fascinating, boring, exciting, dull history.

'Geoffrey's Window', overlooking Priory Street, Monmouth.

My friend Keith Kissack, historian of Monmouth, took me recently to see and sketch *Geoffrey's window*. Surmounted by battlements, flanked by fearsome gargoyles, this exquisite oriel includes two series of six four-centred windows above a range of quatrefoils and a set of cinquefoiled blind arches.

Beneath are three heads, like the oriel, in old red sandstone. They are known as the Knight, the Angel (bearing a shield displaying three lions passant) and the Miller, and might have stepped out of the pages of Chaucer — obviously an after-thought to the oriel.

Now if this was Geoffrey's window his architect must have been three centuries ahead of his time and if *his library* behind it contained a plastered ceiling reminiscent of so many others in Gwent, the pargetter used 17th-century devices and motifs.

For Geoffrey died c.1150 A.D.

Finally, *Brut Dingestow,* published by the University of Wales, is the Welsh text of Geoffrey's History, just as it was discovered in Dingestow Court. The original is now in the National Library of Wales.

THE PRIORY AND CHURCH

Every human settlement in this old land of ours counts one spot which has been holy throughout the centuries. Standing recently in St. Mary's churchyard at Monmouth I was conscious that Christians had worshipped there for 13 centuries.

Our three great saints, Dubricius, Teilo and Oudoceus are concerned in the story. In their name Ilias gave *a mansion and land in Abermynwy for his soul and for the inscription of his name in the Book of Life.* The church built on that land, dedicated to St. Cadoc, probably stood close to the east of the present church, for an old print shows ruins in that position and the charter of the Benedictine priory founded in 1075 refers to the old church of St. Cadoc.

We talk glibly of the 6th and the 11th centuries and, spite of Geoffrey, it is little that we know of that grey pre-Norman period. Yet I find it inspiring to imagine the services held in St. Cadoc's, Monmouth and St. Gwynllyw's — father of Cadoc — above my home-town and many another little stone sanctuary in Gwent, while this island was being ravaged by pagans from abroad.

Founded by Withenoc, Lord of Monmouth, who granted it to the abbey of Saumur in Anjou, Monmouth Priory was consecrated by Herwald, Bishop of Llandaff. St. Florentius at Saumur was a Benedictine abbey and it is interesting to note that while the Cistercians settled in remote spots like Tintern and Llantarnam, the Benedictine foundations, each in the shadow of a castle — Monmouth, Chepstow, Abergavenny and Usk — became centres of industry, commerce, population.

Monmouth Priory was richly endowed, not merely with church gifts. The founder's son, Baderon, presented it with three forges on the Wye, in exchange for land in Hadnock and in the 13th century it acquired land and woods at Buckholt and elsewhere.

At the Dissolution the properties of the Priory were leased to Robert Terghwyt for £6 13s. 4d. per annum.

One of the earliest references to St. Mary's Church, noted by Canon E. T. Davies (*Ecclesiastical History of Monmouthshire*) is in 1289 when Edmund, Duke of Lancaster, granted a rent of 6s. 8d. from a shop in the churchyard to keep a candle burning day and night "before the altar of the Holy Cross in the choir of the parishioners."

That first church (which had a Cappers' chapel) was replaced in 1737 by a new edifice which was described by Coxe as *extremely light and well-proportioned* and retaining the tower and lower part of the spire. In turn this church was rebuilt in 1883 still retaining the tower and spire.

St. Mary's Monmouth, from the Hereford Road.

St. Mary's spire, to me, is sweetly satisfying. A spire is of course a breath in stone — a prayer aspiring — and although Monmouth spire is but half the height of its great contemporary at Salisbury its uplifting influence is felt along every approach to the town. My sketch was done from the Hereford road.

By the way, my motoring friends seeking an interesting run may try *the four spires* — Trellech, Llantillio Crossenny, Monmouth and Ross.

The present St. Mary's was designed by G. E. Street. That fine architect had the grace to build in Early English, and I trust that even the youngsters of Monmouth are grateful for that. I shudder when I imagine what would have been imposed on us by a rebuilding of St. Mary's in 1964 . . .

Visitors should note the enormous Norman pier at the west end of the nave, the canopied sedilia and windows, the painting of the Adoration, the tiles from the priory, and the 16th-century church plate. The eight bells, reputed to have been brought from Calais by Henry V and to be inscribed *Missa De Caelis Camana Gabrielis,* were recast by Abraham Rudhall of Gloucester in 1706.

```
E I N E R N H O J S J O H N R E N I E
I N E R N H O J S E S J O H N R E N I
N E R N H O J S E I E S J O H N R E N
E R N H O J S E I L I E S J O H N R E
R N H O J S E I L E L I E S J O H N R
N H O J S E I L E R E L I E S J O H N
H O J S E I L E R E R E L I E S J O H
O J S E I L E R E H E R E L I E S J O
H O J S E I L E R E R E L I E S J O H
N H O J S E I L E R E L I E S J O H N
R N H O J S E I L E L I E S J O H N R
E R N H O J S E I L I E S J O H N R E
N E R N H O J S E I E S J O H N R E N
I N E R N H O J S E S J O H N R E N I
E I N E R N H O J S J O H N R E N I E
```

WHO DIED MAY 31 1832
AGED 33 YEARS

FRED HANDO, 1963.

Inscription on John Rennie's tombstone, Monmouth.

In the churchyard stands the strangest gravestone in Monmouthshire. My drawing, which demanded the patience of a mediaeval monk, shows the inscription to consist of 15 rows each of 19 letters. The centre of these 285 letters is a capital H, and reading left to right, up or down, with diversions as you wish, the message is the same: *Here Lies John Renie.*

THE CASTLE

Within five years after Hastings, William FitzOsbern, Earl of Hereford, recognising the strategic significance of the site, had raised a fortress in Monmouth. His son Roger was succeeded by Withenoc, who founded the priory and raised St. Mary's. Domesday Book, 1086, names Withenoc's son Baderon as lord of Monmouth, and he was followed by Gilbert, succeeded in somewhat bewildering fashion by his son John, his grandson John and his great-grandson John!

Each of these lords acquired estates which, with Monmouth as its centre, became the *Honour of Monmouth*. When the last John de Monmouth died without male heir he left the Honour to Prince Edward, who became King Edward I.

After eleven years came an event of considerable importance to Monmouth and England. On the appointment of his brother, Edmund Crouchback, to the earldom of Lancaster, King Edward added to the new earl's estates of the *Three Towns* — Grosmont, Skenfrith, Whitecastle — the *Honour, Town and Castle* of Monmouth.

I have told elsewhere of the red roses of Grosmont, symbols of land ownership before the Normans came. To the Lancastrians' love of Grosmont must be added their pride in Monmouth, and it is suggested on good authority (*Monmouth Castle and Great Castle*

House, by A. J. Taylor) that "the noble mullioned and transformed windows, of princely scale and quality" which remain in the ruins of the Great Tower were the work of Henry, first Duke of Lancaster. And, in spite of local tradition, it was probably within this Great Tower that Henry V — Harry of Monmouth — was born in 1388.

That his father, Henry Bolingbroke and his grandfather, John of Gaunt — *time-honoured Lancaster* — lived at times within the castle is certain. Equally certain is it that Henry IV made his headquarters there for his operations against Owain Glyndwr.

It is not my purpose to tell of the part played by Monmouth troops in the Wars of the Roses, the Civil War, or later troubles. Difficult it is now to imagine the appearance of the castle in its prime, but an impression of its strength can be gained by viewing from the meadows across the Monnow.

Surrounding the great mound was a ditch, crossed by a bridge, to the *juliet* as at Tretower; opposite the gatehouse arose the splendid 'Great Tower' or Keep, of the 12th century, which remained more or less intact for five centuries. Adjoining the Keep, but not at right angles, the Great Hall was built in the 13th century. This was where the assize courts were held from early days, for as Mr. Taylor notes, it was referred to in 1370 as *the Steward's Hall beside the Great Tower.*

Great Castle House, Monmouth. The central feature.

Easily the most imposing building in Monmouth is Great Castle House. Built possibly with the well-cut stones from the Gatehouse, it presents the handsome facade, symmetrical, well-proportioned, which we associate with the mid-17th century houses. As I hope my sketch shows, it was erected in 1673 and for two centuries it stood as

26

originally designed, with its three storeys, attics, cellars and string courses beautifully balanced around the columns and devices of the central piece.

Within the house, proportion and space are enriched by the craftsmanship of the artificers in wood and plaster. Elsewhere in Monmouth excellent examples of their work survive, but here the range is from chaste to exotic, from geometrical to flamboyant, from simple panelling to ornate encased beams. The general effect, however, is of an ambitious original plan developed into a scheme plain in parts, exuberant in the main apartments.

The magnificent room on the first floor, formed from five rooms, is a collection of glories and I remember with that the house-high staircase and the hall overmantel with its portrait of Charles II.

In this house the first Duke of Beaufort made it known that he wished his son to be born "near that Spot of Ground and Space of Air where our Hero King Henry V was born." The second duke's mother obliged.

From the diary kept in 1647 by Mr. More Pye, B.A., usher of Monmouth School, I extract two entries:

March 30: Ye townsmen and soldiers began to pull down ye Round Tower of ye Castle and to demolish ye works.

December 22: This day about 12 o'clock ye Tower of ye Castle of Monmouth fell downe upon one side while we were at sermon.

MONMOUTH SCHOOL AND ITS FOUNDER

The almhouses and the free grammar school of William Jones perpetuate the memory of a grand man of Monmouthshire. To read his story is to recognise that it was possible four centuries ago, as it is today, to combine an inborn business instinct with high ambition, a determination to succeed and a warmhearted service, in the name of his Maker, to his fellows.

We were born, he wrote in 1614, *of high parentage without pride* — i.e., of gentle but not noble birth. His arms were those of Morgan ap Meredith, the 14th-century lord of Tredegar, from whom he claimed descent — *argent, a lion rampant, gules* — but Bradney point out that as that famous warrior had no issue, the progenitor must have been a brother of Morgan ap Meredith.

He was born in the 1540's, possibly at Monmouth, probably at Newland, four miles away in the Forest. This was his life according to Thomas Fuller (*Worthies of England*, 1662):

First, his Emptiness — unable to pay ten groats; second, his Filling, flying to London, first a Porter, then (his Brains being better than his Back) a Factour, and going over to Hambrough by his Industry and Ingenuity made such a Vent for Welch Cottons that what he found Drugs at Home he left Dainties beyond Sea. Third, his Refunding; founding a fair School House in the place of his Nativity . . . besides a stately Almshouse for twenty poor folk . . .

Unable to pay ten groats: this with reference, possibly, to the legend that young Will Jones was unable to pay John King, shoemaker, for a pair of shoes. This legend was amplified later by a pretty story of the return of the great man of Monmouth, of his meeting with John King and of a handsome reward. The legend does not fit in with the character of William Jones.

Welch Cottons were probably linen goods. Flax was grown widely. I have described the "retting mill" in the Llanthony valley, and the lovely Forest village of Linton was actually the *linen town.*

It is certain that this country boy made such a success of his business in Hamburg that in 1600 he became a member of the Livery of the Haberdashers' Company, and was already a *Merchant Adventurer of Hambrough*. Haberdash was, it seems, an English rendering of *Habtihr das?* (have you that?) and implied merchandise, various articles for sale. The Company received its first charter in 1448, its armorial bearings (including "two Indian goats argent, two arms embowed," the motto being "Serve and Obey") in 1571, their 'stalls' for the sale of mercery and haberdashery were in 'Chepe' and their Hall, destroyed later in the great fire of 1666, was erected in Gresham Street.

All this, which I have culled from the monumental *History of the Charities of William Jones* by William Warlow, M.A. (1899), is necessary to the understanding of the founding and subsequent development of Monmouth School. We have to imagine this son of Monmouth, with a fortune which in today's values would have made him a near millionaire, living in Hamburg, aged about 65 — *a dark man with fine features.* He had already given to the Company £18,000 for charitable uses.

In his will, dated 1614, the first bequest of this good man is couched thus: *I do bequeath my soul to God that gave it me, and my body to be buried in Christianlike burial, hopeing that, of his mercy, He will, through the merrits of Christ Jesus, raise both body and soul to everlasting life at the last day of judgement.*

The third bequest was in these terms: *Item, I give to the company of haberdashers in London the sume of £9,000 of currant money in England to ordain a Preacher, a Free School and Almshouses for twenty old distressed people, as blind and lame, of the town of Monmouth.*

Under the Statute of Mortmain the King's authority had to be obtained. So, in the letters patent of 1615, it was ordained that the Master and four Wardens of the Haberdashers' Company were to be for ever governors of the school and almshouses.

William Jones had delivered £6,000 of his gift to the Company before his death. In March 1613, representatives selected at Monmuoth five plots roughly of two acres total area, occupied by gardens, tenements, barns and the ground covered with *cinders* (cf. Cinderhill Street) — slag from Roman and Norman furnaces.

Samples of this slag, some from strata deep below the surface, were assayed for me by Mr. Hunter of the Steel Company of Wales. He found the amount of iron oxides to be 63 per cent, indicating a low furnace temperature. No wonder, therefore, that the school authorities found it profitable in 1768 to dig and sell the cinders.

The site faced south and east, with a slope towards the river, which ensured dry soil and it seems fairly certain that William Jones visited and approved it in December 1613.

One of my sketches, copied from an illustration in Warlow's *History* shows the ancient schoolroom, built in 1615. Heath tells us that it measured twenty yards by eight yards; at the upper end was a raised desk for the Master, *in which he sits to hear the scholars their lessons,* and over the lower part was a gallery for the boys' instruction in writing and accounts. That was the room where, since 1615, a number of boys not to exceed 100 had been taught by the Master and the Usher.

In the spring of 1615 the school and the headmaster's house were built, the latter on the site of *a corner stable with the tente adjoining at the corner of Wyebridge Street.* Then were made the first appointments.

Recommended by the lord chancellor and the lord chief justice, the reverend John Owen, M.A., was the first headmaster at £60 per annum with house and garden. Mr. Richard Sedgwick, M.A., was appointed *preacher of the Towne of Monmouth* (following his work as *our preacher here in Hambrou*) with a salary of £66 13s. 4d. and Mr. Richard Owen, B.A., became the Usher at £30. All three were graduates of Oxford. A century later, in 1714, the salaries were £100 for the lecturer, £90 for the headmaster and £45 for the Usher.

The ancient schoolroom, 1615 (From Warlow's 'History').

School opened. The morning session lasted from seven until eleven, the boys coming dressed like the Christ's Hospital lads. At eleven, portions of the New Testament were translated from Greek or Latin into English — this was not apparently regarded as *work*. After dinner, studies continued from 1.30 until 5pm, when the day closed with a psalm and prayers. Each boy brought his own candles for dark days.

Holidays consisted of three weeks at Christmas, a fortnight at Easter and ten days at Whitsuntide. How would our boys react to a six months term lasting from Whitsun to Christmas? Every Monday morning was devoted to *general corrections*. The *birch* was freely used on those delinquents who had committed faults listed and as Warlow hints, *a hard form was not a luxurious resting-place* for the next few days.

The entrance fee was two shillings, or sixpence for *the poorer sort*, and this was divided between the headmaster and usher in the proportion of two to one. The education was in Latin and Greek, and on one day weekly the boys were taught the principles of the Christian religion. Twice annually, the lecturer examined the school and sent his report to the Haberdashers' Company. On every *Sabbath and holy day* the whole school repaired to St. Mary's Church, taking their books with them.

The first two years were inauspicious. Despite his lordly recommendations, the first headmaster was so negligent in his duties that the school fell into disrepute and in 1618 master John Owen, confessing his faults, was dismissed. His successor, Humfrey Crewys, M.A., a man of character and of high scholarly attainments, thereupon led the school efficiently until his death in 1639.

The Civil War began in 1642. Colonel Morgan and the parliamentary forces took Monmouth in 1645 and in June 1646, a new Usher was appointed to the school with the incredible name of More Pye, B.A. Why do I include Mr. Pye's appointment among nation-shattering events?

Mr. Pye kept a diary. That diary survived. In 1859, Mr. W. H. Greene, sub-editor of the *Monmouth Beacon,* copied extracts from the diary which ·was discovered in Overmonnow. Is it possible that the diary, missing since 1859, is still extant?

Monmouth School and St. Mary's from Wye Bridge.

In 1865 the original school-house was demolished and the new school buildings and headmaster's house were raised. 1914 saw further expansion, but during the last three years the school and its grounds have assumed a new look which causes old boys to rub their eyes with incredulity.

I was escorted from the old Wyebridge gate now closed (with a handsome stone tablet), to the impressive wrought iron gates in the wall facing the Wye. These were brought in 1961 from the Haberdashers' Hall, which had been destroyed by enemy action.

Entering the grounds I noticed the raised level within — sure sign that we were within the walled town of old. Eleven steps took us past the new canteens; the ancient mulberry tree, the garden where the boys had conducted their successful excavations, the war memorial and the tall Victorian gothic buildings produced in me that same quietude and calm which I associate with Oxford quads and cathedral closes.

We toured the houses, the form rooms, the labs., the cloisters, the *country house;* we stayed for a time in the lovely chapel with its *shrine of remembrance.* A walk along Chippenhamgate Street from Weirhead house (the old "town house") past the bargemasters' houses took us to the new hall, surely the last word in school architecture.

CLEO HANDO·1963.　　*The School House, Monmouth.*

Five hundred chairs, upholstered in blue, faced the vast stage. Seeming acres of glass gave views of the swimming bath, Weirhead house, the Wye and Penallt hill. One pressure of a button, and quietly curtains slid across the windows while, in imagination, I looked ahead to great occasions when music, drama, opera, oratory will enrich the lives of Monmouth folk in this hall.

I had already seen some of the *extra-mural* houses — St. James and the Grange — and I proceeded now to collect some ideas on education today at Monmouth.

With all the emphasis on science and technology were the humanities occulted? *While we give due weight to the demands of the commercial and industrial future we maintain strength in classical and modern languages — Latin, Greek, French, Spanish and Russian — in art, music, drama, etc. The old emphasis on acts of worship is retained; the day begins with assembly in the new hall; morning service is held on Thursday, we hold two services on Sundays and on Speech day in June the Haberdashers come down in their magnificent robes to join us in service at St. Mary's. Many of the town boys join the country boys for private study in the evenings.*

With far flung sports fields, with the river at hand, with wonderful facilities for cross-country running, it is little wonder that Monmouth men have made their mark in many fields — and streams — of sport. I dare not begin to list them.

Finally, the future development of school buildings will induce a new, self-contained lay-out of the grounds. The range of buildings, now five years old, known to the boys as *the Red Lion* (thanks to the lion passant from the William Jones arms) will extend so as to enclose a satisfying series of quadrangular lawns.

Footnote: The school bell was hung above the old schoolroom in 1716 by the headmaster, the Rev. Andrew Cuthbert. It is inscribed, *Andreas Cuthbert Archididaskalos, 1716, E.E.,* from which we learn that it was cast by Evan Evans, of Chepstow.

31

MONMOUTH SCHOOL FOR GIRLS

The *free grammar school for boys* was built at Monmouth in 1615. In the same year the almshouses, *for twenty poor and old distressed people, as blind and lame,* were occupied by their first inmates, for whom twenty gowns, each with an escutcheon of silver on the sleeve, were provided. Thus the wishes of William Jones enriched the lives of the boys, the poor, the old, the lame.

What made the warm-hearted benefactor ignore the girls? A sex-bar in education seems a contradiction in terms yet, when education was regarded solely as a preparation for livelihood, it is possible that the vocation of women in industry and as wives and mothers, seemed not to demand such preparation. Have we not heard in our own lifetime the boneheaded question, *Why send your daughter to Oxford? She will marry immediately afterwards.*

On reflection I recall the Mosaic injunction about the Sabbath: *Remember the Sabbath day to keep it holy. In it thou shalt not do any work, thou, nor thy son, nor thy daughter, thy man-servant, nor thy maid-servant, nor thy cattle, nor thy stranger that is within thy gates.*

Were the wives to be of less concern than the cattle? Wives and mothers had a seven-day week, the rest of the family six . . .

From 1615 to 1891 no provision from the William Jones Charity was made for the education of Monmouth girls. As in other towns in our country, *private* schools were known, the notable example being the *Castle House* school, recorded in 1800 by Coxe as *the most respectable school for young ladies in this part of England.*

I imagine that the Education Act of 1870 may have turned the attention of the Charity Commissioners towards the education of girls. So it was that in 1891 the Monmouth High School for Girls was established, with £1,000 annually as its endowment, and Miss Nina Luckes, headmistress of the Hereford school, appointed as its first headmistress.

On the 25th day of July, 1892, school opened in Hardwick House, Monnow Street. Five years elapsed while on a glorious site opposite St. Mary's vicarage on the Hereford road a *handsome, commodious school house, replete with every modern appliance and convenience,* was being erected at a cost of £20,000.

Now the patron saint of the Haberdashers' Company was St. Catherine, and on St. Catherine's day, 25th November, 1897, the grand new school was opened by the Marchioness of Worcester and four women — wonder of wonders! — were added to the governors.

The two saints dear to the hearts of Monmouth girls are Catherine and Bride. St. Catherine was the patroness of maidens and women-students, of philosophers, preachers, wheelwrights and millers. Her voice was one of those heard by Joan of Arc; her martydom was designed to take place on a spiked wheel (hence the wheelwrights) but when she was placed on it her bonds snapped, the wheel broke and spikes flew off, killing onlookers. Then she was beheaded. A beautiful St. Catherine window may be seen in Rockfield Church, near Monmouth.

The girls of Milton Abbas, in Dorset, where there is a Norman chapel dedicated to St. Catherine, used to sing — may do so still — in their village games:

> *St. Catherine, St. Catherine, O lend me thine aid,*
> *And grant that I never may die an old maid.*
> *A husband, St. Catherine, a good one, St. Catherine,*
> *But arn-a-one better than narn-a-one, St. Catherine.*
> *Sweet St. Catherine, a husband St. Catherine,*
> *Handsome St. Catherine, rich, St. Catherine,*
> *Soon, St. Catherine.*

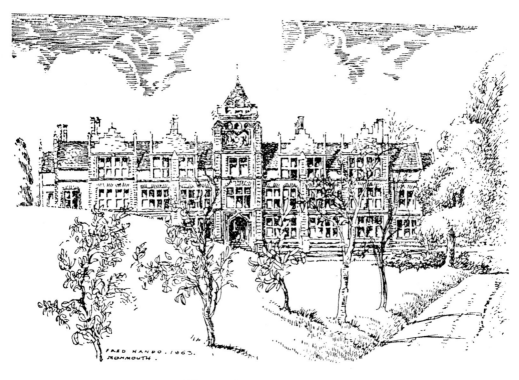

Monmouth School for Girls.

St. Bride has many associations with Monmouthshire, where four or five churches are dedicated to her. In one fascinating legend we read that St. Bride, the pure white virgin saint of Kildare, was commanded by her father to marry a wild Irish chieftain, but refused. When her father repeated his command with threats she plucked out her eyes and flung them on the grassy sward, whereupon her father fled, screaming. Calmly St. Bride replaced her eyes, cut a couple of turves and floated on these to the mouth of the River Usk, where a church in her honour remains to this day.

On the west wall of the tower of this St. Bride's Church you may see a lovely portrayal, in stone, of the saint and above the porch of St. Bride's Church, Skenfrith, a primitive stone head of her.

Among our young friends the many *old girls* of Monmouth School speak of it with affection and pride. Especially clear in their memories is the fact that the impressive front facade of the school was always, in winter as in summer, bathed in sunshine. It is good also to record that they recognise the value of the wide curriculum with its emphasis on modern as well as on classic studies, on skills and sports — yes, even lacrosse — as well as academic pursuits.

In every age the girls and boys have been subject to bitter criticism from their elders. Let me quote some wise, luminous words from a headmistress at the Monmouth speech day in 1927 — a generation ago:

The girl of today lacks, no doubt, many of the virtues of her mother and her aunts, just as those mothers and aunts lacked the virtues of their grandmothers — but she lacks also many of their failings. She is a very delightful person surprising us often by her friendliness, her understanding, her readiness to admit that there may be life and reason in the old folk yet. We, on our part, must be ready to recognise it in her.

33

NELSON AT MONMOUTH, THE NAVAL TEMPLE
AND THE ROUND HOUSE ON THE KYMIN

When the plaque recalling Nelson's visit to Chepstow in 1802 was unveiled on Trafalgar day, 1961, by Mrs. Horatia Durant, many present sought the reason for Nelson's journey to Monmouthshire. A document in the Nelson Museum at Monmouth provides the reason.

It is the first draft of his report, written with the left hand, on the condition of the Forest of Dean from the standpoint of navy timber, in the late autumn of 1802. While he visited other woodlands, it is certain that he regarded Dean as the prime source of oak for his vessels.

He wrote: *If the Forest of Dean were in a high state of cultivation, it would produce about 9,200 loads of Timber fit for building Ships of the Line every year, that is the Forest would grow in full Vigor 920,000 Oak Trees.*

In contrast he reported that, *there is not 3,500 Load of Timber in the whole forest fit for building and none coming forward.* He blamed the foresters for allowing *the generality of trees to stand too long and when good timber was felled, nothing was planted. Deer barked all the self-sown young trees, vast droves of hogs grubbed up the acorns and flocks of sheep bit off the tender shoots.*

He blamed especially *a sett of people called forest free miners who consider themselves as having a right to dig for coal in any part they please.*

Later in his report, Nelson deplores the fact that gentlemen elsewhere who had *from £1,000 to £5,000 worth of timber on their estates, although only half-grown (say, fifty years of age), were obliged to sell it to raise temporary sums, say to pay Legacys.* If allowed to mature, such trees would be worth treble the value.

Nelson recommended that to preserve the Forest of Dean "the Guardian of the support of Our Navy must be an Intelligent Honest Man who will give up his time to His Employment. He must have proper Verderers under him who understand the planting, thining and management of Timber trees. The first things necessary is to plant some acres of acorns and I saw pleanty of Clear fields with cattle grazing in my Voyage down the Wye. In two years these will be fit for transplanting."

I note with surprise that there is no reference in this report to the activities of the charcoal burners.

On one still hazy afternoon I crossed the Wye bridge at Monmouth and took the Coleford road. Rounding the hill bend with care I turned at the finger-post marked *Nelson Temple* and essayed the 700ft. climb, pausing frequently to take the widening views. Where the good tarmac road ended I left the car and walked the short distance to the summit, where I found first the *Naval Temple*, shown in my sketch and then the *Kymin Summer House.*

Kymin is probably *cae maen*, a perfect name for a field strewn with scores of conglomerate boulders.

That grand old historian Charles Heath, writing in 1801, tells how the nation, sensible of the blessings enjoyed from the unparalleled exertions and bravery of its naval heroes, had decided to build a *Naval Pillar* to transmit to posterity the memory of those illustrious heroes . . . In unison with the national effort, a public monument bearing the name of the Naval Temple was now erected on the summit of Kymin and Charles Heath commented:

Long may this Temple continue to record the proud superiority of the British Navy, and the general sentiment confirmed to the end of time, THAT NEPTUNE MAY EVER ACKNOWLEDGE BRITAIN'S KING FOR HIS SOVEREIGN.

In his description of the temple, Heath tells how the building, 13ft. square, stood on a bold ledge of rock, enclosed by a circular wall, rising from 18 to 36ft. from the ground.

Above the two fronts, with seats *for the accommodation of company*, was a broad frieze ornamented on its four sides with medallions of distinguished naval commanders, while the ground on which they were painted, red, white or blue, expressed the flag under which each admiral ranked at those important periods.

The Naval Temple on the Kymin, Monmouth.

A walk, 180ft. long, led from the Summer House through an elegant gate, 10ft. high, to the Temple. The Temple was dedicated to the Duchess of Beaufort, daughter of Admiral Boscawen, for, while the Duke had been *extensively liberal* towards the building, the Duchess had been responsible for the *fine Carriage Road.*

Britannia, 4ft. 6in. high, seated on a rock, surmounted the arch on the pillars of which were fixed two anchors. A white marble tablet, *executed with peculiar Taste,* recorded the erection of the Temple on 1st August, 1800, and the dedication, while a painting representing the Standard of Great Britain waving triumphant over the fallen and captive flags of France, Spain and Holland, decorated the west front. A second painting showed the Battle of the Nile.

I found the arch, the medallions, anchors and inscriptions, after 160 years, as Heath described them. Britannia on her rock, the elegant gate, and the paintings, have disappeared.

From the east front the haze robbed me of the view of Staunton, the Buckstone, Newland and the wide sweep of country from the Malverns to the Mendips and from the west front I imagined *the Prospect that embraces a Semicircle of a Hundred Miles.*

It is interesting to note that during his visit Nelson congratulated Monmouth on having, in the Temple, *the only monument of the Kind erected to the English Navy in the whole Kingdom.*

His column in Trafalgar Square was completed in 1849.

In 1801 Charles Heath was writing his account of the Naval Temple and the Summer House on the summit of the Kymin. He printed his book and sold it *in the Market Place,* with no other motive, he averred, than *to render the efforts of my Mind and Press subservient to the interests of the county in which I reside.*

From Heath's delightful little book I abstract the essential facts about the round Summer House. It seems that, to quote Heath, a select party of friends had made a habit of spending a social day together annually. Choosing a fine summer's day, they would meet at some pleasant spot near Monmouth.

In 1793, they met and dined among the Kymin rocks. *The fineness of the day, and the beauty of the prospect* so entranced them that they agreed to dine together on the same spot the week following. Dinner after dinner, week after week, followed, until at the onset of autumn their "partiality for the spot" was such that they decided to erect a building *as a security from the inclemency of the weather.*

Exactly in the centre of the summit of the Kymin this circular, embattled tower was raised. In 1794 the foundation stone was laid and, before the masons had completed the ground floor apartment, parties assembled almost the whole of the day. When the upper floor was laid, the 'labour of the artificers' were almost suspended, so great was the delight of the innumerable visitors.

Within two years the building was completed. It stood 30ft. high and contained two circular rooms 15ft. in internal diameter. The lower apartment was the kitchen, the upper (reached by external iron stairs) the banqueting room furnished in a neat and convenient manner. In this room was an excellent *Tellescope,* made by Dolland, the gift of Admiral Sir Charles Thompson, M.P. for the borough of Monmouth.

Through that telescope, Charles Heath made a detailed study of the views through each of the five windows. From his almost incredible list of objects seen I select a few:

Window No. 1: The Buckstone, Newland Church, Clearwell, Mrs. Bathurst's summer house above Lydney, St. Briavels, the Maypole above Whitebrook (where "Mr. Grove, of Bristol, has extensive paper works"). On the horizon, Rodborough Hill, near Stroud, the Fleece Inn between Stroud and Bath, Didmarton Church, Badminton Lodge, Oldbury Church, Dundry Tower near Bristol and the Mendips.

Window No. 2: Penallt, Argoed, Windcliffe, "Levox," Lydart; Nicholl's Firs (probably Ty-yn-y-Cae), Graig-y-Dorth ("Shakespeare has laid here a scene in his play of Henry IV").

Window No. 3: Troy House, Mitchel Troy Church, Pen-y-Clawdd Church, the Hill Farm, Pontypool Park; Wonastow, "Dingestow," "Ragland" Castle, Treowen Tregaer and "Brungwin" churches, Clytha, "pleasure house," Llanarth, Llanelen, Llanover, Llantillio Crossenny, Whitecastle; "the three Machen mountains," "Pen-Twyn-Barloom," the Blorenge, the Skirrids, Sugarloaf, Crickhowell Beacons, Hatteralls, Gaer Vaur and Dial Carig.

Window No. 4: The Monnow Valley, Perthyr, Hilston, Garway Hill, Black Mountains, Talgarth Hills, Radnorshire Mounts, Dixton Church, Priory Farm, the Leys, Whitchurch, Goodrich, St. Weonards, to Aconbury, Dinmore, Clee Hill (sixty miles distant), the Doward.

Window No. 5: Beauulieu Woods, Ross Spire, Perrystone Court and hill, the Coppet hill, Symonds Yat Ruardean, May Hill, Huntley Tump, Staunton, Dean Forest, and Littledean, the Malverns, the Lickey (seven miles from Birmingham).

The Kymin Summer House. In the upper room Nelson breakfasted in 1802.

Summing up, he claims to have viewed ten counties: Monmouthshire, Gloucestershire, Herefordshire, Worcestershire, Shropshire (a hill near Bishop's Castle), Glamorgan, Somerset, Brecknock, Radnor and Montgomeryshire. And the present curator informs me that on nights with good visibility it is enthralling to take the circle of lights.

When, in 1802, Nelson, with Sir William and Lady Hamilton, arrived at Monmouth by boat from Ross, their approach was greeted by a salute from the four long four-pounders in the enclosure of the Naval Temple. Trafalgar was still three years ahead, and Nelson expressed surprise at being known *at such a little gut of a river as the Wye.*

A few days later he drove up the Kymin. First he inspected the Naval Temple, and next took breakfast in the banqueting room of the summer house. He admired the five views and then, to the intense delight of the crowds lining the route, walked back to Monmouth.

The Kymin, with its treasures, has been for over fifty years National Trust property. I spent a pleasant afternoon in company with the curator, Mr. Ainscough and his wife. From them I learned that in 1901 the rent of the Summer House was 10s. a year, and of the cottage with its acre and a half of ground 6d. a week.

I heard how during the last century the summit had been developed into a showground, with bowling green, stalls, swings and donkey rides. Transport from the railway station to the summit cost 6d. by donkey and 1s. by pony.

I admired the blue violas in my host's garden, blooming bravely 800ft. up in mid-December. Inside the Summer House I could but marvel at the ingenuity with which the old battlemented tower had been converted, with tasteful extension, into a pleasant modern home, with two bedrooms and a bathroom and a kitchen equipped with electric cooker, refrigerator, electric pump, telephone.

Up the stairs, now converted and indoors, we climbed to Nelson's breakfastroom. The table is now in the Nelson Museum at Monmouth, and one of the five windows is blocked, but, to me, with my memories of his flagship, the Foudroyant, as well as of the Victory, that visit to the Summer House was beyond words evocative.

That the distant views were veiled by a wintry mist was of little account. Thrilling it was to stand where Nelson had stood and to see Monnow coming down, a silver ribbon, from the Black Mountains to join Wye, a broader ribbon from Plynlimmon, at Abermynwy.

ST. PETER'S CHURCH, DIXTON

A footpath from the boathouse at Monmouth leads up the Wye to Symonds Yat. I had heard of the path from friends of mine who made a pilgrimage there every September to pick the autumn crocus.

Less than a mile above the boat-house I came to the ferry steps, to a churchyard lawn which outrivalled the much-vaunted lawns of Oxford and to the lovely white church of Dixton. The conjunction of wooded hillside, crystal-clear river, lawn, and white church with its exquisite tower, was of overpowering beauty, and I was content to sit for many quiet moments and allow the cool harmony of the scene to still my spirit.

Keyed up to a pitch never designed by our Creator, we town-dwellers need at times to loosen our strings. Relaxing thus and slowing down our tempo, we find ourselves open to influences which come to us straight from heaven, healing our bodies, calming our minds and lifting us to realms where old-fashioned things like beauty may play on our souls.

So it was at Dixton. The light trickled through the trees, dappling the lawn and the white walls, the river sang its soft tinkling music, the trees, wonderfully green in their sudden foliage, shut out the busy world and like another Newport man, I found refreshment and serenity in standing and staring.

St. Peter's, Dixton, as my drawing shows, consists of western tower, nave and chancel. In addition to the south porch, there is an entrance on the north side and a vestry built possibly on the site of David, the 16th-century hermit's cell.

St. Peter's Church, Dixton.

In the churchyard are two crosses, the Dixton cross near the tower and fragments of a cross brought down from Wyesham which may have been the cross of the church of St. Thomas, Wisam, one of the four chapels owned by Dixton in the 12th century.

At the foot of the north-west of the tower stands a carved stone representation of an angel bearing a shield, also brought down from Wyesham.

I am indebted for much of my information about Dixton to Councillor Keith Kissack, who lives at the old rectory and who has written a scholarly and beautifully illustrated account of the development of the church.

Dixton was Henllan Tydiuc, the old church of St. Tydiuc. When this little known saint built his cell here the site was a clearing in the primeval forest. No saint or Norman would build a church on ground liable to floods, yet during the 18th and 19th centuries, and recently, St. Peter's has suffered gravely from devastating floods; tablets on the chancel arch show the depth of the water in 1929 as five feet two-and-a-half inches and in 1947 as five feet eleven-and-a-half inches. I am sure that Mr. Kissack is correct in blaming the removal of the forest for the floods.

Outside several of our churches, stone seats are built against the walls, sometimes outside the porch and at Dixton outside the chancel. This seat is called the lepers' seat, just as the little window in our cathedral is called the lepers' window, both without justification, for lepers were not allowed within churchyards.

In the tower are four bells, one of 1876, two of the 17th century, while the fourth, our only *Royal Head Bell,* has the heads of Edward III and his queen, Philippa, stamped as stops. This bell, according to Arthur Wright, was cast in Worcester about 1420.

39

Within the north porch is a portrayal in white stone of the crucifixion, inverted, of St. Peter, realistic to the last nail. Affixed to the wall is a long list of vicars of Dixton beginning in 1257 with William de Conflens, who became Archdeacon of Hereford and later Bishop of Geneva.

He was followed by John de Longford, John Fitzelias, Richard de Sidenhall and, in 1346, *William (an Alien)*.

I understand that the presence of this alien William (a French Guillaume) caused some surprise in London and he was instructed to explain his position before the courts. However, when it was known that he was ill and old, he was excused and allowed to retain his post.

Bishop Herwald, whom we have met elsewhere in the story of Gwent, had consecrated the church in 1068 with Ris as the first priest. But by 1104, when the bishop was 100 years old and feeble, Llandaff lost Archenfield with its 27 churches, including Monmouth and Dixton, all of which remained in the diocese of Hereford until 1844, when Dixton returned to Llandaff for seventy years.

Then in 1914 Dixton with other border parishes voted on the question of inclusion in the Church of Wales and by a large majority decided to return to the Deanery of Archenfield in Hereford diocese.

The church is long and narrow, with the chancel slewed a little to the south of the line of the nave. Up to 1820 the church was furnished just as Clodock is today, with three-decker pulpit, box pews, western gallery and Laudian altar rails.

Today all is changed, but some very early herring-bone masonry has been exposed in the north wall and the memorials to the Griffits, the Bellamys and Admiral Griffin remain.

On a table in the nave are the famous *Dixton bibles*, a copy of which we have in the borough library at Newport. They were compiled by Thomas Bankes (1770-1805) who, Mr. Kissack tells us, enraged his patron, Lord Gage, by obtaining a dispensation of residence, stating that the climate of Dixton was undermining his health. He died from a chill after a short visit to Dixton.

For many another sprightly tale, like the epic battle between the vicar and Miss Griffin, the lay rector in 1860, I must refer my readers to Mr. Kissack's charming booklet.

And charming in truth are the beaten iron candle holders throughout the church. I was not at all surprised to learn that they are the work of my dear old friend John Bryan, the mastercraftsman of Grosmont.

When we stand on the green hillsides of Gwent and look down on a valley church, our hearts grow warm within us. The trees bend in benediction, the rounded meadows are threaded with church-paths, the bells from the grey tower fill the valley air and God is no longer remote.

Chapter Three

A JOURNEY FROM MONMOUTH TO ABERGAVENNY

Visiting the little churches of Wonastow, Dingestow, Tregare, Penrhos, Bryngwyn, Llanarth and Llandewi Rhydderch.

WONASTOW

Many a traveller by road to Monmouth must have viewed with pleasure the church set among trees high on the hill at Wonastow. No finger-post directs to it; there it stands, withdrawn, remote; there a church has stood for thirteen centuries.

The Trothy brook, on its way to the Wye, flows south and then east, forming the boundaries of the manor of Wonastow on those sides. Twyn Gwyn and the adjoining lands are well-wooded with copses named Tell-Tale Wood, Allan's Little Wood, Calling Wood, Whitehill (Twyn Gwyn) King's Ash, Hunt, Lower Magg and Orles Woods. *Orles* is undergrowth.

Wonastow Church and its avenue of clipped yews.

Threading the south of the manor is Jingle Street, the very ancient way to the prehistoric encampment of Clawdd Du at Overmonnow, Monmouth. The church and court stand near Jingle Street.

Wonastow in Welsh is Llanwarrw, but of old was Llan Gungarui on Trothy. In the days of Bishop Trychan of Llandaff 160 acres of land here was bought by Cynfwr and presented *to God and St. Peter, St Dubricius, St. Teilo and St. Oudoceus with all its liberty and Commonage.*

This 7th-century purchase was made in exchange for a horse worth twelve cows, a hawk worth twelve cows, a dog which killed birds with the hawk and was worth three cows and another horse worth three cows. *Llan Gungarui* implies a church at that early date and the saint's name has undergone various changes to Warrw, Warrow, Winwaloe, etc.

On a bright windy afternoon I drove along Jingle Street. I drove slowly, savouring the beauty of a sweet countryside, imagining the jingle of the *octuple tintinnabulators* as the great wains made their progress along the old track. Parking my car at the entrance to the Court I took the field path which led to Home Farm, the school and the church.

My first view of the church set it at once among gracious memories of Rockfield, Skenfrith and the other lantern-towered churches. Screened by big trees, backed by the biggest barn I know, this hillside sanctuary caught my fancy at once by reason of a fascinating avenue of clipped yews which led from the Court-gate past the churchyard cross (with its ancient broached base recessed for votive offerings) to the porch.

And what a porch! At the peak stood the Holy Mother and child; looking up to her in adoration were a couple of angels with Rossetti faces, the three sculptures in red stone; we have nothing like it elsewhere in Gwent, and it is due to a couple of generous Devonians, Sir John and Lady Seale, who came to Wonastow Court from Dartmouth in the 1880s. Seale windows also beautify the nave.

Noting the holy water stoup, I entered the nave to see something most unusual in our land — four pairs of hammer-beams supporting the steep roof.

A screen of extreme beauty though of no great age separated the nave from a chancel packed with interest. In the north wall was the vicar's door — the only entrances to this church are on the north — which was still accompanied by the wall-holes for the draw-bolt.

Among the oak treasures I noted the superb reredos, chancel-wide, pinnacled and crocketed, *peopled* with statuettes. Consecration crosses on the altar slab, a finely embroidered frontal, the symbols alphas and omega and the Chi-ro monogram, the chairs and the general evidence of loving care, made this in truth a holy sanctuary.

'The Faceless Ones'. Monument in Wonastow Church.

On the south wall, imposing by its very emptiness, stood the canopied memorial to George Milbourne of Wonastow Court, who died in 1637, and his wife Christian. Their figures have disappeared, but their four sons and seven daughters are portrayed beneath, rendered faceless by some miscreants.

The black marble slab in the recess, though indecipherable to me, gives their names, according to Heath *(Ragland Castle)* as John, George, Charles and Henry: Lucy, Christian, Margery, Joan, Catherine, Elizabeth and Mary. Some are ruffed, all are reverent in prayer and like similar monuments in Chepstow and Llanmartin, they constitute a charming study in Stuart costume.

FRED HANDO.

Dingestow Church.

DINGESTOW

Two years back the good people of Bryngwyn deplored my ignorance when I pronounced Bryngwyn as *Bringwin*. Surrendering to numbers, I fell for *Brungwyn*.

Now I am told that only inhabitants of Gath and Tiger Bay talk about *Dingy Stow*.

Dingy indeed! ejaculated a well-informed lady. *Let me never hear that pronunciation. You may call us Dingstow or, if you prefer, Dingastow. Otherwise our saint, Dingat, will fry you into pancakes and toss you over Treowen.*

When the saints went marching forth some 14 centuries ago, Dingat pegged his claim in a fair hollow — a real *panteg*. Gentle hills sheltered him, good water flowed for him and he had passable tracks when he went visiting the cells of his brethren.

The Normans, recognising his potent influence after six centuries, retained his name new church. But this was in the dedication of their time after much blood had flowed in the field to the west of the church.

Now, just as St. Patrick was born in four places and Caractacus was buried in seven, the story of the wondrous Welsh bowshot, I am well aware, is located in several Monmouthshire castles. It so happens that I was brought up to believe that the sanguinary sagas I am about to relate happened at Dingestow.

We have seen how the Welsh of upper Gwent were whipped into wild fury when their leaders were massacred after a dinner party at Abergavenny. We have seen how they revenged themselves on Richard De Clare in the black glades of the Grwyny Valley in 1136.

The same chronicler, Giraldus Cambrensis, writing in 1188, tells how that hell-bent butcher of Hereford, Sheriff Ranulf le Poer, while raising a new fortress at *Llandinegat* in 1184, was set upon by a strong force of Welshmen. Giraldus details his injuries with powers of observation worthy of Dr. Kildare:

Ranulf, pierced mortally by a lance, had now his windpipe and the veins and arteries of his neck severed by a sword.

The second saga which I associate with Dingestow concerns a Norman knight on horseback. He is perfectly safe behind the stout oaken door of the keep. He dreams of doughty deeds against the savages of Gwent. He muses on the maidens, the poetry, the drama of his beloved homeland. How he despises this ghastly off-shore island.

A tearing sound; a searing pain; his horse staggers.

The Welsh bowman without has loosed his shaft, piercing the oak door four fingers thick, piercing the knight's armour-clad thigh, killing his horse.

Where did these bloodstained affairs take place? A long jump from the churchyard to the west will land you at the gate of a very queer field, which has the appearance of a giant's shoe. The uppers of the shoe are steep; elsewhere the slopes are gentler, and the hedge marks the foss.

Into that foss, by the way, was hurled the body of the bloodiest villain of them all, de Braose. Yet he survived.

Site of Dingestow Castle.

I walked around and over this relic of early Norman military art. The undulating summit of the mound I estimated in the dim light at about 100ft. by 60ft. with the bailey spread below towards the church. My drawing, done from the mound, should be in colour. The gentle pink and silver of the church stonework was set amidst a glory of tints, of gold and amber, russet and umber, viridian and emerald, and on the distant hillside cottage windows reflected the golden light of the setting sun.

I have left little space for Dingestow church. Its dedication to Dingat, brother of our own Gwladys (wife of St. Woollos), its gift to Llandaff in the 9th century, the unity of its styles and the obvious care bestowed upon it make it a pleasant destination. I found somewhat surprising the flaking of the old red sandstone. Was this Monmouthshire or Worcestershire stone?

Equally surprising was the almost complete absence of the *signs and tokens* which must have made St. Dingat's, before 1864, a treasury of church history. The pretty little window which once lit the stairs to the rood loft is, I think, the sole survival.

Tregaer Church on its prehistoric encampment.

TREGAER

The hexagon of lanes north of Raglan contains many a treasure. Let me recommend for your inspection the comely, unsophisticated hilltop hamlet of Tregaer, near the peak of the hexagon.

Tregaer implies the homestead of the encampment. The church stands within the circular camp, as shown by the circular churchyard and we know from our experiences in the churchyards of our cathedral *(Stow Church)*, Llanwern, Llanhennock, Gwernesney and elsewhere, that a circular churchyard is frequently edged by a trackway and that both are relics from very early times.

In the churchyard I met the vicar, 86 years and a day old, as he informed me. A Welsh-speaking Welshman, the Rev. William Phillips is compounded, inter alia, of vivacity and vitality.

Pointing to the cock on the church tower, I remarked, "An impressive chanticleer you have up there, vicar." His eyes shone with pleasure. "Impressive indeed," he agreed. "Before he was regilded I measured him. He is four feet from beak to tail end and his beak is actually open an inch!"

He left me, but soon returned ringing a handbell. "You must see this. It is the old funeral bell which was rung by the sexton as he headed the funeral procession. Note the Latin inscription, 'Memento mori'."

The masonry and timbers of the porch — lintel, arch-braces and wind-braces — and the oaken seats engaged our admiration. Under the graceful ogee entrance we made our way towards the font, which is surely unique for, while its upper portion, of whitish stone, is patterned with an interlacing of hearts, the lower is obviously authentic, of local red sandstone and inscribed on each of its eight panels with the sacred monogram. The panel facing west has also the motto, *Duw a Digon*, signifying literally *God and enough*.

The upper portion of this font is an afterthought. My thoughts turned irresistibly to the font in the Bryngwyn garden. Could that be the discarded font from Tregaer?

DEFENCE SLIT, RECENTLY OPENED IN CHURCH TOWER.

ONE-STONE WINDOW LIGHTING STAIRS TO ROOD-LOFT

OGEE, QUATREFOILED NAVE WINDOW.

Contrast in windows at Tregaer.

We walked under an early English arch into the tower room. Here we saw the typical E.E. lights, but also an early slit opening which had remained hidden until 1924. The vicar showed how that opening commanded the road from Brangwyn.

Near the west end of the nave north wall I was able, with effort, to decipher a touching memorial to the children, aged ten weeks, three years eight months and 17 years, of the family, a century and a half ago, at *Wern Melling*.

> *Our race we ran so far you see,*
> *This world was not a place for we,*
> *Our time was short, our grief the less,*
> *Blame not our haste to happiness.*

Close at hand are the records of the Tregaer charities, including Good Friday bread and annual donations from the Powells of Llwyn-y-Gaer.

Elsewhere we saw memorials to the Says family of Penrhos. As there are still descendants of that family in the county, it will be of interest to note that their name, Says or Sayce, was originally Sais, indicating a Saxon in a Welsh community.

Facing the chancel, we saw on the left the opening to the rood-loft stairs. When we opened the door, the beautiful little window, 14 inches by four inches, cut from a single stone, was displayed. Such windows are rare, but not unique, in our buildings. Loft, rood and screen have disappeared.

Of the double chancel arch, the lower chamber is pointed and the taller cinquefoiled. As if echoing in a still small voice, the piscina also is cinquefoiled. In the south wall of the chancel is the priest's entrance and near to it the window shown in my small drawing, surmounted by the inscription 1638 M.

Chancel window of 1838 in Tregaer Church.

We walked around the church exterior, noting the contrast between the little windows of the tower and the three-light sandstone window in the nave north wall, with its ogee moulding and unusual quatrefoil top light.

From the churchyard we took the view from the Trellech ridge eastwards to the Black Mountains. Green and glorious, it rolled and dipped with gentle grace, this northern parkland of ours, and we espied not a factory chimney, not a single cubist effort in concrete.

I bade the vicar au revoir at his churchyard cross. The noble steps and chamfered base of the original cross survive and are completed by a cross of octagonal section inscribed *Pax Vobiscum, 1926.* That the cross is of a different alignment from the church may indicate that the cross is the older structure.

PENRHOS

Penrhos implies the high land of the moor. The parish of 2,690 acres contains still many coppices and some woods, relics of the days before timber-felling became a major occupation. Such denudation continues today, but to a lesser degree, among the eastern woods.

My approach to Penrhos was by way of Raglan, the Hands, Pen-yr-heol and the lovely sylvan road which dips delightfully past Poors Wood and then leads westward to Pentwyn. A short southward glide took me thence to the church of St. Cadoc, seven miles from Monmouth, eight from Abergavenny, four from Raglan — as rural a destination as one could desire.

But where was the village? I had asked the same question in Tregaer and was shown the old inn and school. I got the same answer at Penrhos, where the school and the derelict inn are adjacent to the churchyard. This parish-planning is the antithesis of the scheme which produces today the mass-menace which we try to excuse with the execrable term "conurbation."

Truly Penrhos is far-flung. It is as if Cadoc had directed the members of his flock to explode outwards to preach the gospel. Good fun it will prove, I hope, threading tracks with Welsh names like Croes-heol-y-march (cross-lane of the stallion) to places like Llaca-du (black mud) and Great Bottom!

The Old Temple Bar Inn, Penrhos.

I parked my car near the ruinous inn. In the early 19th century this was a hostelry known as Temple Bar — a wonderful addition to our list of Monmouthshire tavern names, worthy of a place among the Goose and Cuckoo, the Drum and Monkey, the Tippling Philosopher and the Ramping Cat. Once there were two inns in the parish; now there are none.

A pleasure it was to perambulate Penrhos church. Evidence of pride and care marked church and churchyard, trees and tombs and the churchyard cross with its massive broached base. Where an extension had been made to provide a north aisle I noted with pleasure that an original three-light window had been incorporated.

The Church of St. Cadoc, Penrhos.

Of the four bells in the battlemented tower the oldest, probably of the 15th century, is inscribed *Sancta Margareta;* the bell of 1672 bears the names of three churchwardens; *Fear God, Honour the King* is the injunction on the 1623 bell, and the latest, of 1904, is in memory of a great vicar of Penrhos, the Reverend William Feetham.

Strange it is to know that when, five centuries ago, the first bell rang in Penrhos, the church of St. Cadoc was already over two centuries old. In one ancient record it is named *Lancaddoc Penros,* in another of 1254, *Ecclesia beati Caddoci de penros* and in 1348 it was *Llancaddoc Penros* . . .

Sensing my interest in the church, a kindly man of the parish obtained the church key, opened the church door, borrowed a ladder and so deciphered the inscription on a stone panel fixed high in the wall of the tower room:

Walter Powel of Llantilio Crossenny in A.D. 1654 left 24 shillings a year to be spent in bread and to the poor, one half at St. Thomas's Day and one half on Good Friday.

Proudly he displayed the carved pew-ends, the work of boys and young men of the parish. One, dated 1901, was in memory of William Ffolliott, missionary to Lake Nyassa, another to the beloved vicar, William Feetham, in 1902 and two others. *Alexandra Coronata* and *Edwardus Coronatus* in 1902. Choir pews, I noted, were surmounted by excellently-carved representations of fishes.

I fear that St. Cadoc's lost heavily during the Victorian 'restorations'. About a century ago the church must have possessed many treasures in oak for, in addition to the normal boxpews, there was a pew in the rood-loft and much oak panelling. The piscina, the doorway and steps leading to the loft, a tiny stanchioned window lighting the stairs, the handsome waggon-roofs and the chancel and tower-arches survive and among the silver, a chalice made in 1659 and the base of a paten dated 1576. I suspect, too, that the simple old table now in the north aisle was once the altar table.

St. Peter's Church, Bryngwyn.

BRYNGWYN

Surrounded by Clytha, Llanarth, Penrhos, Tregaer and Raglan, Bryngwyn is the Welsh centre of a Welsh circle.

Listen to the music of its farm-names: Croes-bychanbach, Wern-y-cwrt, Tynewydd, Llwyn-y-gaer, Nantchwith, Pwll-y-Groes. Little London and Yew-tree Cottage, also in the parish, seem nervously to shrink amid such sonority.

In your labyrinthine wanderings, you lovers of lanes, have you arrived suddenly at an oak tree, surrounded by a stone seat, on a green triangle at the junction of three lanes? This may well have been Bryngwyn; thus I remember it.

Close at hand is the village school built by Archdeacon Crawley — see his name on the stone seat — in 1872. It replaced an earlier structure where, in 1673, the licensed schoolmaster was Aaron Lewis.

Across the road is the rectory, ancient, massive, for some years a farmhouse, but still retaining in its front facade and spacious rooms the characteristic status-look of our Monmouthshire rectories. And here, on raised ground which may be the bryn gwyn, stands the Llanbedr, the church of St. Peter. At the gate is a big five-stepped *upping stone* suggesting that the worshippers' horses were not invariably ponies.

As we walk towards the porch, we note tombs roofed over, the veritable *beddau*, the houses of the dead. The broached base of the churchyard cross is original; the westward view is sublime.

The porch of St. Peter's is a poem in oak. With infinite care the old craftsman contrived curves in his lintel and insets to form an ogee arch between the mighty upright timbers. Not satisfied with the arch-braces which secured his principals, he inserted wind-braces to prevent lateral movement. Stone-seats and a handsome studded oak door complete the little building, confirming that the porch was not merely a way in but also an integral part of the church.

You may remember reading in my articles on Grosmont references to Aeddan, whose tenants each paid one red rose annually for their land. As lord of Clytha, Aeddan celebrated the visit of Baldwin, Archbishop of Canterbury, to these parts in 1188 by founding Bryngwyn church.

Incredible it seems, by the way, that the proposal to replace by a modern structure the ancient Pont yr Esgob in the Black Mountains — which also commemorates Baldwin's visit — seems doomed to succeed!

The ivy on the embattled tower may be picturesque, but should be removed. An inscription on the bell of 1632, *Fear God, Honour the King,* would seem to have been appropriate to those times.

We enter the church, passing the shield-decorated font and stand at the centre of the west nave wall. From this vantage point we see that the axis of the chancel diverges northwards from the nave axis, and we are not surprised, therefore, to note that, on the modern oak reredos, the head of Our Lord falls in the same direction.

A square-headed, two-light window in the south wall of the nave (shown under the eaves of my drawing) and a doorway and stairs in the north wall indicte that once a rood-loft existed above the chancel-arch. Screen and loft have disappeared, but the trefoiled piscina in the chancel south wall, the Early English and Perpendicular windows survive. The north aisle is a modern addition.

BENEATH REPOSES ALL   HERE LIES LAMENTED
THAT HEAVEN COULD LEND   IN HIS SILENT GRAVE
THE BEST OF WIVES THE   A HARMLESS NEIGHBOUR
MOTHER AND THE FRIEND   AND A PARENT BRAVE

In the vestry, I discovered the ancient oaken chest with its three locks and a charming framed poem of the 1870s which gives some of the points of view of the Bryngwyn country-folk.

On the north wall of the chancel are affixed two memorial stones, one of which I copied. The other, ornately bordered, is inscribed:

The body of William Tyler Gent., was buried hereunder the 13 day of December 1695 who left behind him his deare wife Penelope.

Behould the place where I do lye as thou art now so was I but as I am so thou shalt be com wife come deth coim follo me.

The imposing oak reredos recalls the greatly beloved rector and archdeacon, William Crawley, who served Bryngwyn from 1834 to 1896. It was he who planted the oak on the green in 1837 to commemorate Queen Victoria's coronation.

A varied assortment of trees, including one splendid silver birch, surrounds the large churchyard, while a couple of fields away in a marsh is Ffynon Pedr — *St. Peter's Well.*

The Church of St. Teilo, Llanarth.

LLANARTH

Llanarth church was built on the site of a church erected in the 6th century, for in the Book of Llandaff, we read:

> *King Iddon, son of Ynyr Gwent, for the exchange of an eternal country, sacrificed one of his mansions, Lan Garth, and all its territory, which formerly belonged to St. Dubricius, Archbishop . . . to Archbishop Teilo and all his accessors, without any earthly payment, besides to God and the church of Llandaff.*

The church on this land was founded, therefore, between 512 and 566, the years when Teilo was archbishop, and I find it fascinating to stand in Llanarth and imagine the king's mansion, possibly on the site of Llanarth Court and the little wooded church as they were 14 centuries ago.

Llanarth signifies the church on rising ground, or in an enclosure, and from the park the rising ground is evident. The handsome tower is embattled, and surmounted by four slender pinnacles decorated with crockets. Six bells were presented by John Jones of Llanarth, in the year 1800 and an inscription reads:

> *I call in prayer the living to combine;*
> *The dead must hear a louder sound than mine.*

Dedicated to St. Teilo, the church has undergone several reconstructions, as indicated by previous roof marks on the tower and the varied periods of the windows. To the right of the foreground tree in my sketch may be seen an original lancet window, while to the left of the porch the modern cross springs from its ancient base, carved characters on which have tempted some writers to date it from the time of Teilo.

Within the church may be seen the 17th-century font, the steps once leading to the rood loft, which are used now for the approach to the pulpit, the two aumbreys and the piscina in the chancel wall and, on the north wall of the nave, the touching and eloquent testimony to the virtues of his wife, who died in 1737, by William Jones Esq, of Clytha, which, after enumerating her goodness and worth, her gifts in the polite arts, continues:

An utter stranger to every species of detraction she never spoke of her neighbour but with praise and commendation.

Being too good to continue any longer in this world. Elizabeth Jones died aged 58, but her husband's loving words have a message for us all today.

St. David's Church, Llandewi Rhydderch.

LLANDDEWI RHYDDERCH

Llanddewi stands in a valley watered by the Pant brook, which has tumbled from the Skirrid past Bryn-y-gwchyn and Werngochlyn and has received the waters of three smaller brooks, one of which bears the lovely name of *Morlais* — the voice of the sea.

The Pant flows past the village mill (now disused) and old Court Farm, curving gracefully then to join the Trothy, which has refreshed the green lands all the way from its source — Blaen-Trothy — near Campston. Townsfolk who wonder at my concern with the little brooks of our county should realise that Monmouthshire is in many respects the gift of its waters.

This is always confirmed when visitors from dry brown lands, like Texas, comment on our verdant fields. "Oh, honey!" said a sweet Texan lady to her husband as we drove through mid-Gwent, "isn't it all green!" — thanks to its streams.

In alternate showers and sun-caught glimpses now of the Sugar Loaf, now of the Skirrid, in this damp air miraculously transformed as the cloud shadows moved northwards across their slopes. Within two miles the village appeared, tucked into its valley as cosily as a bairn in its cradle. I parked the car outside Church Farm, walked around the corner and saw the beautiful treasure which I have tried to illustrate for you.

Over seven centuries old, this church of St. David, much restored, stands on a slope sheltered by magnificent wellingtonias and yews, one mighty yew being almost as venerable as the church. Part of the many-sectioned trunk of this yew is seen in my sketch to the left of the modern Crucifixion which stands on the original steps of the churchyard cross.

Original, too, is the squat tower surmounted by its timbered *bell-house* — as the belfry was called in 1545. Llanddewi belfry is one of the finest of our timbered towers and as Mr. F. C. Bowler has written recently (*The Timber Belfries and Towers of Monmouthshire Churches*) these beautiful structures are worthy of close inspection.

At Llanddewi a lean-to rests on stout oak supports and bears two series of oak uprights and a pyramidal roof. All this skilled work was undertaken to suspend the bells, the sound of which pealed through the openings. Undoubtedly birds and bats tenanted the tower, which may be the reason why the timbers of these belfries are rarely attacked by beetles.

The one bell in the tower bears the inscription: *William Jones, Robert Hughes, C.W. 1710.*

Within the tower, I noted at once the stout western door secured inside by an oak beam four inches square which slides into holes in the walls. We have seen these door-beams in a number of old Monmouthshire houses.

Four enormous oak uprights, each 1ft. 6in. square, take their share in supporting the super-structure and the lancets of Early English times lend a little light to the ground-floor and bell chamber.

The porch with its two ancient lights and doorways of red sandstone leads to the two steps down into the nave. Lighting is of three periods — candles, incandescent gas-mantles and electricity, each, as the vicar instructed me, having its own function and charm.

On the wands are the mitre, for the vicar's warden and the crown, for the people's warden — symbols of old privileges and duties, which formed the topic of a discussion later, during which I gathered that my reverend friend does not continue the ancient custom of "boar, bull and stallion on his glebeland."

Alongside, the pulpit and Elizabethan doorway leads to stone steps to the rood-loft, all traces of which have disappeared.

On the chancel wall is the memorial to Mr. Seth Powell, who died in 1785, and his wife:

Stop, reader, stand, and lend an ear
Unto the dust that slumbers here.
And when that thou doth look on we
Think on the Glass that runs for thee.

They was charitable to the poor and good neighbours.

Llanddewi implies a dedication to St. David; "Rhydderch" the Welsh chieftain, son of Caradog, who ruled in these parts when the Normans came.

Four lanes meet at Llanddewi Rhydderch. One drops suddenly from the uplands to the 300ft. contour of the village; the others move in sweetly, gently. My favourite approach is, as I have written previously, from the Llanarth road, with the Skirrid and Sugar Loaf ahead.

Over at the crossroads in the village, the church stands sentinel, as it has stood for seven centuries. Church Farm is half as old, as was old Court Farm. Around the village are other ancient homesteads, which I may be able to visit, but I called first at Crispin Cottage.

Crispin and the Peacock.

Post Office, Llandewi Rhydderch.

My drawing shows the cottage — now the post office — which goes to join my growing list of quaint Monmouthshire post offices. Readers may remember the little *posts* at Llangattock Lingoed, Pen-y-clawdd, Whitson and elsewhere; some may recall the unique post office at Cwmyoy, which for years was a vintage Rolls-Royce car perched on the bluff.

Llanddewi post office is a worthy addition to the list. White, clean, attractive, as all civil service edifices should be, it is sheltered at the rear by tall trees and guarded in front by an imposing topiary peacock and hedge. Through the tall trees the Skirrid is seen.

Crispin, as Harry of Monmouth well knew (was not Agincourt fought on St. Crispin's Day?) was the patron saint of shoemakers.

I was not surprised to hear from Mrs. Taylor, the post-mistress, that Crispin Cottage was once the abode of the village shoemaker and, as I made my sketch, Henry's immortal lines came racing back:

And gentlemen in England now a-bed,
Shall think themselves accursed they were not here,
And hold their manhoods cheap whiles any speaks
That fought with us upon St. Crispin's day.

I walked up the Llanddewi Skirrid lane to find the village mill. Powered by the Pant brook, the under-shot wheel had given good service but, like so many of our water mills, it ceased a couple of generations ago.

In the cosy kitchen of Millhouse, Mrs. Taylor and her daughter talked of the joys of life in Llanddewi Rhytherch. Their garden in mid-October was still gay with summer and autumn blooms and beyond we could see the village centre, with a van unloading the schoolchildren, who raced up the hill to see if more *conkers* had fallen from the vicar's chestnut trees.

"There is always something happening as we look out of our window," sang Mrs. Taylor, "but, oh! it's in winter that you ought to see our view. Fields and roofs are all so white and the old church in its trees is like a Christmas card."

Tea at the vicarage included bakestone cakes served hot and short by clever Miss Lewis (who had regaled me at Wolvesnewton). Then we strolled to the church, where the vicar unearthed ancient records and documents which shed light on village life two centuries ago.

The first document, issued by the churchwardens and overseers of the poor in Llanarth (the adjoining parish), 1761, *owned and acknowledged* Richard Ford and Frances his wife to be inhabitants legally settled in Llanarth, followed by a monumental example of alliteration — *whose seals are to the said certificate subscribed and set severally sign and seal the said certificate.*

Such certificates, it seems, were necessary to prevent folk from obtaining poor relief and charities in more than one village, as shown in another document, dated 1764.

Mary Edwards, spinster, lately came and intruded into the parish of Llanddewi Rhydderch endeavouring to settle as Inhabitant thereof contrary to Law not having any ways acquired or obtained any legal settlement therein and that she is likely to become chargeable thereunto, was legally settled in Trostrey parish, therefore the churchwardens and overseers of Llanddewi Rhydderch are required to deliver her over, and hereof not to fail, to the churchwardens and overseers of Trostrey parish.

These certificates, sold by *J. Coles, stationer in Fleet Street,* are legible after all these years. A third gives an idea of the value of human commodities — and money — in 1791:

Examination of Mary Powell, now of Llanddewi Rhydderch, single woman, concerning her legal place of settlement.

She was hired by the year to Edward Parry, of Llangattock-juxta-Usk, Farmer, for the wages of about 26 shillings and that she served the first year and was paid accordingly, but has done no act since to gain her settlement elsewhere.

This, like other certificates, was signed by a *squiggly* mark — the accused's signature.

What do they know of a parish who only the village know? Often I am told by good folk that they know Trellech or Grosmont or Llangattock Lingoed when they have visited the church and the inn of the hamlet.

Little do they realise that the village draws its life-blood from the homesteads of its parish and that in these homes still survive many a treasured heirloom and — which is of greater value — a wealth of culture.

In the village of Llanddewi Rhydderch I heard of houses in the parish with strange names. Women with solemn faces and quiet ways, men with good voices and eyes used to great distances and children with dog-rose complexions united to instruct me how to find the homestead of the Britons (Pentre-Brython), the homestead of the Saxons (Tre-Saeson) and the homestead of the Irish (Pentre-Gwyddel).

"Wait!" I cried, "have you all the united nations in your parish?"

"No, but we have Newfoundland," came the answer, "and Long-house (Ty-hir) and Morgan's Wood (Coed Morgan), and Top of the Park (Pen-y-Parc) and Beech Tree Farm (Ffwyddion) and . . ."

"Whatever you miss" — this from the vicar — "do not fail to find Mynachty-Morlais. That is the Monk's House above the brook named 'Voice of the Sea'."

And as an afterthought: "You might call at the Pool of Beer (Pwll-y-Cwrw) — a cottage, mind, not a tavern."

Ashamed of its previous displays, the sun shone brilliantly as I drove to Llanddewi. I stopped for a word with a plump countryman; a few swallows perched on the wires above us; we listened to their conversation and were amused to hear them ask, "Is our journey really necessary?"

"A grand day," I commented, between puffs of smoke.

"Grand it is, boss," he agreed, "the best bit of summer this winter, eh?"

I drove through the village, up the Abergavenny road, turned right at Croes Hywel, and drifted down the heavenly hill until Mynachty Morlais came into view on the opposite slope.

The new and old monachty, Llandewi Rhydderch.

57

The monks of Abbeydore had chosen a superb site for their grange. Mynachty — the monks' house — still stands in wooded country above the Morlais brook but, as I watched from afar, I realised that I was just in time to see the last of the roof-timbers shown in my sketch.

When Bradley visited Mynachty in 1906 the old house had become uninhabitable and a new one built close by. In the intervening years the monks' house has been used as a barn and will now be demolished.

Tonight is Hallowe'en. Among the spirits which re-visit their earthly homes tonight may be seen, perhaps, the Abbbot of Abbeydore paying a last call at his grange.

I drove to the old house, but found nought of character, except the ancient window in the west wall.

Retracing my tracks, I passed Croes Hywel and turned left for Ty-hir, where Mrs. Lewis showed me the old house. Here, undoubtedly, people and animals lived under one roof and now in one compartment are stored the rosettes and 24 cups won by her sons Bernard and Robert, members of the Abergavenny pony club.

On one wild night during the last war, 16 bombs fell near Ty-hir and all its windows were shattered. It was from the cider-house of Ty-hir that the cider mill was sent as a gift to the Borough Museum at Newport.

Continuing my oddyssy, I took the Coldbrook track.

Down in the valley on my left stood Newfoundland, Pen-y-parc, Pentre-Gwyddel, but time pressed, so I drove on to Upper Farm, where I met Mr. and Mrs. Dando, who directed me down a steep and stony lane to the homestead of the Saxons — Tre-Saeson. Who the Saxons were I know not, but the substantial stone house which now bears the name has beam and window characteristics which speak of 17th-century workmanship.

Substantial, too, is the stone house of Pentre-Brython, which in the stormy days of Titus Oates was one of the Catholic houses of North Monmouthshire.

It was outside Pentre-Brython where I met Mr. Champion of Abergavenny; he told me of his grandfather, John Champion, who walked to Blaenafon from Wiltshire, found work there and took part in the Chartist Riots.

On my way home I called at Coed Morgan, which is the only house in the parish sign-posted. Part in Llanarth, part Llanddewi, Pen-coed-Morgan (to give its full name) is splendidly situated on the ridge, has an impressive Georgian front, ancient ceiling beams, a dove-cote and a farmyard almost as big as a football field.

I regret, however, that I failed to find the pool of beer!

The dove-cote, Coed Morgan.

Chapter Four

ABERGAVENNY, THE GOBANIUM OF THE ROMANS

THE ABERGAVENNY MURAL

In 1907, when workmen removed the partition in the top storey of an ancient house in Cross Street, Abergavenny, they discovered a secret chamber, twenty-three feet by ten feet. On the sloping ceiling at the east end were the remains of a remarkable mural painting four feet two inches by two feet nine inches, apparently representing the Adoration of the Magi. The workmen had come across a treasure which had been hidden for nearly two-and-a-half centuries.

The fresco, with its underlying plaster, was carefully removed, placed under glass in an oak frame, and taken *into private custody*. Other markings, painted on an inner plaster-facing, were carefully covered with glass and documents found under the floorboards were dried and deciphered. So the loveliest mural painting in Gwent was once again lost to view. Inquiries made in recent years were fruitless.

The Adoration of the Magi.

Then Mrs. Barber, wife of my friend Will-o- the hills, while buying sweets in a shop in Cross Street, heard the shopkeeper say that she had discovered a big mural painting behind a dresser in one of her rooms. When Will-o- the hills and I saw it we recognised it at once as the lost *Adoration*.

It is truly, in spite of much flaking in the lower half, a masterpiece. Mrs. Francis, aged 81, who was, and still is, living in the house, told me that when it was discovered in 1907 a certain museum offered £800 for it. Discerning Monmouthshire folk will see at once that its value is beyond rubies.

Under the black roof of the penthouse on the right is the ox, rendered with the poise and forthright technique of a prehistoric cave-painting. Dressed in deep blue, the Virgin Mary, with a circlet halo above her head, nurses the Holy Child, whose halo is more ornate. The star in the east directs its rays towards the Child. On the left is a Wise Man with a hypnotic eye. Where had I seen him before? In William Blake's engravings, created probably two centuries after the *Adoration*.

Where are the other Magi? Maybe their kneeling figures occupied the lost foreground, but there is nothing left which would help us to decide and the vacant space on the Virgin's dress is not wide enough to hold a standing figure.

This, then, was the altar-piece in the secret Catholic chapel in the house of Thomas Gunter, the Abergavenny attorney.

You may see the painting in Mrs. Parry's cafe (part of the old house), just beyond the Swan Inn.

My sketch shows but one of the Wise Men and it seemed to me that we should never know where the others were portrayed.

Mr. John Collett, our borough librarian, set his staff to search among his archives. One of his bright young ladies unearthed in the *Haines collection* a photograph taken of the painting before its removal and on that print, forty-seven years old, we were able to see clearly, behind the figure remaining, the other two Magi, one bearing a gift.

Many of my readers have asked who was the artist. At the bottom right-hand corner of the photograph was some dim lettering. Under a powerful lens and in growing excitement, we studied these letters. Our excitement was dashed when we deciphered the word 'copyright' printed by the photographer on his negative. The artist therefore remains anonymous.

Another mystery is but party solved. How was it that the secret room in the attic was not entered for two-and-a-half centuries? The attic concerned is the room behind the top right-hand window shown in my sketch of the Gunter house. Mrs. Francis, who has been living there for fifty years, assures me that the stairs to the attic were built by Mr. Foster in 1907 and that there was no other entrance.

To solve this problem we decided to circumnavigate the house. We walked up Cross Street, turned into Monk Street and down the lane which was originally *Beili Priordy* (the bailey of the Prior's house), but now Priory Lane. Opposite the Gunter house we opened a door in the high stone wall and entered the very wide-walled garden. The back of the house (which was at first the front), though sadly dilapidated, retains enough character to show what was expected in an attorney's house in the 17th century.

It was possible for us to determine the position of the main entrance; many of the stout window-frames have survived; and in one almost hidden recess we discovered an ancient light, with its small panes and lead complete. Yet of an external staircase to the secret attic there was no trace, so we walked out into the car park.

From this viewpoint we examined what is left visible of the pine-end of Gunter's house. Just above the peak of the intervening cottage roof we saw the lintel of a doorway. This, then, must have been the entrance to the attic, at the summit of a stairway.

Returning to Cross Street, I stood in an archway under a stone boar's head dated 1877 and studied the house. Now three houses, numbered 37, 39 and 41, it was first the home of the Gunters and later the *Parrot*, later still the "Cardiff Arms" inn.

Take away the porch, the shop windows, the *decorative* additions, one bedroom

Gunter's House, Abergavenny.

window and the modern chimneys and replace the 17th-century doorway, windows and chimney and you will have an idea of its original appearance.

Mrs. Parry, whose family occupy the central portion, kindly showed us her first-floor room, which stretches from front to rear of the house. To our great delight, the original ceiling remains, divided into panels bordered with a running pattern of single roses, thistles and pineapples and containing forty-four cherubs' heads.

In the end wall is a doorway of the late 16th century. This room is the only one conveying the atmosphere of Tudor and Stuart days. Knocking at the door of the east wing, we were admitted by Mrs. Francis. We sat and listened while she told us of the reconstruction in 1907.

Mr. Foster, who had taken over the property, decided to give Mrs. Francis an extra room and not only built the stairway to the attic, but also knocked down a lath-and-plaster wall which divided the attic into two unequal compartments. It was then that the treasures were exposed.

First there was the magnificent fresco painted on the steeply sloping ceiling. This was carefully removed, according to a contemporary account, *without damage,* but the *Haines collection* photograph indicates three Magi and now only one remains.

Next a two-faced plaster partition was noticed. When the outer plaster was removed, painted markings were found on the smooth surface of the inner plaster. These still remain and as my sketch indicates are the work of *T.G.* — undoubtedly Thomas Gunter.

These markings were interpreted as the signature of Thomas Gunter over the date, in Roman characters, 1640. I can trace no such date and the hieroglyphics seem to me no more than the drawings and tokens of affection of an adolescent. If this is correct, the markings were made, possibly in his bedroom, by *T.G.* in the 1630's. The framework holding the plaster (now glazed) is fixed in the middle of the east wall of the attic and by standing on a box we were able to see the inner lintel of the entrance which we had viewed in the car-park.

61

The third relic found in the attic was "the mark of the Jesuits." High on the wall above the attic window were painted the letters I.H.S. and a heart coloured red on a green oval surrounded by golden rays and surmounted by a cross. This has in recent years been covered over with a thick and hideous red distemper, but I hope to have that removed.

Who worshipped in the attic? In March, 1678, a House of Commons committee was appointed to consider *the danger the Nation is in by the Growth of Popery and for providing Remedies to prevent the same.*

Among the witnesses called from Monmouthshire were John Arnold, Esquire of Llanfihangel Crucorney, William James of the Lodge, near Caerleon, and Mr. Greenhaugh, Vicar of Abergavenny and Llantilio Pertholey.

They testified that Philip Evans and David Lewis, Popish priests (both executed later) often frequented the house of Thomas Gunter in Abergavenny, that Mass was said in the chapel, that very great numbers resorted to the chapel, that Marriages and Christenings were celebrated there by Popish priests, that Thomas Gunter had declared, *I Kept a Priest in Oliver's time of severity and will Keep one now* and that many times corpses were taken there for interment *with the Formalities of White Crosses upon them.*

My readers will remember how Father John Lloyd was apprehended while administering the Mass at Treifor. Philip Evans, mentioned in the evidence just quoted, was hideously tortured and executed before the eyes of John Lloyd on 22nd July, 1679, and Lloyd was then similarly tortured and executed.

Father David Lewis, the other priest named in the evidence, was arrested on 17th November, 1678, in a house in Llantarnam, tried at Monmouth Assizes and executed at Usk on 27th August, 1679.

A further relic — a figure of our Lord, crucified, was later dug up in the garden of Gunter's House.

AMONG THE RUINS OF TUDOR STREET

Demolitions in Tudor Street have proceeded apace. The houses beyond the town wall have disappeared and, as the visitor threads Nevill Street, Chicken Street or Butcher's Row, he sees ahead an open space, like a bomb site, used now as a car park.

These demolitions have provided the historian with fascinating evidence of the methods and material used in domestic architecture three and four centuries ago. Beams and joists, many beautifully moulded, oak-mullioned windows whose mouldings testified to the craftsmen's delight in decoration, fireplaces in stone or oak (many with massive lintels), impressive stud-and-panel screens (one of which adorns the Welsh kitchen in the castle museum) and wall paintings are but a few of the relics exposed, and carefully recorded by experts.

At the same time, the artists, enthusiastically led by their president, Mrs. Beverley Burton, have depicted on scores of canvases the progress — if that is the correct term — of the destructions.

Doomed houses of Tudor Street seen to the left of the archway from the grounds of the Old Court, Abergavenny.

Standing in the archway of Old Court, with the scarlet creeper painting the tower of St. John's across the open space, I wondered what lay ahead, how this challenging area would be developed. The *new look* demanded in so many of our towns today would be out-of-scale, out-of-taste, devastating, ulcer-inducing in Abergavenny.

I plead that the goddess of beauty should receive as many votive offerings here as the gods of the market place. Maybe a green shrine, an abode of peace, will find a place.

We were a well-mixed party on that sunny afternoon. Music was strongly represented; we saw a harp which may have belonged to Thomas Griffiths, the blind chief harpist to

Edward VII and Lord Llanover and one of our number was herself a harpist; our doctor made, as well as played, violins; there were a couple of artists, quiet, soulful; most of us were golfers, either operative or emeritus; all revelled in the joys of our idyllic county.

And we had come to the ruins of Tudor Street!

The houses which we entered, seen to the left of the archway in my sketch, were doomed to fall on the following Tuesday. Like the adjoining coach-house, which is now the doctor's surgery below and a capacious art studio above, these were outbuildings of Old Court, the handsome stone house behind. Old Court, known to old inhabitants as Beili Baker, must be the subject of a later article but dates, as do its outhouses, back to the early 17th century.

My experiences in other Tudor Street houses were repeated here. We saw excellent beams, one moulded and stopped specimen 24 feet long; ripping off some wallpaper, we exposed an excellent stud-and-panel screen which, with several others, is to be preserved; a stone fireplace with a grand lintel will be also saved, together with a carved oak doorhead; but a timber-framed wall cannot be retained.

Suddenly a memory of a similar exploration flashed into my mind. A couple of years ago a clever young Abergavenny architect invited a few of us to accompany him into a shoe shop in Monk Street. The friendly shopkeeper removed many boxes, exposing a handsome Elizabethan oak door which opened on to a flight of steep stone steps.

Armed with flashlamps and a crowbar, we descended the steps into a narrow passage blocked at the far end. Leaving the lady member of our party to hold the lamp while the architect attacked the end wall, the Bookman and I climbed to the shop and sought the rear of the premises.

There, 12 feet below the street level, we found walls which we were assured belonged to an old prison. While we were examining these walls a stone fell and a beautiful hand and arm emerged — no, it was not clothed in white samite — holding the flash-lamp. The steps had led down to the gaol. And that gaol was within a few yards of the east gate of Abergavenny.

"Is there a cellar to this house?" I asked one of the Tudor Street workmen. Before he could reply an old lady who had joined our group said: "Yes, it was the old prison. One of the prisoners was hanged in this very room — on the ground floor."

We followed the workman down dark stone steps into darkness. The spurt of a lighted match showed on my right a grille, the iron bars of which were still, after long corrosion, stout and firmly set. Just beyond, in the same wall, was a stone doorway, some five or six centuries old, excellently preserved, leading into a cellar perhaps 24 feet by eight feet, with no other exit.

And, of course, this was within a few yards of the site of the great Tudor's gate. The town wall comes behind the Nevill Street houses, is incorporated into Old Court and continues majestically to the castle.

Across Tudor Street was the western gate of the town, about which Coxe wrote in 1800, *Tudor's Gate is a strong Gothic portal, defended by a portcullis, of which the groove is visible. In passing through the arch, the eye catches a perspective view which is much admired . . . and produces an effect which neither the pen nor the pencil can adequately delineate.*

Why were these gaols — if they were gaols — located near the town gates? A similar dungeon was found under the West Gate of Newport. That has been assumed to have some connection with the toll-booth adjacent to the gate.

We were among the last to enter the Tudor Street cellar. Both houses disappeared last week and I assume that the cellar is now filled with debris.

The gaol below the doomed houses.

On most of us, ruins exert a lugubrious attraction. Visit the Colosseum or the Parthenon on any fine summer's day and you will find hordes of rotarians, accountants, townswomen guilders and shale lorry monopolists, all thrilled to their hard cores by the fallen stones.

Me, too. I can't keep away from Tudor Street, in Abergavenny and, when late at night I slip into my bath, a froth of white dust floats around me. For months and months the good people of Nevill Street have found similar dust in their curtains, their soup and their hair.

With the exception of low rear walls, the houses were flat. Those good men, Messrs. Jackson and Thacker, had saved as much as possible, including, to my astonishment, the fine timber-framed gable end wall and, again to my delight, they had earmarked the stone arch of the underground prison for removal to the castle wall.

An Abergavenny lady with her little girl approached. "Could you, could you," she begged, "show me the way you took down to the prison cellar?" Amid the chaos of rubble and dust a black hole yawned. "That, madam," — I struck a Napoleonic pose — "that is the entrance!"

She grabbed her daughter, shrieked, "No, you don't, Elsie!" and I turned as Mr. Alfred Jackson's hand descended on my shoulder.

For the next hour I was regaled with an exhibition of the latest additions to Abergavenny museum. Fascinating in truth they were but, as the museum is closed for the winter months, I will refer to one item only. That is the magnificent Victorian dress in brocade, silk, velvet and lace which, as Mr. Thacker instructs me, belonged originally to Mrs. Davies, second daughter of Mr. Ebenezer Lewis, of the Maindee, Newport.

Now *the Maindee* was the fine stone house off the Chepstow Road which gave its name (maen-ty — the stone house) to the eastern portion of Newport — Newport Ultra Pontem, as it were.

The King's Arms, Nevill Street, Abergavenny.

From the museum I made my way to the King's Arms inn, at the corner of Nevill Street and Tudor Street and therefore close to the site of Tudor Gate.

Carved stone heads of oxen on the upper storey of one of the houses remind us that Nevill Street was once Rother (cattle) Street.

At the inn, Mrs. Barnfield showed me the excellent stud-and-panel screen on the left of the passage and a similar screen separating the two rooms on the left. One upright post had elaborate mouldings recalling the splendid work at Coldbrook in Llandenny. In delightful rooms on the first floor the ancient beams with their simple "stops" were displayed.

But my hostess led me then to her prize exhibit. In the old bar the removal of plaster had laid bare a beam above the fireplace. On this beam, clear as when it was written, I read the following: *Good Quarters for the 15th or King's Hussars, 15th of October, 1817. To Arms for Ever. Jas. Hall, F. Troop 24, S.C.L.E. Berry.*

Military historians among my readers may know how the King's Hussars came to be stationed in Abergavenny in 1817.

ABERGAVENNY MUSEUM

Although less than a year old, the museum at Abergavenny has caught the fancy of the good folk who dwell in the north-west corner of the county.

Treasures hoarded in some instances for centuries have been brought in; the demolition of old houses in the town has provided splendid relics; and the co-operation of the council and the Rotary members, together with generous grants, has enabled the enterprising committee not merely to house the exhibits, but also to show them properly cased and labelled.

Some of the cases — very handsome they look in their turquoise frames — have come from the Victoria and Albert Museum.

The museum buildings rise on part of the site of Abergavenny castle. Few destinations are more attractive than the green castle mound with its majestic views of mountains and river valley, but my readers should note that the museum is open only on Tuesdays, Thursdays, Saturdays and Sundays.

I arrived at the museum and saw the end-product of an exciting act of schoolboy enthusiasm. Mr. Thacker, of White Castle, had rescued from Tudor Street an excellent *stud-and-panel* screen which fitted one of the walls of the museum basement. After three centuries the screen needed cleaning and treating.

"Imagine my delight," said Mr Thacker, *"when a group of Abergavenny Grammar Schoolboys begged to be allowed to undertake the renovation."*

I examined the 'end product,' and now congratulate the boys on the thoroughness of their work. It will take a proud place in a room which Messrs. Jackson and Thacker are planning as a Monmouthshire kitchen. There must be many a kitchen article stored away which would add to the character of this room.

The main room upstairs is a succession of thrills. From 3 Tudor Street came the early 17th-century fireplace lintel which with the accompanying panelling is one of the best pieces. Among the names carved there is that of a nephew of Drake, while the upper panel may have belonged to a merchant company. At hand is a 17th century cauldron.

From Cwm Mawr, in Crickhowell, but typical of the unglazed windows which survive in many farmhouses in Gwent, is the stout oaken 'wide-eye' shown in my sketch. The central mullion is 2¾in. square and the smaller mullions are 1in. square.

In a glass case *Whiskey*, the bright little orange-coloured dog, looked down at me. He had earned his living by a treadmill usefulness, turning the wheel which operated the turn-spit in front of some great fireplace. He came from the old shop in Cross Ash, but his breed is now extinct. As I have noted elsewhere, a wheel similar to *Whiskey's* survives in the Hanbury Arms, Caerleon.

From his pocket, Mr. Thacker took a tiny token which he had found in a stud-hole of a screen in Tudor Street. It was of the 17th century displaying on one side the arms of a Mercers company with the name Thomas Morgan and on the other *TMG Mercer of Monmouth.*

To indicate the wide field from which the exhibits were sent Mr. Jackson showed me a mule-chest and cheese-press from Coed-y-Dias farm, Ffwyddog (near the scene of the Norman massacre in 1136), a 16th-century fireplace from the Bell inn, Tudor Street, and a Welsh dresser from Chapel Farm, Llanvapley.

Within a few weeks this basement room, once a hunting lodge, will remind many visitors of their childhood days, when the bakestone, the great pea-soup saucepan, the shiny kettle, the sway, the bake-oven, the gophering iron and the candlesticks were all symbols of a well-endowed home.

My first sketch shows the coved Queen Anne cupboard. This type of wooden cupboard may have been derived from the coved cupboards set into the thick walls of our ancient houses. I came across such a cupboard in Penygarn house, the early 17th-century home of Mr. and Mrs. F. Richards — evidently it was part of the original fabric.

The oak spoon-rack was designed to store two dozen spoons. Measuring 18in × 9in, it came from Pen-y-Clawdd farmhouse, Llanfihangel Crucorney; my readers may remember the wig-cupboard (also set into the wall) which I sketched when I visited Pen-y-Clawdd.

I should mention here that the long record of wig-making associated with Abergavenny is illustrated so far by only one item — a pipeclay wig curler found in Tudor Street. Other items will be welcomed.

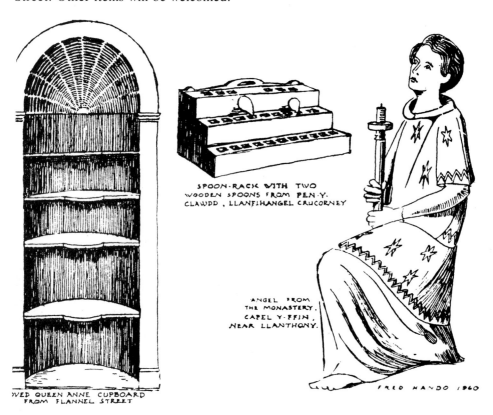

SPOON-RACK WITH TWO WOODEN SPOONS FROM PEN-Y-CLAWDD, LLANFIHANGEL CRUCORNEY

ANGEL FROM THE MONASTERY, CAPEL Y-FFIN, NEAR LLANTHONY.

FRED HANDO 1960

COVED QUEEN ANNE CUPBOARD FROM FLANNEL STREET

My third drawing shows one of the two *Llanthony Angels*. They were candleholders from the altar of the monastery church of Father Ignatius at Capel-y-ffin. When the monastery was dissolved at his death in 1908 the angels were lost. Discovered later in a ditch, they were taken to Walterstone and bought there by Major Foster, of Tamworth, who has now presented them to the museum. The angels stand above the *Ignatius display,* which includes letters, photographs, rosaries, rules and prayers, and a *Breeches* bible, which recall the recluse of Llanthony.

I saw next a copy of the rare *Arithmeticke* of Robert Recorde, the writer of the first important English treatises on algebra, arithmetic, astronomy and geometry. The rector of Tenby has kindly sent me a guide to his historic church in which is a sculptured medallion of Robert Recorde, 1510-1558, physician to Edward VI and Queen Mary. Recorde was born at Tenby and his father was mayor of the town in 1519. When the boys of Monmouthshire learn that Dr. Recorde not only made algebra and geometry available for our schools, but also invented the sign of equality ($=$).

The museum has already 17 old legal deeds, one of which concerns a dwelling-house in Frogmore Street, held on a 99 years lease in 1733 at £4 5s. per annum, *together with two couple of fat hens or two shillings in lieu thereof.*

There is also a fine estate map, on parchment, of Old Court, Llangattock Lingoed, drawn in 1815.

Exquisite pillow lace, made by Miss Walbeoffe Wilson sixty years ago; a Swansea pebble casket; two mediaeval doorkeys from St. Mary's; fine Victorian dresses, including a wedding dress of 1865; Lady Llanover's sealing-set; a Welsh lady's hat in black plush, 14in. wide and 9in. high; a christening pin-cushion bearing the message, *Welcome, Sweet Innocent,* a hoard of hundreds of farthings found in a stocking; and a pot of *Poor Man's Friend,* at 1s. 1½d., which contained ointment guaranteed to cure everything, caught my eye.

I handled a *birding-piece,* 7ft. 9in. long, from Wern-y-Cwm, which may explain the brackets set wide apart above old mantelpieces. Also on view are a typical *Davy Crocket* rifle, a flintlock gun, cannon balls found in the canal at Llanfoist and swords, cutlasses and powder-flasks — ample reward for the young pilgrims to Robert Recorde's *Arithmeticke.*

THE CONQUEST OF THE SUGAR LOAF

From earliest days there have been great adventurers who dared to face the unknown with a cheer. Some have sailed into unchartered seas, some have penetrated equatorial jungles; others, like Daniel Dare, have probed space.

In recent years Mount Everest, 29,002ft. high, and Nanga Parbat, 26,620ft. high, have been successfully climbed. It would be unpardonable if I allowed 1955 to pass without recording a gallant and equally successful climb nearer home — the ascent of the Sugar Loaf on June 10 of this year.

THE SUGAR LOAF.

As Orwell would have said, these three ascents were equally successful, but some were more equal than the other.

It must have been in March, when the oncoming spring was arousing the phagocytes in his blood, that Kenneth Hilary invited Fred Tensing to join him in an attempt to climb the Sugar Loaf.

"We could select Grey Hill, or Machen, or Twyn Barllwm," said Hillary, "but I agree with Kipling when he says, 'Not failure, but low aim, is crime.' Or was it Mrs. Hemans?"

Said Tensing, "Please yourself, O Man of Kent, but get into training at once." He said this with the age-old wisdom of a Man of Gwent. "And 1,955ft. is no molehill," he added.

So it was that K.H. scorned the lift in his office, worried his wife by running upstairs three steps at a time thrice daily after meals and gave up cricket in a devoted effort to get fit. Nay, more, it was noted that from March to June he hardly tasted water.

Tensing's wife tells me that her husband changed his way of life not by one jot or tittle, but she noted that as June approached his eyes became more and more glazed.

Just as Himalaya means *the abode of snow,* so *Sugar Loaf means the abode of the sugar-plum fairies.* The legend of little footprints on the foothills has as little foundation as the Abominable Snowman legend, for the little footprints were traced to a winter's ramble by the members of a Women's Institute.

Many a pleasant hour was passed in planning the upward route. Fred Tensing, who had too much bone above his chin, persuaded his companion not to take the easy way.

"Leave the Rholben Col to lesser men," he cried. "We will tackle the big brute on his blind side, up the West Cwm!"

Kenneth Hillary was easily led, but he, too, could be dogmatic. "We'll take ropes and aluminium ladders, tents and ice-axes, gloves and high-altitude boots if you insist," he growled, "but oxygen I will not take. We are sure to find some on the spot." Good-natured Tensing gave way.

By June 8, all the equipment, down to the last matchbox, flagon and sleeping-draught, was ready and the following day was occupied by the wives in preparing the vast supplies of food for the expedition.

Now mountaineering is not really more hazardous than many other sports, provided the proper precautions are taken. You can break your neck just as easily on the wall of death as you can on the fearsome slopes of the Sugar Loaf.

Our two pioneers, however, had overlooked one essential precaution. They had taken no account of the weather and at the end of May the monsoon came over from Pontypool.

Warm, wet winds emptied their contents over the Sugar Loaf, and yet Fred Tensing, that bone-headed native, saw not the inevitable result.

The great day dawned, still and hot. At 10.30 they left their wives and the plains and drove to the foothills, where they parked their transport at advanced base, Llwyn-du, Fred Tensing surrounded by a million flies, went ahead, smoking, steaming; Kenneth Hilary followed, blithe, humming an air on the G-string.

Suddenly his stretch of bridle-path subsided and the gallant fellow glissaded down the brown slope to the brook. Why was he not roped to Tensing? Verily there must have been some Gadarene answer. Tensing, in that dogged fashion of his, was forging, aye, blasting ahead.

Changing gear, Hillary overtook. The heat and humidity were intense, the flies intolerable. Tensing flagged but, egged on by Hillary, he unflagged.

"Keep at it, brave heart," cried Kenneth. "Above the ferns, somewhere, are the eternal snows." Thus encouraged T. wrung out his braces and advanced upwards, ever upwards, through the giant ferns.

Hour after hour of titanic effort passed and then, when there was little left for the flies to bite, open country appeared and with two stentorian sighs these relics of manhood dropped on the turf, fragrant with wild thyme, smelling like dawn in paradise — the thyme, not the men.

Of their further incredible efforts, of their incredible lunch, of the effects of the sleeping draught on Fred Tensing, who slumbered while Kenneth Hillary completed the climb, of their return down the Via Conia (the rabbit's way), I have no space to tell, but in my talks with them I gathered that both men felt a little hurt that their feat had received no notice in the Press or the BBC news.

Sugar Loaf and Skirrid Fawr — old engraving.

It was good to be afoot on that joyous afternoon; birds were singing, my pipe was sweet and as the track wound this way and that, but generally downwards, I gave way to the old enchantment of Gwent and revelled in the delights of this green upland.

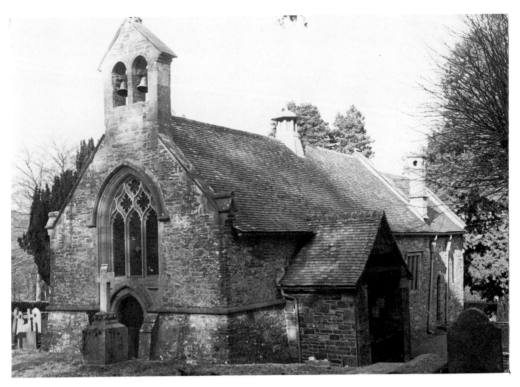

Llanfoist Church   *Chris Barber*

Llanfoist Wharf   *Chris Barber*

Chapter Five

A JOURNEY TO USK

Visiting the little churches of Llanfoist, Llanover, Llanfihangel Gobion, Llanfair Kilgeddin and Kemeys Commander.

LLANFOIST

The name *Llanfoist* has been derived by various writers from ffos (trench), Foyle, Faustus and Gwys. Bradney tells us that the church was perhaps founded by Ffwyst, a priest of the college of Seiriol in Anglesey.

One of our most hilly parishes, Llanfoist extends from the Usk to the Torfaen (Afon Llwyd), but what an extent it is! Yet, when the Brecon and Abergavenny canal was cut through the parish, the company of Thomas Hill, who owned the ironworks at Blaenafon, made a tramroad from Blaenafon to the side of Cwmcraf, *where pulleys, wheels and iron chains liberated the trams, loaded with coal, iron and limestone, down the terrible slope to the canal, while the empty ones are pulled up the steepy heights.*

The boats were then laden, and hauled down to *the port of Newport-on-Usk, to meet the ships which sail from pole to pole to all the harbours of the habitable globe.*

My quotations are taken from an essay written by Thomas Evan Watkin *(Eiddil Ifor)* of Llanfoist, in 1834, who was one of the founders of the society known as Cymdeithas Cymreigyddion y Felli. At the first eisteddfod encouraged by the society in 1834 a prize was offered for a history of Llanfoist. Eiddil Ifor's entry — the only one — was awarded the prize.

The essay was published, in Welsh and English, in 1822 by Y Brodyr Owen, Gwasg Minerva, at Abergavenny and was entitled *Hanes Llanffwyst,* which seems to confirm Bradney's derivation. I am obliged to Mr. Robert L. Williams, of the Old Schoolhouse, Llanfoist, who lent me his copy of the booklet.

In the heights above is the Punchbowl (in Welsh Taren Cwm y Disan*), whence Cromwell's men descended, as legend says, on the Royalists at Llanelen and in the neighbouring districts are many *carn* place names. *Eiddil Ifor* lists Carn y cadnaw (the fox mound), Carnddyrys (entangled mound), Carn y Blawreang (Blorenge mound), Carn y defaid (sheep's mound), Carn y clochdy (steeple mound — to which we shall refer when we come to Trevethin) and Carn diffaeth (the desert mound).

He tells how in time of persecution people were taken to the top of Cwm Craf, *the height of which was found, in 1787, by an air weighing machine, to be 1,607ft. 5in,* how they were placed in a wooden barrel, tied and closed up, the barrel penetrated with nails and then rolled topsy-turvy headlong down to the bottom.

Eiddil Ifor asserts that a village inn was built on the ruins of what was once considered to be an old monastery. He describes a field of the Maerdy Farm named Cae'r Bedd (field of the grave) and gives the *oral tradition* that victims of the plague in Abergavenny were conveyed in wagons and buried in their clothes, *just as they appeared when death came on the scene.*

I walked to the church of St. Faith at Llanfoist. It was restored in 1873 by Mr. Crawshay Bailey in memory of his father, the great iron master, who had lived at Ty Mawr (now Llanfoist House). He was buried at Llanfoist. The church retains a few of the old monuments, while in the churchyard are some immemorial yews, and the column and base of a fine cross.

The porch contains a memorial stone of some interest, as my sketch shows. An Elizabethan — or early Stuart — lady is portrayed with ruff and praying hands, while her feet, under a front view, turn left. I wonder if we have here another masterpiece by

Old Llanover.

FRED HANDO.

OLD LLANOVER

The cool sunlight of a March morning silvers Old Llanover. Set against the backcloth of clouds and great hills, church and cottages dream. The church glows between a vast yew tree on the one side and a weeping willow and lone pine on the other. A sparkling nant-y-mynydd joins the Usk under the arch of Ty'r Afon, the fishing-cottage, Muted jade-green, the river flows strongly.

In this soft mystic light, the lovely hamlet seems too etheral for this bustling, go-getting age. Can it survive? With all the slighting and despoiling of beautiful places, what can be done to retain this other-world sweetness of Llanover? We can schedule ancient monuments and places of historical significance. Before the horrid thing known as *development* deposits petrol-pumps and roadhouses in this shrine of ours, will some enlightened authority take appropriate action?

Less than eight years ago, Old Llanover was in danger from the mightiest form of vandalism. It was actually proposed to erect an enormous generating power station, covering 180 acres of rich agricultural land and to raise four cooling towers, 200 feet high and four chimneys, 300 feet high, in this vale of tranquility.

The vandals misjudged the men and women of Gwent. Led by that redoubtable Ancient Briton, Mr. D. L. Jones, OBE, our forces met the invader in full strength and, after a series of battles, our sacred soil was saved.

As I stand on the river bank on this bright morning my imagination reels at the thought of Llanover shadowed by a pall of smoke and the exquisite river poisoned and ruined by the wastes of industry. The battles fought for Llanover and Machen Vale are among our finest gifts to posterity.

To cross the river, I use *Mr. Pim's Bridge.* Built by my dear old friend, the late Henry Smith, this pretty suspension bridge enabled Mr. Leslie Pim, MP — greatly beloved Mr. Pim, to whom all the country folk took their troubles — to visit the old church.

In the churchyard lies buried the lady who gave character to Llanover, who restored the ancient arts and crafts of Wales to their rightful level, who reintroduced the love of beauty into country life. Lady Llanover was escorted to her grave by twenty maidens dressed in Welsh costume and on her coffin lay a wreath of white roses sent by the Duchess of Teck, who was to become in years later Queen Mary.

Inside the church are inscriptions which, as Coxe pointed out in 1800, are clear evidence of the Welshman's pride in his lineage. Wiliam Prichard and Matthew Prichard, father and son, *of Llanover, Esq,* are commemorated, *lineally descended from the Bodye of Cradocke Vraich vras Earle of Hereford and Prince between Wye and Seaverne.*

A proud claim this, for Cradock was a Knight of King Arthur's Round Table!

The Richards' lived at Llanover Court. The daughter of Matthew Prichard married a remarkable man, Judge Walter Rumsey, of Usk. It was Judge Rumsey, so Bradney tells us, who invented the provang, an instrument for cleansing the throat and stomach and wrote a pamphlet on *Diver's new experiments on the virtue of tobacco and coffee.*

You may see the Rumsey memorial near the Prichard stone. Without attempting to compete with the immortal memory of the Prichards, it yet claims that Walter Rumsey *was descended from the body of Sir Walter Rumsey, Lord Baronet of the Lordship and town of Rumsey, in Hampshire.*

The memorial to Walter Cecil, marked in contrast by a factual simplicity, seems to have disappeared. This is sad, for it bore the shield of arms of the Cecil family, as far as I know identical with that borne by the Marquis of Salisbury. Walter Cecil lived also at Llanover.

From the church, I drive to *Hen-bersondy,* their handsome old vicarage, the middle portion of which dates from the 16th century. Dormer windows, the unusually quaint portal with its *ceil de boeuf* above and the great brown roof, combine with the trees and the view of church and distant hills to make *Hen-bersondy* a delectable home, as Lady Mary Herbert found when she came here during the war.

Hen-bersondy, the old vicarage at Llanover.

LLANFIHANGEL GOBION

With one great arm of the Usk half encircling it, the hamlet of Llanfihangel Gobion dreams into springtime. On this still bright March morning, cold in the shade, tepid in the sunshine, the sheep and lambs vie with the birds in heralding the vernal equinox.

No traffic, no motor-horns, no belching stacks, no modern architecture; all is country peace, country beauty.

FRED HANDO .
GOBION . 1962 .

St. Michael's, Llanvihangel Gobion.

The parish name is really Llanfihangel-nigh-Usk. A walk across its meadows shows that of old the church was much nearer the Usk. The original river-course is clear, almost washing the churchyard boundary and the old forge which gave the name *Gobion*.

This is a reversal of normal river habits, for the Usk has since forsaken the shorter way and established a meander which swings majestically under Pant-y-Goytre bridge to Aberffrwd and then completes a graceful 'S' by turning southwards towards Llanfair Kilgeddin. Or was the meander the original course and the short cut a mere interlude?

Massive, handsomely chamfered, but in need of attention, the churchyard cross base with its stump rests uneasily on three steps.

Purple crocuses at gate and porch open wide as if chanting a welcome. Porch inscription tells how *to the glory of God this church was restored by William George Buchanan Esq., Lord of the Manor.*

76

And there is nobody left to earn fourpences by trapping the 'ants' in the churchyard!

Perambulating the exterior of the church I come at once to the extraordinary sculptured stone set at a height of about eight feet at the south-west corner of the nave. It has been described as showing two priests elevating the Host during Mass; other writers see various symbolisms depicted; all take the figures as priests.

Sculptured stone.

Careful examination — the carefulness of the artist — elicits that the figures are angels. My sketch shows their wings, and shows also that lovely naivete of the ancient sculptor (which we have seen elsewhere in Gwent) which empowers him to give a front view of face and body but side views of feet. I am unable to interpret the burden which the angels are carrying. Is it, perchance, a soul on its way heavenwards?

Symbols of industry and holiness above the north window.

The walls of the church tower are 'battered' at the base and in excellent repair. In the north wall of the church is a unique window which I illustrate.

The splendid stone which forms the ogee arch above the cinquefoils has three sculptures which demand attention.

In the left spandrel are carved an axe and a pair of pincers, obviously tools of the blacksmiths of Gobion, indicating that the church regarded as significant the tools of the craftsmen, worthy, in fact, of consecration.

In the other spandrel is carved a heart and this symbol is repeated within the church. For instance, each face of the octagonal font bears a sculptured heart and the sacred monogram, while a slab, possibly 13th century, in the floor, contains two hearts, one within the other.

At Gobion, as at Tregaer, where we noticed a font of the same type and decoration, I felt the font to be an intrusion; but where is the original font?

Gobion. The entrance.

The lock on the interior of the church door is within an oak baulk 1ft. 9in. long, while a more massive door swings within a heavy oaken frame and under a depressed arch into the tower-room. Viewing eastwards from the tower-door, I noted how under the seven arched braces of the roof the church was filled with light from its cinquefoiled windows.

Of especial charm and interest to me was the quaint little north aisle, one of the smallest in Gwent. Five oak columns supporting a beam twenty feet long form the arcade and each of these timbers is gouged and chiselled to produce the rich decorative effects which I described in Gobion manor house.

Alongside the pulpit the doorway to the rood-loft stairs has been filled in and there is no trace of loft or screen. The chancel has the usual piscina, a two-light window and the vicar's door in the south wall.

Not for these details shall I remember Gobion church. I shall see it always shining in the morning light, guarded by one mighty tree and stereoscoped against a background of smaller trees. And, if you wish to see it portrayed against its more distant background of hills, seek it among the exquisite wall-paintings in its sister church of Llanfair Kilgeddin, near the river.

LLANFAIR KILGEDDIN

Every Monmouthshire motorist knows the lovely road from Bettws Newydd to Clytha, with its superb views towards the Black Mountains. I am asked frequently "What is the name of the tiny church peeping out from its trees across the river? How do we get there?"

To find Llanfair Kilgeddin take the Abergavenny road from Chain Bridge and turn right as you approach the Usk bridge at Pant-y-Goitre. The lane leads direct to the church and you may park on the green space at the bend of the road.

I love to see Llanfair in the morning. On my last visit the year was young, the day was young and the birds filled the air with their ecstatic singing. Between the road and the river I was conscious of neither, only of the profound peace of this exquisite and hallowed place.

Llanfair Kilgeddin. The church with the sgraffito murals.

A yew tree with a spread of fifty feet arose on my left. Other yews and grand beeches, still bare in mid-April, formed a handsome backcloth to the church, while on the right a modern cross stood on its ancient chamfered base and four steps.

Morning sunshine illuminated the good stonework of the church and threw long shadows over the close-cropped lawn. Was it on a morning like this that the good Gethin, fourteen centuries ago, lighted on this sequestered retreat and decided to build his cell here?

I walked through the churchyard noting the burial places of the Mather Jacksons and the Crawshays. Among the Crawshay memorials was a touching tribute to Jessie Louise Dallimore, who died aged 81, "for 52 years the beloved companion and friend of those who rest with her." She was the first governess of Captain Geoffrey Crawshay.

The walls of the church are battered and, in answer to inquiries, that implies a leaning back from the base. In these beautiful walls, windows of various types survive, most of them cinquefoiled, some with square, others with *decorated* hood-mouldings, while the two-light window in the west wall is cinquefoiled but has a quatrefoil set in above.

The bell-turret has three stone projections and a couple of nicely-placed quatrefoil decorations. In 1809 the bells were described as *without wheels, the larger about 200lb. and the lesser, 150lb.,* and that most careful investigator Arthur Wright *(Church Bells of Monmouthshire),* after examining the Lombardic capitals and stops on the older bell, suggested that it appeared to be by Robert Hendley, 1450-1500.

There is a niche for an image over the porch entrance and a semi-circular doorway within. Standing at the centre near the west end of the nave I confirmed that Llanfair Kilgeddin is an outstanding example of the deflected chancel axis.

Nothing will convince me that the pronounced bending of this axis from the direction of the nave axis was an accident. I aver again that this was and still is, a poignant symbol of our Lord's head, fallen sideways in death.

A two-light window once lit the stairs leading to the rood loft, but stairs and loft have vanished. The perpendicular screen is dainty with its formal ornamentation; the roodcross is modern, while the piscina and stone slab cross in the chancel are 12th or 13th-century relics. Possibly older still, the original Norman font rests behind the later font which is a mere three centuries old.

The wall-decorations are unique. Three years after his wife's death in 1885 the stricken vicar commissioned Mr. Heywood Sumner to illustrate selected passages from the Benedicite as a memorial to Mrs. Rosamund Lindsay and the work was carried out in sgraffito.

I have told before how this ancient Italian process was practised at Llanfair. On the well-damped surface white plaster about threequarters of an inch thick was laid, and over this the requisite coloured plasters were quickly applied. When all was set a third layer of white plaster formed the upper surface, into which outlines were cut exposing the colours.

The nave-panels convey the spirit of the Benedicite. One of them, in true Italian Renaissance style, uses the Blorenge, Sugar Loaf, Skirrid and Gobion church as motifs for *O ye mountains,* and *hills, bless ye the Lord.* The chancel walls display the apostles and epistles and finally above the chancel arch is shown Christ in Glory.

Sgraffito decoration in Llanfair Kilgeddin Church.

Kemeys Commander.

KEMEYS COMMANDER

We turned aside from the Usk-Abergavenny road at a little white cottage with blue window-frames and a couple of almond trees in pink blossom. This was not the direction for the Black Mountains, but I felt the call of Kemeys Commander, with its old houses, its happy people and its dear little church.

Not for us the main entrance to the churchyard; we use the Parson's stone stile, made for the direct approach from the old vicarage, 15th-century home now of Farmer Ben Griffiths — whom I have never seen without his smile.

It was in Ben's ancient house that the *Stuart Lady* was discovered under the whitewash on the oak screen and another smaller face — possibly that of her baby — near at hand.

In the churchyard we read the inscription on the tomb of William Richards, Gent., who died in 1830:

> *This tomb is not to be unbound*
> *Till the Archangel's trumpet sound.*

We admired the crocuses and tulips, the lilies and forsythia, the countless daffodils on the graves; we gave a glance at the ancient cross; we lingered in the picturesque timber-porch, admiring its craftsmanship.

Inside the church of All Saints we made first for the screen — a simple, severe structure surmounted by the beam of the rood-loft which was lighted of old by a very small window in the south wall.

In tune with the rest of the sanctuary was the altar-slab of stone, resting on four stone supports. An embossed waggon-roof ran the whole length of the church.

With good taste the villagers had kept the floral decorations for Easter to white, gold and green. White tulips and jonquils on the altar, daffodils, narcissi and catkins on the screen and daffodils arising from ivy and yew on the windowsills expressed perfectly the spirit of Easter.

81

Chapter Six

USK, OTHERWISE KNOWN AS BRYN BUGA

The River at Usk is at all times beautiful. Upwards towards the bridge and castle-crowned hill, with the backs of the houses in New Market Street making a pretty and varied pattern; downwards towards Llanbadoc where of a still evening the reflections of hills and meadows, trees and swans defy expression in words or paint.

While dawdling here on a late and golden evening one September I saw a skein of swans — five in a line — flying down-river; it was a superb swan-river ballet, which Tchaikovsky (and Markova) would have loved to see.

It was a cold morning, grey, still, when I left Newport. The fields of Gwent, under the frost and thin cloak of snow, bore that creme de menthe appearance which my sweet-toothed wife adores and which provides so satisfying a complementary hue for the ochre of our sheep.

As I turned the corner at Llanbadoc the old town came into view — green river, white houses, bridge and castle suddenly illuminated by floodlight from a break in the pall of grey cloud. Once again I groaned because my sketches have to be in black and white.

Usk Bridge and Castle.

After crossing the bridge I turned right into New Market Street. At once I became aware of the spaciousness of the old-time town planning — as if the planners wished to introduce a French grand place touch to offset the narrow cross-streets. This is of course even more noticeable in Twyn Square.

The ditches edging the road have long since gone, but the old wide cobbled sidewalks survive. Between the road and the riverside fields, a number of interesting old houses caught my eye. I called first as Ynys Hafod.

Ynys Hafod river-meadow summerhouse. Usk.

Ynys means an island or a rivermeadow, Hafod a summer-house. This delightful name — *Rivermeadow Summerhouse* — caught my fancy, especially as I saw through an opening a little hexagonal stonehouse, obviously on the edge of the river. It must have been this little edifice which suggested the name of the big house in New Market Street.

Big undoubtedly it is. It is divided now into two homes, Ynys Hafod and Min-yr-Afon (river brink). At Min-yr-Afon I was welcomed by Mrs. E. J. Lewis, whose late husband was high sheriff; she had moved there from Bedwas.

Amid the grace of modern decorations and furniture is a staircase lighted by a barred window. At the foot of the stairs a ceiling-beam with "stop" is visible and here, as we turned, a long passage was entered under an archway made in the days of the first Elizabeth.

This arch is first-class craftsmanship. Along the passage, however, is a quaint recess cut, I imagine, by an apprentice mason, whose amateur efforts, preserved for some sentimental reason, gave us much amusement, and prompted the suggestion that one of the Rumseys might have *tried his hand* at masoncraft.

At the side entrance of the house we met Mr. Richards, who lives in a third part of the house, now named *Henllys* (old court). Stepping gingerly on the frozen path, we walked to the summer-house where half a dozen semi-circular steps led up to the first-floor entrance. Ignoring a pencilled note, "Bar open Thursday", I inspected the interior, with its views in every direction.

My sketch was done on the river-bank and shows as well as the summer-house the little *arbour* with bucket at the base, the splendid beech which shades the bank in summer, and a glimpse of the rear facade of Ynys Hafod.

In a state of deep freeze, I walked then to the strange stone entrance of the big house, guarded by three heraldic beasts above the porch. Large, well-proportioned rooms retained the stone fireplaces of old, but the circular stairway which led to the first-floor and then to the attic has disappeared. The attic, by the way, runs the whole length of the house.

Mrs. Brain and her daughter Carolyn, took me into the kitchen (now the breakfastroom). In the ceiling was an array of six big hooks for suspending breadracks, and twenty-three smaller hooks. Standing on a chair, Carolyn unhitched from a hook the original front-door key, over 14 inches long.

Most of the bedrooms (as in the Cross Keys inn) lead off a corridor, but one — a handsome apartment known as the Tudor room — occupies the upper floor of the wing. The window in this room has six lights, with some bottle-glass panes; the mouldings of mullions and transom are of the early 17th century.

The house next (towards the bridge), which looks so modern, is the coach-house of *Ynys Hafod* and is an attractive and clever adaptation.

Interesting it is to read in Bradney's *History of Monmouthshire* that Ynys Hafod was the home of the Rumseys, whom we have come across in various parts of Gwent and Breconshire.

It seems that John Rumsey, a Somerset rector, was brought to Usk by Roger Williams, of Llangibby, in the 1550s and that Rumsey married Ann, the daughter of Thomas ap David. Ann's brother was lord of the manor of Huddlehay, which Bradney suggests may have been the original name of Ynys Hafod.

Various families have owned it since — Hill, Wheeler, Rogers and Nicholl; for a time it was used by judges and during the last war by girls of the Land Army, but the name Ynys Hafod will always conjure up for me the view through an oak-framed window of a white summerhouse on the bank of a green river set against a backcloth of wooded hills.

In New Market Street, Usk.

Twyn Square, Usk.

TWYN SQUARE

My drawing, with which I have taken liberties, shows the view from Twyn Square, Usk. Sardonic, imperturbable, the castle surveys from Buga's Bank the traffic surging along the Raglan road. "Step on it," it seems to grunt, "I'll be here long after you have gone." The great trees nod assent.

This afternoon Twyn Square seems like a harbour with the town clock as its lighthouse. All the spare space in the harbour (empty in my drawing) is packed with cars, moored here away from the main stream.

Their owners make Usk a talking-place and rest centre. Their owners have come from farmhouses with splendid Welsh names; their jolly clean-shaven faces are red, like the good red lands of mid-Gwent which they work. Of medium height, there is no giant or dwarf among them.

Talking of giants, I must introduce Buga, for in colloquial Welsh Usk is Brynbuga. Bradney tells us that Buga was one of the traditional giants and with Bwch, Clitha and others founded castles in these parts.

Usk was known also as Caer Wysg (Usk fort) and, to the Romans, as Burrium. That there was a settlement here before the Romans came seems likely, for the hill on which the Norman castle was raised was a typical hill-fort site and a bronze-age axe and brooch (now at Cardiff) have been discovered in the town area.

Twyn Square has a tradition of a *tump* or twyn in its centre. Though it has no walls, Usk, like Monmouth, has its Clawdd Du (black dyke), an earthen rampart of Roman origin, on its south and east. Its main streets also are roughly at right-angles; the Roman road which has come up from Caerleon along the east bank of the Usk rejoices in the name of Maryport Street and, beyond the centre, Porth-y-carn as it leaves for Gobannium (Abergavenny); at right-angles is Bridge Street; the Roman road to Monmouth leaves by Pont-y-cleision over the Olwy brook, skirts Llandenny and Llangovan and climbs gloriously over Pen-y-clawdd.

Actually, Maryport Street ran through the site of the present gaol. In 1852, when the foundations were being laid, traces of the road were found and coins, tiles, bronze and iron articles and pottery were unearthed. Even today, Roman coins are found in gardens along the line of the old road.

Norman Usk centres around the de Clares. My readers will remember how Richard de Clare was ambushed and massacred by Morgan of Caerleon in the Grwyney Valley in 1135 (commemorated by *Carreg-y-dial,* the stone of revenge). This Richard was one of the first lords of Usk and is buried in Gloucester cathedral. Another Richard, the fourth earl, signed Magna Charta in 1215 and by this time their castle on Brynbuga, with its square keep, and the round towers, was well on the way to completion.

During the war waged by Edward I against Llewellyn, 180 houses in Usk (and 35 in Llantrisant) were *void and burnt* in 1295.

In 1381 died Edmund Mortimer, Earl of March and Lord of Usk, who had presented Adam of Usk to a studentship at Oxford.

In 1402 came Owen Glyndwr to *destroy* Usk, Caerleon and Newport castles and in 1405 Owen's son, Griffith, attacked Usk castle (now repaired).

In the words of Adam of Usk: *Lord Grey, Sir John Greyndour and many others sallied forth leading their men through the river Usk to the mountain of Upper Gwent, slew many both with fire and sword and drove them through Monkswood where Griffith was taken.*

And their captives, to the number of 300, they beheaded in front of the said castle near Pontfaldum.

I understand that scores of skeletons were found when a pond north-east of the castle was drained during last century. This may have been the site of the mass execution.

Other lords of Usk included Richard, Duke of York, killed at Wakefield in 1460, his son, Edward (reputed to have been born at Usk castle), who became Edward IV, Elizabeth, queen of Henry VII, and so, down through the centuries, to Valentine Morris of Piercefield, the dukes of Beaufort and the later holders.

During the reign of Richard II a charter was granted to Usk by Roger Mortimer, Earl of March. Dated 1398, it was lost during the attack on the town by Owain Glyndwr, but it was confirmed by Roger's son, Edmund, in 1416, who styled himself *Earl of Marsh and Ulster, Lord of Usk, Trellegg, Tregricke, Carlion, Edlogan and Lebenith in Wales.*

In this charter he confirmed unto the bailiff, commonalty and burgesses all liberties, franchises and customs used and enjoyed from the time of Elizabeth de Burgh, *former Lady of that Town.* The bailiff of Usk was given the powers of a magistrate, to try civil and criminal cases occurring within the borough.

Long before this, however, Usk was a corporate borough. In 1323 the burgesses of Usk, by royal charter, were for ever *quit of toll, murage, pontage, pavage, lastage, stallage, pickage, tronage, keyage, landage through our whole kingdom and our duchy of Aquitain and our land of Ireland* (See footnote).

In a deed of 1539 there is a reference to a port-reeve and two bailiffs, and in 1598 Henry, Earl of Pembroke, granted to the port-reeve, bailiffs, burgesses and tenants a piece of land in New Market Street for the building of a market house.

It seems therefore that the town was governed by a port-reeve and one or more bailiffs. The port-reeve was elected at a court-leet, served for a year and was eligible for re-election. He presided at the court-leets, committed offenders for trial and, in petty cases, confined delinquents within the house of correction. He was returning officer for the borough and was entitled to tolls amounting to £7 annually.

In his book *Usk Past and Present*, James Henry Clark gives the form of warrant to summon the leet, the charge and the oaths taken by the foreman, jurymen, port-reeve *(you shall do equal right to the poor and rich after your cunning, wit and power)*, constable, bailiff and burgesses.

In the charge, reference was made to forestallers, ingrossers and engrossers. A forestaller bought goods coming in the way to market; an ingrosser bought corn, etc., in a market and sold it again in the same market or within four miles; an engrosser bought corn, etc., in large quantities with intent to sell again. All three enhanced the price of provisions, took a successive profit and made the market dearer.

Perambulations of the borough, beginning at the Bell, Llanbadoc (now a private house), included the Island below Llanbadoc church and the waste land at Pontsampit. The boundaries in 1630 began at the *farthest middle stone peer of the bridge . . . the river of Uske to the uttermost syde of the mill pound entring into the river of ukse mearing to the hedge-rowe of Walter Reynolds,* and so on.

Among the customs and privileges of the burgesses were the *pawnage of their swine within Wyeswood, Gwehellogge and Glascoyd by the payment of one penny for every swine to the woodward,* and the *underwoods and windfalls of the said woods for their ffewell by payment of 1d. in a quarter of a year.*

Monmouth, Usk and Newport sent one member *(Monmouth Boroughs)* to parliament. Until 1832 these burgesses were the only people in Usk who could vote and they, of course, have been nominated by the lord of the borough.

I have a boyhood memory of *Monmouth Boroughs*. In one of the general elections the Liberals decided to hold a cycle ride from borough to borough. Before Usk was reached many of the tyres were punctured by tin-tacks placed business-end uppermost in the road.

The following week saw a "broadsheet" on sale, beginning *They tax the sugar, they tax the beer, They tacks the road to Usk.*

In 1886, under an order from the local government board, Usk ceased to exist as a corporate borough and so ended a corporation which had begun in 1323 in the reign of Edward II. The last of the port-reeves was James Henry Clark.

Some confusion exists in connection with the bridge at Usk. Clark says that formerly a wooden bridge crossed the river nearly opposite Llanbadoc church, for which the present bridge was substituted. Another writer states that the stone bridge of four arches was built by Morgan Thomas, of Laleston, Glamorgan, in 1836.

The name *Bridge Street* in ancient documents indicates that from early days a crossing existed where the present bridge stands. That bridge, with its five arches, must have been built, as Clark indicates, c.1752 and was narrow and steep, with recesses on the piers into which pedestrians leapt to avoid injury.

In 1836 the bridge was widened four feet on each side, enabling paved footpaths to be laid down, but it is still a major operation to manoeuvre a wide load along Bridge Street and over the bridge.

My sketch shows the bridge and castle as seen from the upper room of Mr. Etheridge's garage on the Usk-Newport road. Usk bridge is an ideal place on which to stand and stare, not at the traffic but up and down the lovely river.

One gentle remonstrance, however. Will the appropriate authority consider the construction of a riverside walk, in place of the unsightly dump in the withies which disfigures the west bank of the river.

At the dissolution of the monasteries in 1535, Roger Williams of Usk became by royal grant the owner of Usk Priory, of one hundred acres of land within the borough of Usk, and lands in Llangibby and Llanbadoc. Although he enlarged the old castle at Llangibby, according to Bradney he did not live there; he was high sheriff in 1562.

Now in Old Market Street in Usk still stands a big, gaunt house with walls like cliffs. So big it is that it houses six families.

Although 19th-century miscreants robbed it of almost all its external glories, of its magnificent stairway up which four people could walk abreast, and of almost all its woodwork, this, am sure, was the house which the newly-enriched Roger Williams built circa 1545 on the hundred acres. Soon afterwards he must have built Ynys Hafod in New Market Street for John Rumsey, the Somerset rector, who was to act as his secretary.

Did Roger Williams live at Ty-mawr? At number 27 Mrs. Powell, a sweetly courteous old lady, showed me into her passage, where the decorated ceiling indicated that this must have been part of the hall and the door at the other end is a robust example of early craftsmanship in oak.

"Here, to the left of this door," said Mrs. Powell, "arose the wonderful staircase."

We turned right and soon entered the hall which, although reduced, is still an impressive apartment, with its ceiling decorated in geometrical plasterwork with Tudor roses and other floral devices.

Progress: How the twentieth century has treated the sixteenth century early Tudor window at Ty-mawr, Usk.

On the floor above are two bedrooms which, judging by their decorated ceilings, were formerly one and in their original state, with the four-light windows, must have constituted a beautiful room. The unusual barrel-ceiling in the attic was a further example of good workmanship.

The ceilings in Mrs. Powell's portion of Ty-mawr are probably typical of the ceilings which formerly glorified all of this *great house*. They are the only surviving ceilings.

What of the windows? I called at number 17, where Mr. Saffin took me through his house, which is completely modernised, to the garden. Here, on the *hundred acres,* which stretch to Clawdd Du, we surveyed the vast wall, some 63ft. by 40ft., which formed the original front facade of Roger's house.

I was tempted to reconstruct Ty-mawr and show it in its former splendour, but life is so short. Suffice it that it is still possible to discern the four-lighted windows (see smaller sketch) each surmounted by its moulded dripstone and relieving arch and each bearing the graceful curves of early Tudor work.

From Mr. Saffin I heard of the legendary secret way from an opening in his cellar-wall to the castle and of a window high in the east gable-end which was pierced as an escape hatch for Charles I, if he perforce had been hidden in the attic.

My readers will remember a similar escape-device in the attic of the Gunter house in Abergavenny.

My conclusion, then, after inspecting the surviving relics, is that this was undoubtedly the home of Roger Williams, his wife (a lady from Clearwell), his two sons and three daughters. What Roger would ejaculate could he see his house today is beyond the range of my Welsh vocabulary.

From Ty-mawr I walked along Old Market Street to the market house and left into Baron's Lane, named after the lords of the castle. On the left is the malthouse, comparable in size with Ty-mawr and suggesting that in the old days the good folk of Usk must have known full-scale thirsts.

At the end of the lane, to my delight, I espied another 'house with a wooden leg', companion to the hilltop house at Llanhennock, which formed the subject of the first article in *Monmouthshire Sketchbook.*

"The house with the wooden leg". The Willows, Usk.

By the way, Mrs. Fred Harding, who saved for us the Llanhennock house with the wooden leg, is now busily and skilfully restoring the picturesque school-house there.

As my sketch indicates, the *leg* of the Usk house is now in part oak, but the lower half is stone. It is one of a number of stout timbers at the entrance while the entrance arch suggests an early 17th-century origin. This, however, I cannot confirm, as the rest of the house has been modernised.

I was welcomed by Mrs. Lewis, the wife of my old friend Jack Lewis, who owns Allt-y-Bela (to which I shall refer later). We toured the spacious rooms, all flooded with light through the big windows and then walked out into the garden, which is part of the riverside *ynys*.

The family were somewhat weary after attending during the previous night to lambs new-born in bitter weather. Fifteen lambs had already arrived and many more were expected.

Surveying the placid scene, I pointed to the graceful elm which I have depicted at the left of the drawing. "Under that tree ten months ago," remarked pretty Isabel, "was born my foal, 'April Love'."

The fresh green of the meadows, the shadows of the wooded hills towards Llanbadoc and the curve of the river, coursing so sweetly Severnwards, made a picture which I shall not forget.

GREY FRIARS

Between the Yspitty and the river bridge at Usk, an imposing "Norman" gateway gave admission to the grounds of a very old building. This gateway was demolished in 1876, but the old building, although much altered, still stands in 1959. Judging by the impressive stone doorway, shown in the centre of my drawing, this ancient house was of the early 14th century.

Writing in 1800, Archdeacon Coxe announced that the *gothic* doorway on the south of the house still existed and that another on the north side was filled in. Actually the doorway is on the east of the building and there is no trace of another.

Traditionally this was a house of Grey Friars. To find it I sought permission from the kindly grocer, Mr. V. E. Jones, for whose shop the old building acts as a store; together we inspected the stone doorway and the relics of Tudor window dripstones front and rear.

By 1630 it had become a "House of Correction held by the justices of the peace for the use of the inhabitants of the county of Monmouth". Here, in 1679, Father David Lewis (also known as Charles Baker) was incarcerated after his arrest at Llantarnam, where he had been preparing to say Mass.

The Jesuit David Lewis, like the Benedictine Augustine Baker, was a native of Abergavenny, born in 1617, son of Morgan Lewis, the "scholemaster" of the Royal Grammar School. At the age of 19 he became a Catholic, and was sent by his father to the English college at Rome; a priest in 1642, a Jesuit in 1644, he then set out for South Wales, where he toiled as a missionary, visiting afoot the persecuted Catholics.

Among his ports of call was the Gunter house in Abergavenny, where mass was regularly celebrated. Witnesses at his trial averred that he had preached in English and Welsh and that at the Gunter house more people were present than in the parish church. In the little attic room of the Gunter house, hidden under the distemper, is reputed to be a Jesuit sign.

We have full particulars of the trial and death of Father Lewis, including *A Narrative of the Imprisonment and Tryal of Mr. David Lewis,* written by himself while a prisoner in the House of Correction at Usk.

Greyfriars doorway. House of Correction, Usk.

It seems that after his arrest at Llantarnam (maybe at Ty-coch) six men conveyed him to a house at Llanfoist and thence to Mr. Arnold's house, Llanfihangel Crucorney Court. On the following day, escorted by constables, he rode to Monmouth gaol and some two months later was taken to Usk where he remained until his trial at the Monmouth assizes in March, 1679. There was never any doubt about the verdict. Having passed overseas and taken orders in the church of Rome, and having returned to this country for forty days and more, he had committed high treason.

Punishment for this crime was carried out on August 27, 1679, at Usk. From the old house of correction — once, let me repeat, a friary — Father Lewis was dragged on a hurdle to a gallows on the land now known as the Coniger (rabbit warren) or the island (from ynys — an island or river meadow).

Here, in English and Welsh, he avowed his innocence, forgave his accusers and persecutors and was hanged, with the subsequent horrors. His body was buried in Usk churchyard.

When John Howard, the prison reformer, visited Monmouthshire in 1779, he called at the *County Bridewell* (the *house of correction*) at Usk, and recorded that on the ground floor were a room for men and another for women. The keeper's wife told him that many years before that time the gaol was crowded, and that she, her father, and others had "the gaol fever". Howard noted that the prisoners had some allowance, that the spinning wheels were not provided by the county, and that the keeper had all the profit of the work. There were seven prisoners.

In 1842 the present gaol was built and by 1851 there were eighty-two prisoners.

The Roger Edwards Endowed Grammar School.

THE GRAMMAR SCHOOL

In mediaeval days all education was in the hands of the Church. Frequently the school was held in part of the church building — a room above the porch, the vestry, or a room above the vestry. The schoolmaster was a clerk in orders; the school was controlled by church courts.

That there was such a school in Usk seems probable. We know that John Rumsey, the Somerset Rector whom Roger Williams installed in a new house in Usk in the 1550's, was soon in charge of a school, for Bradney quotes evidence given at a case in 1589: *Mr. Jo'n Romsey of Uske, schollmaster, being a very learned man and a grate friend of the said Roger Williams.*

As we have no record of the founding of a school by John Rumsey it is likely that he took over a school already in existence. Then and for centuries afterwards, that school was held in the vestry of the church and the room above the vestry, both on the north side of the chancel.

Is it too fanciful to suggest that in this school Adam of Usk, priest, chronicler and lawyer, was a scholar when Edmund Mortimer, Earl of March, presented him to a studentship in laws at Oxford?

Conjectures retire, however, by 1621, for in that year Roger Edwards endowed his school at Usk. Who was this Roger Edwards?

In 1599 Roger Edwards, living in a low building named Allt-y-Bela near Gwernesney, decided to build an extension to his house which should incorporate all the latest ideas, even to the extent of glass in the windows, contemporary mouldings, cider cellar, parlour, bedroom and loft.

The oft-told story tells how this rich and cultured old squire found, on setting out for a ride, that his sons had cut his saddle girths, hoping that he might fall and be killed.

Sending for the notary, Roger Edwards drafted a new will in which he left most of his property for the founding of alms-houses in Coed-cwnnwr and a grammar school at Usk. And although he left legacies to three nephews, his sons were not mentioned.

Roger Edwards died in 1624. His will was proved at Llandaff in 1636, and twenty-seven years later, as J. H. Clark records, it made an appearance in Chancery.

From then until 1772, nothing is known of the administration of the charity but in 1700 the schoolmaster's salary was £30 a year, his house was valued at £6 a year, and a scholar leaving for Oxford received £5 a year.

In his will Edwards made no provision for a schoolroom. This strengthens the belief that there was already a school at Usk, a school which was held in the church. The schoolmaster's house was on the site of the present school in Maryport Street.

As the years passed troubles ensued. Grants for scholars were misapplied, school property was leased for purposes other than educational, and it is small wonder that by 1745 (see *Monmouthshire's Schools and Education by Canon E. T. Davies*) the school *had declined to nothing, for there are only two Latin Scholars where there used to be Six Score. At present it is in a very ruinous condition and must if not speedily prevented fall down.*

Canon Davies reviews the changing fortunes of the school and the changes in its curriculum. By 1850 the master, the Rev. W. H. Wrenford, was able to offer Latin, scripture, Greek (optional), reading, writing, spelling, English grammar, mathematics, history, geography and French, taught by himself and one other.

Long before this the school had been transferred from the church to a schoolroom near the master's house. This, in 1836, was like *a cart house, or small stable and was cold, ill furnished, nasty.*

It was little improved by 1860, when *it had every defect of ventilation and comfort which the most ingenious architect could have contrived for the punishment of children.*

In an entertaining paragraph, Canon Davies tells of the walnut trees in the headmaster's garden. One of these five trees, uprooted by the wind, lay on the ground for two years. In 1863 the headmaster sold it to a builder who agreed in return to add a plaster arch to the house entrance from the hall, a cornice around the hall and an ornament in the ceiling for the gas light.

News of this brought a storm. Should, a schoolmaster barter school property for the enrichment of school property? Tumultuous meetings.were held, but at last Mr. Wrenford was cleared of all guilt and today, as my friend the present headmaster showed me, the plaster decorations of 1863 look down in virginal purity.

In the records many references are made to boarders. In 1826 there were twenty boarders and in 1858 there were 48. Manifestly they could not have been housed in the Maryport Street premises, but a little research reveals that in 1826 the headmaster rented the Priory for the purpose of boarding and there, I assume, the boarders were accommodated until the school lost its status.

St. Mary's Priory Church, Usk.

PRIORY CHURCH OF ST. MARY

I stood in Old Market Street, Usk, and watched the centuries roll back. For 800 years the gatehouse to the priory has stood on guard, while the tower and some of the fabric of St. Mary's date back to the 11th century. My view point was one of the most evocative in our old, old land.

To get an idea of St. Mary's in its glory I walked through the churchyard. From the road to the east I sketched the tower, with its Norman windows above and lancets below.

Clearly marked to this day, the roof-lines on the tower indicate the heights of the choir and the two transepts and now I could visualise the church with its tower borne on four arches forming the focal point of a magnificent cruciform structure. As such it was raised, according to tradition, by Tristram Fitz Rolfe, Lord of Usk, standard-bearer to William the Conqueror, when the battle of Hastings was a recent memory.

In his *Historical Tour of Monmouthshire,* Archdeacon Coxe printed a charming picture of St. Mary's in 1800, showing the tower with pinnacles, the north transept with its chimney and external steps leading, apparently to a gallery above the north aisle.

He wrote, *The tower communicated with a transept and choir, which no longer exist,* but this reference must be to the south transept.

Coxe adds in his characteristic prose, *The porches in gothic style, are not inelegant.* These porches, of the late 15th century, I noted, have groined roofs, bosses, niches for saints, armorial bearings in the north porch and an interesting stoup surmounting a head in the west porch. I am disposed to call them elegant.

Now, almost all of our parish churches have their main entrances on the south. Why are the porches at St. Mary's, Usk, on the north and west? The answer, I assume is that the south transept projected into the grounds of the priory and that the six Benedictine nuns made their entrance in that part of the building. This would take them into the conventual portion where they would be hidden from the parish worshippers by the rood screen.

The west porch leads into the north aisle. Over the external doorways of each porch is a graceful floriated label of the same design as the labels I noted at Caldicot and Llangattock (Crickhowell). An interesting stone within the church near the west door is quaintly inscribed:

Water Iones I doe him prayse a valian sovdiovr in his days vnto the wars wovld he goe to fight against his forraine foe to advavnce a pike before his qveene the which Elisabeth have seene his sword and speare he did advavnce and then he tooke his way to France and landed in the Ile of Ree where his desire was to bee and to the Lord he gave the prayse that he came home to end his dayes and whilst I in my grave doe sleepe I pray the Lord my sovle to keepe Water Jones deceased the 14th day of Febrvary 1656.

(Bradney records the recutting of a stone in the churchyard to Philip Mason, who died in 1772, aged 52 years, weighing 554lb. — 39 stone 8lb!).

The north aisle and the nave arcade are early 13th-century work, but as the floor level has been raised the bases of the columns are hidden. The eastern column marks the boundary between the parochial and the conventional churches; the screen, of typical 15th-century style, is graceful in spite of modern attempts to reproduce in part ancient colours.

On the screen is fixed the famous brass to Adam of Usk. Measuring 19in. by 2in., it is inscribed in ancient Welsh which has produced a goodly crop of translations. The 15th-century poem was apparently mis-read by the English engraver and this has complicated the task of translation. All authorities, however, agree that the brass commemorates the virtues and attainments of *adam yske* who died in 1430.

The other, smaller brass, commemorates *Margareta Baskervyle,* second wife of Henry Rumsey, son of the Reverend John Rumsey, *scollmaster* of Usk.

In the chancel which is, of course, the ground floor of the tower, the clustered columns, the rails and the altar table, once the refectory table of the Priory, add grandeur. Close at hand are the Jacobean pulpit and the oaken chest of 1538 which once had four locks.

Two restorations were effected in the last century. The galleries were removed and the nave extended in 1844 and extensive repairs undertaken in 1899 when the organ of Llandaff cathedral was installed.

I have no space to deal with the chapels, chantries and the many monuments of St. Mary's, but as I stood near the simple font, I closed my eyes and listened to the whimpers and lusty yells of the thousands of babies, royal, yeoman and peasant, who had been baptised there.

I thought of Adam Usk, of Father Baker, of Roger Edwards, of "Happy Dick" of Dingestow, and the others lying in the churchyard. And finally, I thought of the good men and women who over nine centuries, through wars and storms and pestilence, as through quiet years of peace, have kept burning bright the lamp of God in Usk. Shrine of holiness and beauty, St. Mary's had quietened my mind and enriched my soul.

THE PRIORY

The Normans who conquered our land were an interesting study in mediaeval personality. Having raised their castles and cowed the country-folk they turned their thoughts to the next world. The churches which they now built bore little relation in size to the population; rather were they an offering, a propitiation, to God, on the basis that the more glorious the church the greater would be the chance of eternal felicity for its builder, his family, his retainers. If, in addition, a group of monks or nuns could be housed near the church, their prayers for the soul of the founder would strengthen his chance. So it was that at Usk the prioress and her five nuns prayed daily for their founder, Richard de Clare, his son, Gilbert, his grandson, Richard and later benefactors.

An early charter was quoted in 1330 by Elizabeth de Burgh, who confirmed in her own charter the endowments granted by her grandfather, Richard.

These included the tithes of St. Mary's, Usk (among which the ninth fish was especially noted), of Llanbadoc, Llangeview, Raglan and Glascoed; their property was widespread, with such items as *27 acres at Trostrey, near the hermitage* and *30 acres near the hermitage at Trosty* which, says Bradney, might have been Estavarney.

Offerings to images in St. Mary's and in the chapels of St. Radegund and St. Mary Magdalen, belonged also to the priory. The chapel of Radegund is recorded by Adam of Usk as being within the walls of the monastery. Like the priories at Chepstow,

The priory and the tower of St. Mary's, Usk.

Abergavenny, Monmouth, Bassaleg and Goldcliff, Usk priory was of the Benedictine order and, as Adam wrote to the Pope, *in this monastery only virgins born of noble ancestry were wont to be received.*

From the 12th century to 1536 the nuns continued their prayers and ministrations. In spite of their rich endowments, they were reduced by misfortunes of war to poverty so that in 1404 Adam of Usk wrote to the Pope an account of their straits.

Owing to the burnings, spoilings and other misfortunes caused by the wars, he wrote, *the same monastery has come to such want that, unless some remedy be quickly provided by your holiness, the same nuns will be forced to beg for food and clothing.*

He suggested that the worshippers who visited on festival days the chapel of St. Radegund within the walls of the monastery and *stretched forth helping hands* should receive an indulgence from the Pope.

The Pope returned his letter, signed, with the footnote: *So be it as it is asked.*

I called at the priory on a day of storm and sunshine. Raindrops bejewelled hundreds of crocuses, snowdrops and aconites massed near the gatehouse and, as I approached the house, the sun shone on a heavenly drift of pale blue crocuses growing between the priory and the church. From this standpoint the south wall of the tower showed the roof-line of the vanished south transept. Without doubt the transept extended along the present tarmac drive to within a few yards of the priory, and I was not surprised to find in the north wall of the latter an ancient doorway now blocked up. This was the portal through which the nuns made their way to their doors in the transept and so to the conventional portion of the church.

The tower from the east, showing roof-lines and arches of the vanished choir and transept.

In the absence of the owners, Colonel and Mrs. Barnwell, their daughter, Mrs. de Montfort, who had lately come home from Ceylon, took me around the ground-floor rooms. It was obvious that the oldest part of the house was in the centre, for here in the south wall (masked now by a projecting wing) is a stone arch of the 13th century, which was probably the other entrance of the priory. The many extensions and restorations have been carried out to preserve the 16th and 17th-century atmosphere.

And the ghost? Over cups of tea, my young hostess and I talked of secret passages to the church and castle and, suddenly, she remarked: "I should tell you that my godmother who lived here some years ago saw the priory ghost, who appeared, in the full habit of a Benedictine nun, in the old part of the house."

WHITE FRIARS, NOAH'S ARK AND THE HEALING WELL

In pre-reformation days Usk housed at least three religious orders. Near the bridge lived the Franciscans or Grey Friars, in the priory the Benedictine nuns and opposite the east end of the church the Carmelites or White Friars.

The house of the White Friars was part of the priory property *granted* to Roger Williams soon after the dissolution.

FRED HANDO · *The house of the White Friars, Four Ash Street, Usk.*

I found White Friars (scheduled as a house of historic interest) in Four Ash Street, off Twyn Square. Evidence of its age survives in front, where three small windows (one beautifully cut out of a single stone) and signs of the original entrance remain, and at the rear in two more small windows, a projecting shaft, a big chimney, and (behind a shed) a 14th-century window.

Mrs. Marfell invited me to see the western half of the house. Her bright and charming

98

diningroom displays in its eastern wall two 16-century doorways, now boarded up, which once led to the other apartments. Why doorways of different sizes were necessary I know not, unless the smaller one, made first, raised too many bumps on the brothers' tonsured heads.

From the stairs I looked through the single-stone window which has now a glass pane 9in. long and 3in. wide. I am no stonemason but the piercing and chamfering of this boulder seemed to me excellent craftsmanship.

The eastern half of the house has been extended and so the external chimney running up the gable end is now hidden. Mrs. Marfell's pretty diningroom shows no signs of the doorways which led into it from *next door*. I asked her what had happened to the piscina which Bradney noted half a century ago.

"It was too big for a piscina," she replied. "I saw it once and am certain that it was a font. It was carved with monk-like figures and traditionally my diningroom was called the 'christeningroom'. Unfortunately, before we came here, the font was sold to a travelling antique merchant."

Should any of my readers know its subsequent history I shall be glad to hear of it. (My sketch shows the rear of the house. I removed one of the lean-to sheds to reveal the 14th-century window).

On several occasions in Usk I was advised to see the *healing well* and when I asked for its situation my informants, with a sweet smile, said, "Near Noah's Ark". "And Noah's Ark?" I asked, "Near Pont-y-Cleifion," was the information.

Pont-y-Cleifion — the bridge of the sick — spans the Olway on the old Monmouth road. I called to see Mrs. Taylor at the cottages behind the Olway inn.

"Is this Noah's Ark, Mrs. Taylor?" I asked. Her calm face broke into a sunny smile as she answered: "It was when we came here fifty years ago. Why it was so-called I never knew. The cottages were oh! so pretty, with their little latticed windows, but the agent of the owners thought the name undignified and changed it to *Olway Cottages*."

The healing well near Pont-y-Cleifion, Usk.

Mrs. Taylor directed me across the field to the healing well where, she told me, the women of Usk and beyond until recent times used to fill their bottles with the water for healing their eye-troubles.

I found and sketched the well on the sloping ground in the middle of the field.

The stone at the entrance is worn concave, there are no recesses for votive offerings, and although it was *Chapel Well* I saw no signs of a chapel. The water is clear and inviting. Standing there and looking towards the cottages, I solved the mystery of *Noah's Ark*. Over the flood water of the field between, the cottage seemed to float, ark-wise.

USK CASTLE

High on its bluff, the castle is more or less, according to season, out of sight of the through roads. Impregnable on the north-west and south-west, where the approaches resemble the Heights of Abraham, the fortress (which may have been raised on a prehistoric site) was guarded originally on its remaining bounds by a wooden palisade and ditch. The total area is some three acres.

On a grand March day, I climbed the hill off the Raglan road to view, once again, the noble relics of the fortification. Snowdrops on the steep bank, crocuses and daffodils in the garden blossomed gaily, while the fat buds of the magnolias promised *magniflora* splendour in May.

Usk Castle — the twelfth-century keep.

Jolliest of our hilltop denizens, the Humphreys clan welcomed me as if I were their long-lost cousin. A few words with the ladies, bless 'em and then I was whisked off by Richard, who downed tools on a busy afternoon in order to conduct me around his castle.

Clearly, the rectangular keep seen in my smaller sketch was the first of the stone buildings. It towers over the gatehouse (itself tall) at the south-east of the hilltop and is of the late 12th century; traces of battlements remain in the south wall and semi-circular-headed windows in the west wall. It was entered by a door on the first floor.

William Marshall's contribution to the defences consisted of the curtain wall with its eastern gateway and the round towers, all of the early 13th century.

The fine new castle played its part during the wars of the barons when, in 1233, Henry III descended on it from the north. Stout resistance induced the king to parley and, whether by subterfuge or not, he took temporary possession. In 1265 Simon de Montfort attacked and captured it.

Usk Castle — the garrison tower and curtain wall.

Walking along the green past the Garrison Tower, we came to the steps leading to the walk along the curtain wall. Here, we got the view which satisfies all visitors. Almost vertically below us was the main road and beyond it were the shops and houses, the river meadows and river, while the shadowed wooded hills formed the skyline. To the south-west I made out the pines on Ty-yn-y-Cae, the geographical centre of the county and was delighted to hear from Mr. Humphreys that, following his motto, "Plant a new one when an old tree dies", he has planted more pines on that famous summit.

We returned to ground level to inspect the 14th-century hall and chapel — sure indication that Usk castle was now a residence of importance. This is an impressive corner of the ruins and my host assured me that the hall is a magnificent sight when the mass of pink hydrangeas is in bloom.

That the gatehouse, where possibly Adam of Usk was born, was raised in the same period as the hall is doubtful. It appears to be early English. A previous and careful owner used stone from Worcestershire in his repairs. Effective as it is, its colour, however, is blatant in comparison with the chaste and aristocratic hue of our own "old red".

The last engagement, it seems, was in 1405, when Owain Glyndwr's son, Gruffydd, attacked the castle but was heavily defeated, leaving 1,500 dead on Pwll Melyn.

But, while we stood chatting in upland peace, I recalled two other visitors who paid a peaceful visit to the castle in 1188. *On this green quadrangle, still surrounded by its palisade and ditch,* I mused, *and with the great keep frowning in its new strength.* Baldwin, Archbishop of Canterbury, supported by the Bishop of Llandaff, preached the Third Crusade. How does Giraldus record the result?

A multitude of persons, influenced by the archbishop's sermon and by the exhortations of the good and worthy William (of Llandaff) were signed with the cross. Among them, to the astonishment of the spectators, were many of the most notorious murderers, thieves and robbers of the neighbourhood.

Without doubt, these ancient miscreants chose to join the army and see the world rather than being confined in the Usk *house of correction.*

Twyn Square, Usk.

USK TOLLHOUSES

Some day, when I have more time, I must record the surviving tollhouses of Monmouthshire. I come across them in and around our towns and villages as well as in the less populated parts. Strategically placed, with windows directing on the converging roads, they are still an evocative item in our county scene. How many mad drivers, haring along at 12 miles an hour, must have cursed the toll-keepers who held up their hell-for-leather progress!

Usk was guarded by five tollgates. At the Three Salmons interesting black and white illustrations of these gates were shown to me by Mr. Butcher.

The Monmouth Gatehouse, Usk.

Monmouth gate shows a picturesque hexagonal house with dripstones over its shuttered windows and the woman toll-keeper walking over the cobbled road.

This house still stands, as my sketch shows, at the junction of Castle Street and the Monmouth road. "When houses were two-a-penny," my host said, "the Monmouth gate house was sold for £25. Later, when the scarcity came, the same owner sold it for £750."

Four Ash Gate shows the toll house backed by three ash-trees with the well on the left, the church tower on the right and the old old road leading off via the gate shows another quaint little house and gate under the castle-crowned height, the railway bridge in the distance bearing a tall-funnelled engine. This gate was on the road to Abergavenny.

Four Ash Gate, Pontsandpit Gate and Porthycarne Gate are on Roman roads.

The Bridge Gatehouse, Usk, built 1837.

Bridge Gate is a spirited drawing of the toll-house erected in 1837, the year of Queen Victoria's accession. I have sketched the little edifice as it is today, with its dripstones and porch, and windows looking towards Newport and Pontypool, but the artist of the plate in the Salmons was not satisfied with the building alone.

He has presented in the foreground two asses, named Bradlaugh and Honk Secretary, in belligerent poses, while the toll-keeper smokes his pipe in hope of excitement. It is good to see that this gatehouse is being repaired.

FISHING AT USK

J. H. Clark, writing in 1869, recorded that for the previous twenty years many of the inhabitants gained their living during a great part of the year by fishing. During the season, ten or a dozen fishermen might be seen carrying their coracles, shaped in section like walnut shells, 5ft. long, 4ft. wide, with a seat placed across the centre.

The *dexterous navigator* might often be observed to work his paddle with one hand, conducting the net with the other and holding the line in his teeth. He tells how, in 1855, the fishery was taken over by the Trostrey Weir Association, who controlled all the fishing from Trostrey Weir to Usk bridge.

Their rules, too long to quote here, prohibit *all netting or other fishing (except fair rod and line fishing) and all night lob worm or salmon paste fishing.*

In 1869 the river teemed with salmon and Clark writes of a 62lb. fish caught in the previous century.

Thomas Churchyard *(Worthiness of Wales)* reported in 1587:

> *A thing to note when fammon failes in Wye,*
> *(And feafon there: goes out as order is)*
> *Than ftill of course in Ofke doth fammons lye,*
> *And of good fifh in Ofke you shall not mis.*
> *And this feemes ftraunge, as doth through Wales appeare,*
> *In fome one place are fammons all the yeere.*

THE CROSS KEYS INN

Long years ago, on the north side of Bridge Street, Usk, near the bridge, stood an yspitty. The name *yspitty,* so non-euphonious to English ears, is redolent of kindness and generosity to all Welshmen, for it has the same connotation as *hospitality.*

Yes, *yspitty* — the ancient *hospitiam* — gave refreshment, without payment, to the traveller and. his horse. The name is frequently found in association with an old-time trackway, just as in England a similar association concerns *Coldharbour.*

Strangely the Welsh and English rest-house names are found near each other inside Newport borough. I wonder how many of my Liswerry friends connect Yspitty Lane and Coldharbour with rest and refreshment for travellers on a weary journey.

The Cross Keys Inn, Usk.

The yspitty at Usk adjoined the House of Correction, so it seems fair to conjecture, therefore, that the fine old tavern known as the Cross Keys was built on the site of the yspitty and continues (though with payment) its tradition of hospitality. I find a reference to the inn among a list of 14 Usk alehouses compiled in 1856 by James Henry Clark (who became the last Port-reeve of Usk). The Cross Keys was kept then by John Prosser.

The present innkeeper, Mr. Hoffman, showed me first the fireplace in the bar-parlour. Behind the carved oak lintel-front the great lintel-beam, 8ft. 6in. long, survives, although a modern fireplace fills the space beneath. In the recess to the right, unique in my experience, is a smaller fireplace, above which the stonework and some of the bricks are stained brilliant red, as if with oxide of mercury.

To the left of the fireplace, in the thickness of the wall, a flight of oak stairs leads to the first floor, from which baulks of oak form an extension stairway to the attic. The two doorways to the stairs, on the first floor, are of late Elizabethan period and give, as my sketch indicates, an authentic *old-world* character to the inn, emphasised by four windows almost as old.

Elizabethan doorways on the stairs at the Cross Keys Inn.

Like the arrangement in the Horse and Jockey at Llanfihangel-Pontymoile, the bedrooms at the Cross Keys lead off a long corridor. One of the bedrooms contains a decorated ceiling, of which, lying on the bed, I made a rough study. The motifs in the design recall a ceiling at the White Hart inn at Llangibby, although there is, I believe, no dove representation there. Interesting it is to imagine the clever craftsmen who made the plaster ceilings of our bigger houses spending their leisure hours practising their arts in wayside hostelries.

Mine host showed me next the room which caused recently so much interest. "You will note," he said, "that the door is prosaically modern yet, if we latch it at night, it springs open in the early hours, even when there is no draught. Invariably now we leave it open."

In answer to a question, he added, "The children sleep in this room."

Taking note of the tiny diamond mullioned window en route, we climbed to the attic floor, to find many mighty roof-timbers untouched by time.

On the ground floor again we saw ten transverse beams in the front bar and a couple of carved stone corbels on the fireplace wall, the purpose of which is in doubt. At the rear of this room we walked down stone steps (one of which bore a carved design) to the cellar floor which is on a higher level than the original floor.

Decorated ceiling at the Cross Keys Inn..

A strange old window with two iron mullions gives on to this cellar and has aroused the pretty theory that the cellar was a penitential cell, the occupant of which could be observed through the window.

My large drawing shows that two of the chimneys retain their original bases, that the first entrance to the inn was central, under a taller porchway than the present one and that the Cross Keys possesses one of our most monumental mounting blocks.

As I crossed the bridge on my homeward journey, I recalled J. H. Clark's account of the 24-day frost in February, 1855: *a continual frost with occasional snow, the River Usk was frozen over, excepting in two or three places of small extent, where the current was exceedingly rapid, from Llanbaddock church to the Long Bridge on the road to Abergavenny, and hundreds of men and boys amused themselves in sliding and skating on its surface.*

THE THREE SALMONS

When I was six — Beatrice was in reminiscent mood — "my father who, as you know, was a sea-captain, took me in a growler to Usk. Sitting well-cushioned alongside the driver I looked down with pity on the people of Maindee who were not going to Usk. The growler pulled up at the Three Salmons where my father ordered a sumptuous dinner which I remember ended with almonds and muscatels."

Yes, for many travellers memories of Usk centre around The Salmons. *Praised be the habitation of the Salmons in Uske, cries Arthur Machen: thither we all hasten after we have crossed the bridge, for we see the shield from afar, azure, three salmons nayant in pale argent.* There with his company of Silurians he held synod, while the tankards and cans and cups foamed up, and foamed again, and the company silurianised till the flames leapt up through the chimney-top.

Wondrous ale they drank, *so concocted that it smelt like a garden of spices of Arabia.* For their constitution as the Society of Cwrio Dda, headed by the Lord High Tosspot and the Tankard Marshall, how they traced their Benefice of Free Sokage back to Arthur's Round Table, and how that accounts for the number of *houses* in Carleon, I must refer you to Arthur Machen's *chronicles.*

For my purpose today, which is to describe some of the impact of an Usk inn on our county literature, I must include his dictum that if you wish to learn Silurian wisdom

107

you should go to Usk and spend *a few hours and a little money at the Salmons, taking the seat between the fire and the window which looks out on a fair open space.*

The Three Salmons at Usk.

Among the other authors who have recorded sojourns at the Three Salmons I select Percy Thoresby-Jones, who wrote *Welsh Border Country*. He is still remembered at the inn, after twenty years, as the writer who made all his journeys afoot or by bicycle. Indeed, his careful surveys of the ridges of our Black Mountains were made on his bicycle.

To Thoresby-Jones, Usk was the natural jumping-on centre for trips to Caerleon, Abergavenny, Monmouth and Chepstow. He found the old borough of considerable historic interest, but what was more important to the wayfarer was that Usk contained *one of the most comfortable and intelligently conducted hotels in all the border — the veneral Three Salmons.*

In season, he tells us, he was offered fresh Usk trout for breakfast and a choice between Usk salmon and Severn salmon for dinner. The beds were soporific and *if you do — after salmon — remain wakeful you will find a judicious selection of books in your bedroom.*

There was also a paragon of parlour maids named Patricia.

It seems that until salmon fishing became *the thing* the old inn was known as the Golden Cross. This may well have been, for it stands where the Roman roads cross, one facade on Bridge Street, the other on Porthycarne Street. Like all big, solid Silurians, its hands are warm, and some of my pleasant memories are of meals at the Salmons after driving many miles in mid-winter.

Indeed, its reputation for cosy warmth was the reason why for many years the autumn sessions would adjourn to the inn when the court-house was too cold.

Today, with its entrance lounge, two bars, three diningrooms, a TV room, 12 bedrooms, a ballroom and a vast cellar in three compartments (used as an air-raid shelter during the last war), the Three Salmons makes a happy port of call for the traveller, the historian, the artist and especially the angler.

Here I draw my brief survey of Usk to a close, conscious that I have left many of its treasures unrecorded and equally conscious that I am deeply indebted to the warm-hearted folk of the ancient borough who opened their doors to a stranger and spent so many hours educating him in the love of Brynbuga.

Chapter Seven

A JOURNEY FROM USK TO CAERLEON

Visiting the little churches of Llanbadoc, Llangibby, Tredunnock and Llanhennock.

LLANBADOC CHURCH

Motorists sometimes ask, "What is the church with the leaning tower which we see on the bend of the road just south of Usk?" The church is Llanbadoc, but it is not the tower which leans. It is the motorist's car on the cambered road.

Until 1758 the road ran between the church and the river and remains as a pretty pathway. Llanbadoc, which may yet mark the crossing to a by-pass road around Usk, was a place of importance in prehistoric days as shown by the traces of a hill-fortress *(Twyn Bell)* on the high ground behind the church.

St. Madog's Church at Llanbadoc.

The church, dedicated to St. Madog, a 5th-century saint, was restored in 1877 when the north aisle was added. Slim and plain, but quite upright, the tower is original.

When I visited St. Madog's I passed at once from the furious flurry of the main road traffic into a riverside haven of rest. Red hawthorn and chestnuts were in full bloom, the wellingtonias and yews shadowed the pale rose walls and the cedars (planted by Shelley's friend Edward Trelawney) held out long green arms of benediction.

As I walked towards the porch I saw on the right the ivy-clad steps of the ancient cross, out of which a yew tree grows. That ivy should be removed, for the steps may be as old and just as sacred as the church.

Above the outer archway of the porch is an interesting ogee moulding, similar to the decorations at Caldicot and Crickhowell and above the inner archway is a niche which doubtless held once the image of St. Madog, portrayed now in a coloured window.

Down two steps, I entered the nave with its original square font, three arches opening into the aisle and an Early English arch into the chancel, the screen under the latter arch surmounted by figures of Christ, St. Mary and St. John. Screen and figures are modern, as is the reredos, but on each side of the reredos is a tall niche of the same period as the priest's door, the piscina and the arch in the north wall.

A fine chalice is engraved, *1577, the parishe of Llanbaddow. David William John propreters* — officials who appear to have been responsible as "procurators" for the entertainment of the bishop and other visitors.

The tower contains two bells. To find their inscriptions I turned again to Arthur Wright's valuable book, *Church Bells of Monmouthshire*. The first reads, *Soli Deo Detur Gloria, W.I.: R.M.: 1635*, the second, *Walter Morgan: Ambers Williams, church wardens, 1677*.

(It was with sorrow that I read of the death of Arthur Wright, whose work has enriched the lives of many Monmouthshire folk, young and old).

Now a mystery surrounds a church bell of Llanbadoc. The reach of the Usk at the village is named *Bell Pool*. The inn was, until recently, *The Bell Inn* and the hillside fort is *Twyn Bell*. All we know is that a bell from the tower fell into the river and was "miraculously recovered."

I crossed the road from the churchyard and climbed the steep path, pausing at intervals to admire the view downwards. The sun, swinging around behind the hill, gilded the upper portion of the slim tower and lit up some of the branches of the churchyard trees. All else was shadowed and threaded most beautifully by the pale blue river — as fair a sight as any in this fair county of ours.

LLANGIBBY

Fourteen centuries ago, when Gwent was lost in wickedness and poverty, Cybi came over to us from Cornwall. With his monks, he pitched his tent on a field near the Usk — a field which has ever since been known as the Priest's Meadow (Waen y 'ffeirad) — in which a standing stone marks, according to legend, the site of his small encampment.

The heathen King Ethelic and his wild men descended upon Cybi, when suddenly the King's horse fell dead and Ethelic himself was struck blind. Kneeling before Cybi, the King prayed for forgiveness. The dead horse awoke and pranced around the meadow, while the dark curtains arose from the King's eyes.

In deep gratitude and faith, Ethelic gave the holy man a site for a church on land above the river flood-level. On that site the first Llangibby Church was built, and just below stands St. Cybi's well, which supplied the village, until recently, with unlimited supplies of water.

Llangibby.

The church, built on sloping land, consists of porch, nave and chancel. Three steps lead down to the porch, and five from porch to nave. The ancient stone steps up to the rood-loft survive on each side and are lighted by the original small windows. At the west end of the nave is a gallery which now contains the organ.

Llangibby village is always associated with the squires of the castle. Their memorials enrich the walls of the church, from Sir Trevor Williams, who died in 1686, to Lieutenant Addams-Williams, killed in action in 1915. Sir Trevor was the highly complex character who, on the outbreak of the Civil War, used his wealth and influence on the side of the Royalists but soon changed and supported Parliament. After being arrested and allowed out, on bail, he attacked and captured Monmouth and Usk for Cromwell.

Yet, in 1647, we find him in company with his uncle, Sir Nicholas Kemeys of Llanfair Discoed, Mr. Thomas Lewis of St. Pierre and Mr. William Morgan of Pembridge taking part in a successful surprise attack on the Roundheads' headquarters in Monmouthshire — Chepstow Castle. After the recapture of Chepstow, Cromwell, who was in Pembroke, wrote to Colonel Saunders, requesting him at all costs to capture Sir Trevor.

He is a man, wrote Cromwell, *full of craft and subtilty: very bold and resolute: hath a house at Llangibby well stored with arms: his neighbours about him are very malignant and much for him.*

This chequered war-time experience of Sir Trevor Williams had as its sequel a pardon when Charles II came to the throne and the Knight of Llangibby represented his county in parliament from 1667 to 1681.

At the other end of the line, Lieutenant Donald Addams-Williams, of the South Wales Borderers, after being thrice wounded, died while gallantly leading his men into action in the Dardanelles in 1915.

.Facing the main road in Llangibby is a wonderful L-shaped hostelry — the White Hart. A legend, strongly held in the village, expressed the view that the White Hart was a rest-house owned by the Commandery of St. John at Dinmore. I am assured by the St. John authorities that there is no truth in this legend.

My friend, Mr. J. R. Gabriel, points out the irony of the situation when the White Hart — the badge of King Richard II — is the sign of the Llangibby inn, for the Rector of Llangibby was one of those who had most to do with Richard's deposition.

The inn retains much of its original character — I had almost written *many of its original characters* and, indeed, I know no country *house* with more salty habitues! The great beams and fireplaces, the cosy nooks and pretty windows of the ground floor are matched by the plaster decorations of the bedroom ceilings. Up in the great attic, so the genial old village blacksmith informed me, worked for many years three cobblers.

Some years ago, a few of us saved the White Hart from desecration. A great beam from the fireplace had been removed in readiness for the introduction of a modern atrocity. Fortunately, some enlightened directors stepped in at the right moment and saved a 16th-century relic. I hope that the splendid old inn of Llangibby will remain untouched, to recall for us the days when men knew how to build for posterity.

My sketch was drawn in the field to the south, above the village. I had always thought that Llangibby looked at its best at the meet on Boxing Day but, on this July afternoon, when the hamlet lay embosomed in the varied greens and browns of its magnificent trees, when the church tower glowed as if of ivory and the old inn slept so sweetly under its brown roof, when the distant hills rose and dipped gracefully to the horizon — this, I decided, was the ideal time to view one of our most characteristic villages.

TREDUNNOCK

At the hill-top I paused. In the Homestead of Ferns (Tredunnock), I entered the churchyard, saw once again the memorial stone to Julius Julianus of the 2nd Augustan Legion, and then sought out the tomb of Isabella Gill, only child of Sir John Franklin, discoverer of the North West Passage. The inscription, now indecipherable, read:

Far from a much-loved home, from whence she came in quest of recreation and health, here lie the mortal remains of Eleanor Isabella, wife of the Rev. John Philip Gill (incumbent of St. John's, Notting Hill, in the County of Middlesex). In faith and charity and holiness she adorned the doctrine of God our Saviour, and fulfilled her vocation in His Church as a teacher of good things, a trusty councillor in the work of the ministry and a kind and sagacious friend to the sick and needy. As she was the only child, so also did she inherit the character of that brave commander, Sir John Franklin, first discoverer of the North-West Passage, who died on duty 11th June, 1847, within the recesses of the frozen ocean. For the spirit of self-sacrifice was hers, both by nature and by grace, and the contagion of a deadly malady, from which her care had rescued a suffering child, was the means of her translation to eternal rest on the 30th August, 1869, at the age of 36 years.

Tredunnock at twilight enshrines idyllic peace. The birds in the great trees sing their vespers, but all else is still. Colour fades from the sky; the first star gleams. 'On such an evening,' I muse, 'when the world was young, the magician changed the cows into ferns, giving the village its name. Later came the Roman troopers, living their exiled lives, burying their 'beloved dead'. For half a millennium,' I remembered, 'the country-folk of Tredunnock have worshipped in their lovely brown church. Welshmen, Romans, Saxons, Normans, loved this place; all of them are with me in spirit. My dead friends live on in this starlit haven and when they and I are long forgotten, the men of the new, swift-moving ages will come to Tredunnock and in its green shadows drink from the well of peace.'

Tredunnock Church.

Tredunnock possesses a quiet charm which is infinitely restful to a town dweller. The little place seems always at peace, church, well, rhododendron hedges and old houses diffusing an atmosphere of serenity and loveliness.

Tredunnock Church is part of its own landscape, for its red stones were quarried out of the Llanhennock ridge. The tower is probably built on the stock of an old Roman watch-tower, while the church itself dates back some six hundred years. On the north wall of the nave the Rector showed us the famous Roman memorial stone, discovered three feet below the ground near the foundations of the church. The inscription is as follows:
and has been translated thus:

> *To the Gods below.*
> *Julius Julianus, a soldier of the*
> *Second (Augustan) Legion, of*
> *18 years' service and 40*
> *years of age, has been buried*
> *here at the charge of a*
> *beloved wife.*

113

Roman memorial stone at Tredunnock.

The Legion referred to is the Roman force which in A.D. 75 subdued the Usk Valley. On the same wall, a few feet away, is a memorial to two lads who lie *in Flanders fields,* victims to the same lust for world-power which brought the Roman troops to our quiet Gwent vales...

We inspected the font with its inscription and date, 1662; and then emerged into the sunshine of the churchyard, with its fine cross, rhododendron hedge, and lych-gate.

The bridge below Tredunnock was, a hundred years ago, a comparatively busy spot. Here came, overland, the bar-iron manufactured at Trostrey Forge beyond Usk, to be sent down the river to Newport for shipment. But today Newbridge is forsaken by industry, unless that be the quality possessed by the many fishermen who haunt its river banks. The bridge was built by the famous architect of Pont-y-pridd, whose son constructed Newport Bridge.

Newbridge-on-Usk.

LLANHENNOCK AND THE HOUSE WITH THE WOODEN LEG

There were two roads in the old days from Caerleon to Usk. The more picturesque followed the river from Ultra Pontem, past Bulmoor, under Kemeys Craigs, to Llantrissent, Llanllowell and Usk.

From Caerleon itself the "main road" crossed the Afon Llwyd upstream from *Pont Satwrn,* climbed the hill as a hollow way to the south of Penrhos (where once stood a Roman villa), dipped into the valley of the Soar Brook past *Miss Arthur's Cottage* and then, still as a hollow way, climbed the hill to the right of the present road to Llanhennock, continuing thence to Toll Bar.

Travellers along the present roads mistake the old road for a hedge. But if they will look under the hedge they will see the hollow track, much of it dry in the wettest winter, much of it 6ft. below the field levels. Maybe they will try to imagine, as I do, what happened when two vehicles met on such a road.

The house with the wooden leg, Llanhennock.

Llanhennock, once a village on the main Usk road, is now a pretty but decaying relic. It is sad to see neglect robbing us of one of our most charming hilltop hamlets.

Henog, one of our 5th-century Saints, may have loved this upland retreat, and good men throughout the years have sought its peace when *the world has been too much with them.*

Llanhennock has character. For a small village, it possesses remarkable powers of attraction. Hence it is that motorists making for Usk find their cars suddenly diverted uphill to the right. Hence it is that hikers seeking Glenusk climb the steep pitch for the sheer pleasure of seeing the old school, the *house with the wooden leg*, the grey church and then taking the field walk past the ruined oak, as ancient as the church.

See Llanhennock in winter, when the sun shines on the rounded snow-clad fields and when the river-valley viewed from the churchyard seems filled with the white beauty of holiness. Visit it in high summer, when the garden of the village inn is gay with frilled marguerites and the old-fashioned sweet peas.

Gather your blackberries here in September and your coral-coloured spindleberries in October. Best of all, choose your evening with care around harvest time and watch the sunset change from flame and scarlet to gold, while Mynydd Maen glows a royal purple. Then, from the churchyard (where a famous Newport rugby forward sleeps), see the moon rise in silver majesty over Wentwood.

As my sketch shows, the *House with the Wooden Leg* is, for these parts of the country, unique in design. The vane and the handsome chimneys, the decorated barge-boards, the slated upper walls, the pretty windows, the *leg* and wooden frame at the entrance and the coach-house at the west end present a picture at once attractive and melancholy.

Attractive undoubtedly is the old hostelry — for this was once the famous *Mackworth Arms,* in coaching days the only "pull-in" between the *White Hart* at Llangibby and Caerleon — but there are ominous signs that unless repairs are carried out immediately the effect of the hilltop weather on the fabric will be serious.

In my view, and in view of one who has travelled the world, the Llanhennock *House with the Wooden Leg* should be regarded as one of our treasured relics, scheduled as an ancient house and saved for posterity.

Similar remarks apply with equal force to the delightful old village school opposite. The timber of the bell-turret is rapidly disintegrating. I was glad to learn that the bell is preserved in the church.

Some of the windows were blocked up long ago to evade the window-tax but it is quite evident that the ancient school was modelled on the lines of the more ancient inn.

When I was invited to see the interior, imagine my pleasure at the sight of another *wooden leg,* this time a post less than 6ft. in height supporting a great beam in the ceiling of the livingroom and bearing notches cut to record the annual growth of the children.

Nothing is left to indicate which of the rooms was used for a schoolroom and no school has been held there within living memory.

If these charming old buildings were situated in the home counties they would be cherished as they deserve. May I repeat the hope that the appropriate authority will step in during this Coronation year and preserve the Llanhennock inn and school?

Before leaving the village I strolled into the churchyard. Near the entrance is buried Gladys Corner, whom her parents knew and loved for one brief year. She died in 1885, but their faith shines through their grief as brightly now as then:

> *She is not dead,*
> *the child of our affection*
> *But gone into that school where*
> *She no longer needs our poor protection*
> *And Christ Himself doth rule.*

CAERYDER OAK AT LLANHENNOCK

I have written previously of the great oaks of Monmouthshire. Records exist of the Golynos giant, 9ft. in diameter, yielding 2,426 cu. ft., which was felled in 1810; within memory a *Foresters' oak* in Wentwood burned for a week before it was finally consumed.

The noble oak at Llanfair Grange, Colonel Harry Llewellyn's home, is still hale and heart-sound. To these I add with delight the magnificent old veteran of Llanhennock — the Caeryder oak — once the greatest in the county. In 1876 the spread of its branches was 126ft., its height was 70ft. and the circumference of its trunk one foot from the ground was 38½ft.

Between storms, I went up to Llanhennock to take the measurements of the Caeryder oak.

The Caeryder Oak, Llanhennock.

Near Pencrug I met the lady of Woodbank, who insisted on taking a hand in the survey and who was not perturbed when we found that between the stile and the oak was a *bogulated quagmire* holding scores of little pools made by the hoofs of a dozen Guernsey cows who had sought the company of the oak. My companion tripped lightly over the slough; I wallowed in her wake.

Holding the 12-yard tape a foot above the ground, we found, after a double check, that the distance around the "knees" of the oak is now 48ft. Taking into account probable erosion, I find such growth amazing.

Back on the road, we watched while the low afternoon sun floodlit the ancient tree against the indigo of the clouds. Every crevice, every crack in the mighty structure was lined with moss which clothed trunk and branches in a brilliant acid green while the shadows held purple and brown. One enormous scar marked the breaking away, two years ago, of one of the biggest branches.

While the oak is known generally as the Caeryder oak, I had heard it named also the *Coronation* oak. This was explained when Colonel Dean showed me at Glenusk a coloured print showing the celebrations held under the oak in 1837, when Victoria ascended the throne. Following a clue, I called at Lynton Cottage above Llanhennock where Mrs. Edris Davies showed me the original drawing, obviously the work of a master.

On a chair near the trunk sits a harpist, in bardic robes, who may have come from Llanover. The men, several of them waving their hats, are dressed in tight-frocked "two-button" coats, but they are merely a foil to the graceful women, each wearing a "Dolly Vardon" hat, shawl, bodice and long skirt.

At the left is a shelter decorated with ferns and surmounted by two poles bearing garlands and flags; the table within suggests that this may have been the 'bar'.

I have sketched a few of the figures, but my drawing gives only a slight idea of the original, with its canopy of foliage, its air of restrained gaiety and the beauty of the surroundings, Penycaemawr rising in hazy distance.

The countryfolk tell me that their tree is giving them cause for anxiety, that it is becoming *shaky at the knees.* Those knees appeared stalwart enough when we measured them and I fancy that the Caeryder oak, which was probably a stout sapling when the first Elizabeth came to the throne, will last for many years of the present reign.

From the great oak I crossed the road to Pencrug — once the imposing home of an important family but now robbed of its character — and to Little Pencrug, perched at the top of the green crag, with thrilling views up and down the Usk valley.

How Arthur Machen would have thrilled to that view, for on that afternoon Usk brimmed with flood-water and was indeed, in his words, *tawny as the Tiber.*

It was here also that I was shown a little walled garden, white with hundreds of snowdrops; I place them with the Beechwood crocuses among the fairest February sights in Gwent.

Coronation celebrations under the Caeryder Oak, 1837.

Footnote: Exiled long ago from Crumlin to Oswaldtwistle, Mr. J. M. Day asks: "How did the leek come to be the emblem of Wales?" On March 1, 693, according to legend, the Saxons attacked the Britons, disguising themselves in the British dress, whereupon King Cadwallon gave a leek to each of his men — *a trophy bright and green* — and this enabled them to distinguish friend from foe.

Chapter Eight

CAERLEON, THE CITY OF LEGEND
AND HISTORY

Caerleon, city of history, city of legend . . . What pageantry it has seen. What piety has it known. What paganism put to flight. So old it is that even the 11th-century Norman tower of St. Cadoc's is a relatively modern upstart on the historic landscape.

But let us go back to the beginning — to the beginning of recorded history that is. For who knows how many unwritten chapters preceded even the coming of the Emperor Claudius and his Roman legionaries. That, according to Tacitus, the Roman historian, was between AD 50 and AD 75, a hundred or so years after Caesar's reconaissance visits to Britain in BC 55 and 54.

At first the Second Augustan Legion (Legio II Augusta) had their work cut out to subdue the wild and warlike Celts of South Wales — Silures, the Romans called them.

But, when the worst of the fighting was over, the invaders set about making themselves at home. They built themselves comfortable, centrally heated barracks, equipped them with baths, added an arena for their sporting events and rounded off the work with a basilica or temple in which to worship their gods. It is now established beyond reasonable doubt that the site for that temple was the spot where St. Cadoc's stands today.

Here, then, in their togas, came the warriors of Rome. Theirs was not the worship of one god but of many, as is proved by the numerous altars that have been found at Caerleon. Among these were Jupiter Dolichenus, originally a Semitic thunder-god, often shown in Roman sculpture standing on a bull, dressed in a suit of mail and holding a double axe and a thunderbolt.

Bonus Eventus and Fortuna, gods of good luck, were also popular and doubtless they were the recipients of as many prayers as the promoters of the modern football pools. Another special favourite was the sun-god Mithras, whom the Romans had taken over from the Persians. He was a warlike creature to whose cult no woman was admitted. Then there was Diana, or Artemis, goddess of the moon and goddess of fertility, in whose name were many ritualistic orgies carried out at Caerleon.

Meantime, long before the Romans left Britain, in the 5th century and long before the hordes of Saxons and Jutes and Norsemen reached our shores, Christianity came to Caerleon. Legend has it that it came with Joseph of Arimathea, who is said to have founded a university in Caerleon, the *Academia Legionensis*. The same legend says that Joseph brought with him the chalice used for wine by Christ at the Last Supper and that in it Joseph had caught some of Christ's blood as He died upon the Cross.

Out of this early story grew the legends of the Holy Grail, the miraculous vessel which inspired the poets of the Mabinogian and played so important a part in the mediaeval tales of chivalry centring around King Arthur.

But, leaving legend on one side for a moment, we find in the Book of Llandaff a record that in AD 156 Lleurwg, King of the Britons, sent letters to Eleutherius the Pope asking that he and his people might be received into the Christian Church. Whereupon the Pope ordained Elfan, one of Lleurwg's ambassadors, a bishop and sent him back to Wales with two missionaries, Fagan (who founded St. Fagan's) and Dyfan (founder of Merthyr Dyfan). On their return, they christianised Britain, making Caerleon the metropolitan See of Wales and Lleurwg built the Cathedral at Llandaff, of which Elfan was the first bishop.

A few years later, in AD 185, according to Matthew of Westminster, the church of Caerleon was made the third Archiepiscopal See in Britain, the archbishop having authority over all the country west of the Severn.

The Roman garrison at Caerleon continued to worship their own gods, but it was obvious that their cults were losing ground before the onslaught of Christianity. In AD 303 the Emperor Diocletian, becoming suddenly aware of this situation, ordered the wholesale massacre of Christians.

Among those martyred were Saints Julius and Aaron, two citizens of Caerleon, *who, according to the 7th-century historian Gildas, when they had endured sundry torments and their limbs had been torn after an unheard-of manner, yielded their souls up, to enjoy in the heavenly city a reward for the sufferings which they had passed through.*

The two martyrs were later canonised and churches erected over the spots where they suffered for their faith: St. Aaron's, to which was attached an order of canons was at the camp of Penrhos, half a mile north of Caerleon, while St. Julius's (corrupted to St. Julian's), where there was a choir of nuns, was situated near old St. Julian's House, home of Sir William Herbert of Cherbury. The two saints are commemorated in the stained glass east window in the chancel of St. Cadoc's.

Before the close of the 4th century, or at all events early in the 5th, the Roman Legionaries, who for so many years had brought animation and prosperity to Caerleon, were recalled to defend a crumbling Roman Empire.

Caius and Baebius and Flavius were heard whistling about the streets no more, the shouts of gladiators died away in the amphitheatre and the temple of Diana in time became used for Christian worship.

Then, in the 5th century, a Caerleon priest named Morgan, more widely known as Pelgaius, caused a stir throughout Christendom by declaring that man was a creature endowed with free will, that the doctrine of original sin was therefore complete nonsense and the State of Grace a further anomaly.

The Pelagian heresy caused a big split in the Church and was the occasion for convening the Councils of Jerusalem and Carthage and gave rise to a prolonged spate of religious polemics.

It was not long after this that King Arthur held sway at Caerleon. Arthur, Gwenhwyvar, Lancelot, Elaine, Peredur, Merlin, Viviane. What wondrous tales of chivalry the very names conjure up.

What a tremendous hold they have had upon the imagination of poets and story-tellers and musicians ever since. The Mabinogian, Malory's *Morte d'Arthur,* Tennyson's *Idylls of the King,* Wagner's *Parsifal* and his *Tristan* all owe their origin to Arthur's Court at Caerleon.

But, of all the literature which that period inspired, nothing has ever quite equalled the marvellous cycle of mediaeval poems composed by the French troubadours when they came to Britain at the time of the Conquest.

The nostalgic romanticism of the Celts whom they had conquered swept over Europe, and lords and ladies in their chateaux along the Loire and the Rhine liked nothing better than to hear how.

> *A Pasque por sa cort tenir*
> *A Carlion con maintenir*
> *Volt le rois la costume lors*

At Easter the king came to the same place in Caerleon to hold his court, according to the custom of those times.

One of the features of Arthur's Court was its insistence on piety, and the knights, splendid in armour, together with their ladies — some with long tresses yellow as the sun, others with locks as black as the raven and complexions *like crimson blood upon the snow* — must have come regularly to worship at St. Cadoc's.

The old Welsh Triads say that St. Cadoc was one of Arthur's *three wisest counsellors* and one of the three keepers of the Holy Grail. Another tradition says the Holy Grail was kept at the Abbey of Llantarnam, two miles away. There is a connection between Llantarnam and Caerleon, though it comes much later than the Arthurian era.

Early in the 12th century Howel's son Iorwerth sought to establish a Cistercian community at Caerleon, and caused an abbot and 12 monks to come from Strata Florida to found a priory there. When they arrived, however, they evidently discovered Caerleon was more urbane than they had been given to understand — for by the terms of their order the Cistercians are a farming community. So, after a very brief stay within the city walls, they moved to Llantarnam. From 1189 their monastery was officially known as the Convent of St. Mary's, Caerleon and it was not until the 14th century that it was described as the Abbey of Llantarnam.

Did the monks take the Holy Grail with them to Llantarnam? When the Dissolution of the Monasteries took place in 1536 and they had to flee back to their original Priory at Caerleon, it was not among their treasures, nor was their precious manuscript, the *San Graal,* any longer in their possession.

Some say the *San Graal,* after incredible adventures all over the world, found its way to the home of the Powells of Nanteos, near Aberystwyth, not far from the Monastery of Strata Florida. Here it was called the Cwpan Nanteos and it was known to be in existence up to a year or two ago, still, so they say, retaining its miraculous qualities, still a source of mystic healing power . . .

The upheavals of the Middle Ages did not spare Caerleon. The castle was frequently contested and some horrible deeds were done by those who laid claim to it. Sir Howel ap Iorwerth put out the eyes of the rightful Lord, his uncle Owen ap Owen Wan, and mutilated him. Yet this same Sir Howel founded the Abbey of Llantarnam and his crest, a castle triple towered, has been incorporated into the arms of the Council.

Already in 1235 the castle, burned down by Morgan ap Howel, was *utterly ruinated.* Whether St. Cadoc's came unscathed through that particular disaster we do not know, but it almost certainly underwent trial by fire at the hands of Owain Glyndwr, for the 15th-century arcading suggests that the church was restored after his passing.

In Tudor and Stuart days the Lordship of Caerleon had come into the Herbert family, who owned not only land but also *the waifs, estrays, felons' goods, treasure trove, wreck and deodands within this manor.*

Although Lord Herbert of Cherbury, Lord of Caerleon in the reign of Charles I, declared himself on the side of Parliament, *Carline* was Royalist.

Many a man of St. Cadoc's must have taken part in the victory which was wrested from the Roundheads in the streets of the city on January 25, 1646 and many a terrified woman, no doubt, looked on from an upstairs window.

One parishioner at least who is buried in St. Cadoc's could have witnessed this battle when he was a tiny child — Thomas Morgan, of Penrhos, whose epitaph is a Welsh acrostic of his name:

TREFNUS A	MWUN
HARDH	OSTWNGEDIG
OEDTH	RODGH
MEWN	GADEDIGI
AARFAN	ARGHONDH
SWUDHOG	NEFOL

(Orderly and elegant was he in arms, a gentle, humble officer; the kindly gift of the Lord of Heaven).

Two years before this, Thomas Morgan died; in 1672 his brother Edmund fought a duel with a relative of theirs, Charles Williams of the Castle. Edmund was killed and Charles fled to Smyrna where he made a huge fortune. The deed evidently weighed on his conscience, for when he died he left £4,000 to found a school and £3,000 for the repair and adornment of the church and roads.

That fund still fructifies and the donor is commemorated in a beautiful series of stained glass windows in the austere modern beauty of the Lady Chapel and in the magnificent rhodium altar ornaments. But Charles Williams does not lie in his native Caerleon; his bones are interred in Westminster Abbey.

It is, of course, impossible to see much of Caerleon in one short visit, but three hours on a warm July evening were packed with interest.

The Roman amphitheatre at Caerleon.

Standing on the north bank of the amphitheatre, we tried to set its stage in place and time. It was built just outside the defensive ditch which surrounded the legionary fortress and completed circa AD 80. From our standpoint on the bank we examined the skyline: Christchurch, eight centuries old and St. Albans, built on the traditional site of a martyr of Roman Caerleon, lay to the south. Northwards loomed Belinstock, now Lodge Camp and I imagined Tom o' the Lodge commenting in his deep Silurian voice, "The ancient amphitheatre! My dear fellow, my trenches and tumuli swing back in time probably as far before the Romans as we are ahead of them."

(I believe that excavation will prove Lodge Camp to be of about that period. The habit of naming every hilltop camp as of the Iron Age cannot be justified and my own view is that Lodge Camp and Llanmelin were the prehistoric hilltop precursors of those *cities of the plain,* Caerleon and Caerwent).

Grey-blue to the left arose Twyn Barlwm, mocking the stripling Norman Christchurch and middle-aged amphitheatre and so, realising that the Roman invaders had come to an old old land, we proceeded to examine the hollow where the Romans used to make holiday.

This hollow is an oval. The major axis, 1,864 feet long, runs roughly north-north-west and the minor axis is 136 feet long. A wall 12 feet high surrounded the arena, while the outer wall rose 32 feet.

A drain, into which the gutter surrounding the arena discharged, ran under the arena joining the chief entrances and then continued to the river.

The six other entrances led to the seats and were also vaulted over their outer halves. Of these six, those at the ends of the minor axis of the main oval retain the most interest. In each of these entrances, at the bases of the steps, a small apartment was erected opening on to the steps and the arena. Over the vaulted roofs of these rooms were the seats of the VIPs of those days, reached by special stairs.

The erection of the amphitheatre was allocated to the companies of the Legion. When each task was completed, a record was cut in a stone which formed part of the unit's work. Four of these inscribed stones were laid bare during the excavation of 1926, but weathering has destroyed two of the inscriptions. North of the main western entrance you may still read on a pink stone the remains of the record of the tenth cohort and to the south of the same entrance, on a stone which has been replaced in an inverted position, what is left of the record of *the century of Sadius Tiro.*

Next year's excavations on the adjoining racecourse will add much to our picture of Roman Caerleon. Maybe we shall have to think of the amphitheatre not merely as a holiday centre *without the city walls* but also in its position amidst a later and vast suburb extending far down the Usk Valley.

And let us not think too hardly of the task of our Roman invaders. Bloody combats between men and men, or men and animals, martyrdoms and the rest which formed some of the attractions at the amphitheatre, were mild in comparison with the bloodbaths of our own century.

Leaving the amphitheatre, we spent a fascinating hour in the legionary museum, now so well-arranged that it was possible to examine in comfort the priceless relics and to understand their significance with the aid of the excellently printed labels.

How I envy the newcomers to Gwent who are seeing our treasures for the first time!

The church of St. Cadoc, Caerleon.

ST. CADOC'S CHURCH

Standing before the lovely Bethlehem in the south aisle of Caerleon church I allowed my fancy to take rein. I saw Jerusalem in enemy occupation when the Babe was born.

Precursors of the Roman troops there had journeyed half a century before to our land. Their grandsons may have been among the Second Legion who fought their way later to Siluria and founded Caerleon, building their headquarters on the ground where St. Cadoc's church now stands.

Some five centuries later a babe was born, possibly at Caerleon, to the pagan Welsh chieftain Gwynllyw and his saintly wife Gwladys. This babe, Cadoc, grew into holiness, won his father for Christianity, built a monastery and became in those dark days a beacon-light shining for his Master.

Is it too much to conjecture that in the old Roman city the faith which had inspired the Caerleon martyrs, Julius and Aaron, was kept alive throughout the five centuries? We have chronicles recording an archbishopric there and I am prepared to agree that on this same spot worshippers heard the voices of St. Teilo, St. David and St. Cadoc.

Five centuries more and the Normans arrived. They travelled along the old roads, pausing at strategic points to set up their mottes, to lay out their baileys. Sometimes they used old mounds, as at Caerleon and as soon as they were certain of their conquests, they raised churches.

A casual observer, visiting Christchurch, the cathedral and Caerleon might conclude that the churches were originally built in that order. There is, however, one relic preserved in the fabric of St. Cadoc's which tends to show that the Normans tried their *prentice hands* there first.

124

Original Norman arches in St. Cadoc's; early English arch inserted.

This relic is to be seen in the lower portion of the tower-wall facing the nave and is without doubt one of the arches of the first nave arcade. Roughly semi-circular, resting on stout square piers, it rises in line with the present arcade, while the pointed arch within it corresponds to the entrance-arch into the tower.

The smaller arch above is a mystery; it could not have been, as suggested, part of a triforium. Near the modern font at the west end of the south aisle is a most venerable font. Octagonal above, cylindrical below, of crude workmanship and unusual porportions, it is possibly the oldest relic in the church.

The first Norman church, then, was built in the early 12th century. It was rebuilt about four centuries later as the impressive perpendicular nave arches testify. A further rebuilding in 1867 saw the retention of the nave arcade and tower, while in this century the chancel has been lengthened and a Lady Chapel added to the south aisle.

It is interesting to compare the towers of Caerleon and Christchurch. At Caerleon the corbel-table is surmounted by a battlemented parapet, whereas at Christchurch the parapet has no battlements.

The square-headed upper lights of the tower suggest a later date than the lancets below, yet, as my sketch indicates, the relieving arch above one of the lancets shows that a square-headed light originally existed there.

Two items of the church repay close examination. The perpendicular arches recall the grace and beauty which we used to associate with the nave arcade at Christchurch while every pier, base and capital contributes to the feeling not only of unity, but of aspiration.

The second item renders St. Cadoc's unique in this county.

When Charles Williams, native of Caerleon, died, aged 87, he left a part of his vast fortune to the church at Caerleon *for mending and adorning the inside*. At the rebuilding a century ago the legacy was drawn upon to replace the old windows with stained glass which should depict the life of Christ from the Annunciation to the Resurrection.

And in 1953, as if applying the Christ-story to Caerleon, the lights of the east window were filled with portrayals of St. Cadoc, St. Julius, St. Aaron and St. Gwynllyw, with the risen Christ in the centre. I note that St. Cadoc's martyrdom is shown carried out by Saxon horsemen, while a Roman swordsman kills St. Julius and St. Aaron is being led to his execution.

In addition, the window above the primitive font is an appropriately beautiful tribute to a lady of Caerleon who devoted her leisure to exquisite needlework some of which adorns St. Cadoc's church.

It is pleasant to report that the devotion of Elizabeth Williams to her church is being continued in the lives of her successors. St. Cadoc's reflects the loving care of its parishioners.

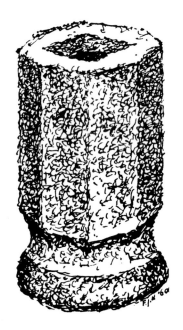

Primitive font in St. Cadoc's Church.

THE PRIORY

The narrow old road now named Bridge Street but once Heol-y-Coyty separates The Bull from a massive house, the facade of which is pierced by suspect Tudor windows and a stone porch. This house retains traces of the original Caerleon Priory.

Historians have boggled over this priory. Well they might. The *Abbey of Karlyon* was Llantarnam Abbey and that alone has caused packets of confusion. In addition, we read of Cistercian monks from the community at Strata Florida setting up their house here in the 12th century — a house valued at £18 8s. 4d. in the *taxation* of Pope Nicholas. It seems that credit for its foundation should go to Hywel ap Iorwerth, who later founded the monastery at Llantarnam.

Caerleon Priory — the garden facade.

At the same time we should recall The Bull addressed by Pope Honorius the Second to Urban, Bishop of Llandaff:

Honorius the Bishop, Servant of the servants of God, unto Our venerable brother Urban, Bishop of Llandaff, greeting and apolistic benediction. Winebald de Baelun has arranged to give the land of Caerleon to the monks of Montaign (Benedictines) for the good of his soul; and therefore we commend your fraternity to grant that land to the aforesaid monks, saving the rights of your Church. Given at the Lateran on the 16th of the Kalends of July, 1128.

Winebald de Baelun was one of the Norman conquerors of Gwent and was founder of the Cluniac *cell* at Malpas — another *alien* establishment.

There should be records of Caerleon Priory, but so far we have no list of priors, no accounts except in the one *taxation*. Monks were there in the 12th century and Mr. J. R. Gabriel (whose authority as the historian of Caerleon is unchallenged) tells us that at the time of the Dissolution the few remaining monks met the Commissioners in this house.

From 1450 onwards the owners of the Priory were the Morgans of Plas Machen, of Langstone and Pencoed and later of Penllyn Sarph and Plas Bedwellty. For the Plas Machen family this was their town house because, even as late as 1480, for instance, Caerleon was the *town* and Newport its *outport*.

Archdeacon Coxe, writing in 1800, shows in his plan of Caerleon the Amphitheatre in the *Round Table Field,* separated from *Miss Morgan's Lawn* by the Roman Wall.

He quotes Tanner in ascribing the *Terra de Cairlion* of Winebald de Baelun to the ground on which Malpas cell was raised. He records that the Roman wall on the south-west side is parallel to the Usk *and skirts the lawn of the abbey, now Miss Morgan's house, where part has been rebuilt with the Roman facings and part remains in its original state.*

That is taken to imply that the *abbey* — our Priory — was refaced on the Bridge Street front with stones from the Roman wall. The arch in the Roman wall, so often referred to as a Roman arch, was raised at the same time. I ought to point out that Coxe's description might have referred to the wall and ties discovered at Caerleon. Coxe notes *have been removed. The only specimen now remaining are a few coins in the possession of Miss Morgan which, on account of her absence, I could not inspect.* Those may have included the coins which, 162 years later, I did inspect.

Strange it is to read that the archdeacon had talked to *Pritchet the shoemaker* on an earlier visit to Caerleon. Master Pritchet, who had discovered and disposed of many coins and rings, was 85 when he died in 1798 and so had lived during the reign of Queen Anne!

Among the many noteworthy people who lived at the Priory was Mr. John Edward Lee. Historian and artist — his *drawing on stone* adorned many of the publications of the Monmouthshire and Caerleon Antiquarian Association.

Mr. Lee, of the Priory, with his friends Octavius Morgan, Thomas Wakeman and, later, Mr. and Mrs. F. J. Mitchell, was responsible for the remarkable upsurge of interest in local history in this country from about 1860 onwards.

Lee had been a geologist before settling in Caerleon. Life at the Priory had given him a powerful new interest. I can imagine the thrill he felt when he discovered in the roof of his ancient house the letter which read:

Captain Thomas Morgan — You are to remain with the Train Band under your command in the town of Chepstow, to secure the said town and not to permit any of the firearms to go out of the said town. Also, of the four pieces of ordnance which are there, you are to dispose of two of them for the defence of the town of Monmouth; and for so doing this shall be your warrant.

Dated at Ragland the 28th day of March, 1643.   *Ed Herbert*

As author of the Catalogue of Caerleon Museum, Lee had applied his keen mind to the translation of some baffling Latin inscriptions. One tablet, displaying above the inscription two imperfect figures representing *Fortunae et Bono Evento,* had been taken as a sepulchral memorial by their wives to *Castus et Julius Belisimnus.*

Mr. Lee's comment is delicious: *I never can believe that two Roman-British ladies would have erected a monument to fortune and good luck on the death of their husbands.*

My drawing shows the garden facade of the Priory. On the gable to the left is seen an early Tudor window, reset at some *restoration*. The small sketch is of the cap stone over the entrance gable. On the right is a flower, the stem of which is held apparently by a hand; the face on the right comically resembles Mr. Charles Chaplin (or Napoleon), but I was unable to interpret the remaining portrayals.

Imagination boggles at the thought of this handful of holy men holding up the banner of their meek and gentle Master amid the ruins of the Roman city, while fierce Welshmen and powerful Normans struggled for the *lordship*.

But it is only imagination that we can use. We have no records. A lively young student suggests that there must be references in the Vatican library. History graduates seeking a title for a thesis, please note. My reference to the *Bull* of Pope Honorius the Second was obtained from the *Book of Llandaff* — not from the Vatican!

I come now to a consideration of the Priory house, home for so many years of Miss Ethel Radcliffe. It must not be taken as disparagement of this beloved and bountiful lady of Caerleon, from whom every good cause at some time benefited, when I record that the new owners have effected within the house changes in layout and colour which have substituted for Victorian dignity and sombreness a sprightly and luminous new look.

Some of my readers will raise their hands in horror. "How can you justify such treatment in an ancient house?" they will cry.

During this last decade I have admired the way in which young wives have introduced light and colour into their houses, new or old. From Mrs. Harry Llewellyn at Llanfair Grange to the latest bride in her 1962 sun-lounge the accent has been on brightness and pure colour. And the psychological effect on husbands, I am informed, is noteworthy!

Mr. and Mrs. Terence Williams took their courage in four hands. They wanted space. The Priory gave them space. They brought to that space the blithe outlook of the young decorators who find virtue in luminosity.

So it was that as we took coffee in the one-time kitchen the sunshine without over *Miss Morgan's lawn* was echoed by the brightness of the big rebuilt room. Difficult it is to give a simple account of the plan of the Priory. On the first floor, for instance, are 12 bedrooms, three bathrooms, two dressingrooms, a boudoir and a room which will become the library.

These rooms, like the rooms on the ground floor, are massed around the most enchanting courtyard, known, for some abstruse reason, as the *Nun's Walk*. Entering the Priory through the porch, with its stone seats occupied by lion and unicorn doorstops, I was thence led under groined ceilings along passages which edged this courtyard. Through delightful windows five or six centuries old I caught glimpses of this lovely retreat, surely the most impressive and evocative survival in the Priory.

I spent a charmed hour in the *Nun's Walk*. The name has the whimsical touch I should associate with John Edward Lee, who would have revelled in the comment made last week by a dear lady — "Of course they must have had special ladies' days when the monks of Caerleon invited the nuns of Usk, those glamorous 'virgins of noble birth'!"

Forget that. In utter silence I stood with the old red sandstone walls rising like cliffs, pierced here and there by windows of several periods, each with its simple, double or triple dripstone.

All the windows had been filled with varied leaded lights and those on the ground floor contained fascinating painted panes portraying many of the Caesars, each with its accompanying quaint verse.

Vespian was treated thus:

> *When Rome with sword and famine was opprest,*
> *This Caesar came to bring them joy and rest,*
> *The father of his cuntrey he was namde,*
> *For piety and virtue both enfamde,*
> *Great honours to his Cittey this man gave,*
> *For which a tombe he had and peacefull grave.*

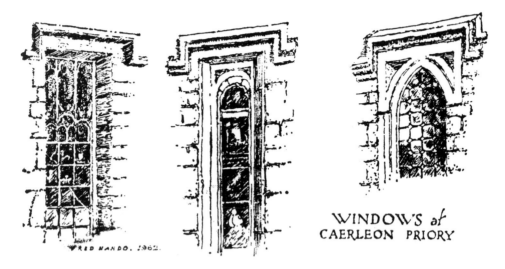

WINDOWS of
CAERLEON PRIORY

FRED HANDO. 1962.

Overlooking the "Nuns' Walk".

My sketches show three of the windows but give nought of the quiet peace which broods over the courtyard. It was difficult to realise that an arterial road to the north bearing its incessant traffic lay not twenty yards distant.

I have space to refer to but three of the remaining rooms. In the diningroom a delightful frieze rang a bell in my memory. Here were the Tudor rose and Arragon pineapples which we know in our Newport *Murenger's House* — a pretty tribute to Henry VIII and his Spanish wife.

The famous Flemish mantelpiece has been retained in the drawingroom. That will attract all eyes, but Mr. Williams and I were drawn downwards to a fireback hiding in the shadows. We made out the inscription:

M

H   M

1761

which by a piece of swift research on the part of my host proved to be the initials of Henry Morgan, Clerk of the Peace, and his wife. The beautiful oak room, with its panelling brought in 1622 from Homerton, has two windows of absorbing interest.

One, Jacobean (J.R. 1622) has rich curtains embroidered C.R. 1630; the other, matching it in colour and design, is the coronation window of 1952. Both repay careful and detailed inspection.

Graceful and light, the staircase of the Priory rises beneath an unusual but attractive segmental ceiling. On the wall, to my delight, hangs the portrait of Miss Radcliffe by Margaret Lindsay-Williams. Freed from the inhibitions of royal portraiture, our gifted artist has revelled in the exquisite beauty of her sitter, flooding figure and background with a silvery light and a subtle range of colours which render the canvas truly radiant.

THE BULL INN

The jolly old face of *The Bull,* with its six eyes and three horns, greets you as you journey from the bridge through Caerleon. Cocked quizzically, delightfully, the upper left-hand eyebrow seems to quip, "What's your hurry? Call in and see us!" The Bull's mouth is around the corner beyond the left-hand horn.

The Bull Inn stripped of its plaster in 1925.

It was not always thus. During the reconstruction of 1925 the removal of the plaster revealed some of the original door and window openings. My sketch, made at that time, shows the positions of these openings and also the line of the old porch-roof on the Cross Street front, together with the Bridge Street openings. There, too, was evidence that the good door to the right of the present inn replaced a further entrance.

During that reconstruction I climbed through a trap opening in the upper sittingroom ceiling. Stepping on the rafters I came to a shaft, about 3ft. 6in. square, which seemed to be almost full of rubbish. In those days I knew nought about such shafts and was pleased to find fragments of pottery. My readers will know that this vertical shaft was part of the equipment of early sanitation.

Under a floor near the shaft we discovered a newspaper dated 1847 and an almost complete pottery bowl, beautifully decorated, obviously hidden there by an unfortunate domestic who had broken it.

The reconstruction of the inn was followed by an attempt at a "new look." To my horror, vertical and horizontal boards were fixed on the exterior to give the appearance of a half-timbered house. Those boards, though creamed over, survive. They do not appear in my sketch. I plead that such a ridiculous travesty may be removed.

The Bull is entered from Bridge Street, which leads down to the Roman bridgehead near the Hanbury Arms. This ancient street was in 1574 known as Heol-y-Coyty — a name which suggests that it led to a wood containing a house. By the way, a street now named Backhall Street, reached via Cross Street, was of old Black Hall Street.

How did the Bull get its name? We know that it was owned by one of the Morgans (of Pencoed) in 1525 and in her excellent book on Monmouthshire, Olive Phillips reminds us that among the coats-of-arms of the Morgans we find the bull's head arms

131

The Bull Inn, Caerleon.

of Bledri, their remote ancestor. This seems a more acceptable explanation than the theory that Bull Inn was a cryptic way of naming a tavern after Anne Boleyn (Bullen), the beauteous but unfortunate wife of Henry VIII.

When his house closed on a recent afternoon the kindly innkeeper, instead of taking his well-earned rest, showed me around the various rooms. As I remembered it, the old hostelry was a typical country pub, ready but somewhat rough and drab. In the process of modernisation the main bar, facing Cross Street and extending along the whole facade, has become a spacious and comfortable place, retaining much character.

To the left, behind the Bridge Street front, I was ushered into three *retreats* — very pleasant reminders of the monks who dwelt in the Priory across the way. I was glad to see that the ancient arch and corbel in one of the walls had survived.

Upstairs, behind the priceless early 16th century windows, window seats and original beams (some resting over windows) gave an authentic old-world atmosphere. The central bedroom was separated on the one side by a partition and on the other by a stone wall on which the Medusa head has been allowed to remain. I knew that head in 1925. Behind the *cocked-eye* window the room has a floor parallel to the dripstone of the window, indicating that a beam-subsidence affected wall and floor.

In their pretty upper lounge I asked Mr. and Mrs. Thain to indicate the trapdoor which I had used so long ago. When I saw it I was (a) pleasantly reminiscent of my former slim figure, and (b) content to rest on memories.

"Our son found your shaft," I was told. "It had been cleaned out and he was able to descend a considerable distance with the aid of the *footholes* in the wall."

THE HANBURY ARMS

Until the *Caerleon road* was made in the 1820s there were only two roads from Newport to Caerleon. The less direct way, which was used exclusively when Newport bridge was being built, was past Malpas Church to the Pwll Mawr road, and so, under Lodge Camp to Caerleon. The better course was by the main London road to the finger-post at Christchurch down what is now *the Black Ash Path* into Caerleon Ultra Pontem and across the bridge at the Hanbury Arms.

This as the bridge-head shows was the site of the bridge in Roman times. In Anglo-Norman days the bridge was strongly guarded and the gate-house forming the entrance to the castle works, according to Archdeacon Coxe (writing in 1800), stood a short distance up the road. The inn is built to an old round tower called the Constable Tower.

The Hanbury Arms, Caerleon.

The bridge as described by Coxe was supported by ten piers and was divided by posts and rails into *rooms,* each twelve feet in length. It was one of these *rooms* which, on a dark night of October, 1772, broke away on a violent ebb-tide and bore Mrs. Williams and her candle-lanthorn downstream. Her screams awoke the occupants of St. Julian's, but her candle was now extinguished and they could see nought; her *room* was broken into beams and planks by its impact with Newport bridge and poor Mrs. Williams, now hoarse with screaming, bestrode a beam and prayed, *O Lord, I trust in thee. Thou alone canst save me.*

A mile below the bridge she espied a barge and renewed her cries; after much effort she was saved by the master of the vessel.

Little is kown of the early days of the inn. It may have been a *house on the quay* for the prosperous monks of Llantarnam Abbey and there is little doubt that from Roman times considerable river trade was carried on to and from that quay, constructed as it was just below the bridge. That trade continued within living memory, when the produce of the Eastern Valley, brought along the tram-road to the quay, was taken to the Newport wharves by sailing boat. *The Bristol boat* enabled the Caerleon ladies to travel to Bristol for important shopping.

The beautiful *open window* — a veritable wind-eye — visible across the courtyard of the inn from the road, is not, in my opinion, in its original position. In Prout's lithograph of 1838 it is shown — or a replica — in the south-west gable-end of the out-building beyond the Constable's Tower. If, as I believe, it is the same window, it must have been removed from its position in a *weather-wall* and fixed into the newer wall in the courtyard. The interesting head inserted in the wall above, with its curiously elevated ears, is assumed to be Roman. As the windows on the river-front of the house, I place them, with the windows of the Bull Inn, among our best Tudor relics.

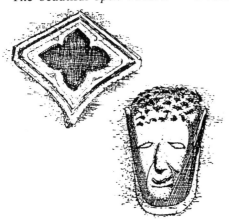

'Open' window and Roman head
' at the Hanbury Arms.

At the Hanbury Arms, on a golden evening in June, I and my friends John, Will o'the Hills and the Bookman talked over flagons of ale with mine host and some choice men of Caerleon. We talked of the Constable's Tower, into which the *drunks* were led, awaiting trial in the Magistrates' Room; of the Mari Llwyd and other strange rituals; of the old school and its boys and master; of the duel between Charles Williams and Tom Morgan; of Hanbury Williams; and, at last, of Tennyson.

Our friendly inn-keeper showed us the room — the *Magistrates' Room* — where Tennyson mused and planned his *Idylls of the King*. We saw his chair*. Standing in the lovely bay window we enjoyed, little changed, his view across the river of Ultra Pontem and the hillside. Very beautiful were the sunlit cottages and the still, full river, seen through the small panes, and into our memories floated idyllic music:

> *For Arthur on the Whitsuntide before*
> *Held court at old Caerleon upon Usk.*
>
> *but in scarce longer time*
> *Than at Caerleon the full-tided Usk,*
> *Before he turn to fall seaward again,*
> *Pauses . . .*

Elaine, the lily-maid of Astolat, made a pretty history to herself of every dint and scratch on Lancelot's shield —

> *this cut is fresh;*
> *That ten years back; this dealt him at Caerlyle;*
> *That at Caerleon; this at Camelot.*
> *And later Lancelot himself speaks of his great battles at Duglas,*
> *Bassa, Celidon the forest, Castle Gurnion —*
> *And at Caerleon had he helped his lord,*
> *When the strong neighings of the wild white Horse*
> *Set every gilded parapet shuddering.*

Almost a century has passed since this music flooded the English-speaking world. Adoration of Tennyson has long since given place, in the sad and darkened modern circles, to disparagement. Yet for us whose youth was spent in or near Caerleon few other poets can hold us, as Tennyson holds us, in an inescapable spell.

Tennyson's Window in the "Magistrates' room" in the Hanbury Arms, Caerleon. Here in 1856 the poet wrote: "The Usk murmurs by the window as I sit like King Arthur in Caerleon."

Yet it is the Tennyson window in the magistrates' room that attracts most visitors. Crowning an external projection which rises from ground level, it remains as it was in Tennyson's days, and indeed — as one of his illustrations indicates, as in 1800, when Archdeacon Coxe knew it.

Tennyson must have spent much of his time here, in September, 1856 and while he did not write his "Idylls" in Caerleon, he planned them and mused over them in this window.

Windows at the Hanbury Arms, Caerleon.

135

Chapter Nine

NEWPORT, OTHERWISE KNOWN AS CASNEWYDD

NEWPORT STREET AND DISTRICT NAMES

"Newport" implies the out-port of an old port. The out-port developed downstream from the new castle (Casnewydd) and bridge, while the town sprouted new streets from the one through road which became High Street and Stow Hill.

Across the river, the district between the through road and the Usk belonged to the Herberts of St. Julian's; south of the road were two farms, Fairoak and Ffynnon-Efa (Eveswell). Later, a good stone house gave the whole district the name of Maen-ty, now Maindee.

Our most evocative district name, a challenge to the non-Welsh, is Pillgwenlly. The Pill (tidal ditch) of Gwynllyw was by tradition the mooring place of our 6th-century pirate-prince's long fast ship before he became our patron saint. Our businessmen and sportsmen claim added prestige if they are known as "Sons of Pill."

King's Hill was the triangle of valuable land bounded by Stow Hill, Charles Street, Vicarage Lane and Commercial Street. It belonged to Newport. In my opinion it should still, with all its perquisites, belong to Newport as it did in the centuries following 1410.

Baneswell took its name from Ffynnon-maen, the stone-lined well in Pump Street. Eveswell in Maindee was named after the well in Batchelor Road. Famous Tudor houses are recalled by the district names of Crindau and St. Julian's, while East Usk comprised the area near a remarkable decoy duckpool known to us as the Muxon.

Part of the through road, named appropriately Church Road, separates the cathedral city roads named after London, Bristol, Hereford, Exeter, Liverpool from a colony of streets with the ecclesiastical nomenclature of Lord, Bishop, Dean and Canon streets.

These stone houses were built over a century ago by a missioner named Philip Barnard, who on a journey to West Wales was appalled by the hovels which he found on this site and dedicated his life to the rehousing of the inhabitants of what in his honour became known as Barnardtown, a name which survives, I believe, in the post office. Barnardtown school has since changed to Church Road and later to Fairoak.

The through road, known in 1783 as the Swansea to London toll-road, climbs beyond Duckpool Road as Christchurch Road. Of the branch roads I must select Victoria Avenue for special mention. Old inhabitants still call it George Hill and indeed the popular inn at the foot is The George.

Parallel to George Hill was Summerhill, but a royal romance effected a change to Albert Avenue and Victoria Avenue, joined, please note, by Crown Street. Social climbers in Newport noted these changes as also the substitution of Shaftesbury Street for Marshes Road and Severn View for the Rookery.

The advent of immigrants with the Lysaght works enriched our street names with Dudley, Walsall, Lilleshall and other examples of Midland nostalgia. And when, in 1932 the new development schemes around Ridgeway were set afoot, a splendid Elizabethan relic, Ty-llwyd (Grey House) was demolished. Ty-llwyd Road is its only memorial.

That this town site of ours was settled in pre-history is proved by our magnificent hill-fort which gives its name to the various Gaer streets. Not far away were the Caerau — the tumuli of Stow — and at the other end, in what is now Clevedon Road, rises the iron age hill fort known there as the Camp.

Newport in 1818.

Crossing Newport Bridge, we pause for a few moments to watch the coming and going of vehicles at the busy five-lane crossing. The name of an inn — *The Old Green* — causes the centuries to slip back and, in imagination, we see the Castle Green in the "dip" between the bridge and High Street, extending some distance down Dock Street and to the foot of Mill Street.

We are on debatable ground here and must record with care. That there was an East Gate — the Bridge Gate — into Newport seems certain, for Leland mentions "a great stone gate by the bridge" and there is still extant in Abergavenny a small oil painting showing the archway in 1800.

The hinge pivots on which the gate swung survived for many years after that date, but I must note that these pivots were the only items of the East Gate that Coxe described in 1798-99.

The stage coach from the east, then, would descend from the bridge into the "dip." The horses, urged by a touch of the whip and a rousing obligato on the "yard of tin," would race up the slope to the High Street and soon the equipage would stop at the pull-in of the King's Head Hotel. Gates and pull-in are no more to be seen at the King's Head, yet you will find the gates — King's head complete — at the modern pull-in of the Westgate Hotel.

The "post" was deposited and collected opposite the King's Head. Hence the reason for the siting of the post office. Hence also the siting of the railway (as opposed to the roadway) station.

In 1752, High Street was "Market Lane." The middle of the "lane," near the site of the present post office, was occupied by the Market House, with its brown roof, gable ends, gate and doorways.

Much of the town's business was conducted in the Market House, while the stocks and whipping-post within its gates and the bull-ring just outside, must have contributed somewhat to the entertainment of the townsfolk.

Crindau as it was a century ago.

Crindau House, now situated in a quiet backwater off Redland Street, was once a country home. In 1924 Arthur Machen wrote to me: *You give me one shock. I remember the old house on the Malpas hillside in its original condition before it was defaced by some ruffian in the 70s of last century. But it stood clear of Newport in the fields and you talk of streets!* On the splendid porch of Crindau you will find in the spandrels of the arch the letters M and H and, above, the inscription *Anno Domini 1580*.

This has been taken to imply that the house was built in 1580 by Humphrey Morgan on his marriage to Katherine Herbert, but the house itself is far older than the porch, with its late Tudor arch and windows. I am glad to report that the present tenants take great care of their ancient home.

THE MURENGER HOUSE

Picture High Street, Newport, two centuries back. A narrow ditch of a road left the Bridge Gate at the Castle, dipped into the Castle Green (have you seen *The Old Green* tavern hereabouts?), climbed to the Market House, passed the handsome town-house of the Herberts of St. Julian's and dipped again, narrower than before, with small houses and taverns edging it, to the Murenger's House opposite the *muddy chasm* of Skinner Street and so to the West Gate and the Cardiff road leading to Stow village and the west.

Yes, there were but three buildings of any size between the Castle and the Gate. The Market House in the middle of the street (called *Market Lane* in 1756) was a brown gabled structure raised on pillars, and contained within its gates the stocks and the whipping post. In June, 1977, Alice Morgan, found guilty of breaking down part of a hedge, was stripped from her waist upwards, and whipped *with thirty lashes, till the blood issued forth.*

The bull-ring was embedded in a stone in front of the Market House. Here, on a spot between the sites now occupied by the Post Office and the King's Head Hotel, our forebears indulged in the art of bull-baiting.

The *Murenger's House,* a large, venerable structure, decorated (like the West Gate) with the Stafford coat-of-arms, stood, it is assumed, on the site of the National Provincial Bank. It must have been, at the latest, of early 14th-century construction, for the office of Murenger became extinct when Edward II granted the burgesses of Newport their Charter.

Every fortified town kept its walls in repair by means of wall-tolls. These *murages* were collected by an officer known as the Murenger and his existence in Newport is evidence that Newport was a walled town. Further evidence was the *West Gate.* Now, of course, comes the problem: if the Murenger's duties lapsed circa 1324, and we have still an old building in Newport dated 1541, how can that building be named the *Murenger House?.*

The answer is that it was never called by that name until the mid-19th-century. This picturesque Tudor dwelling place was the town-house of the squires of St. Julian's and, as such, should, with Crindau House and St. Julian's, be regarded with pride and reverence by every son and daughter of Newport.

Crushing the temptation to dilate on our neglect of our other Tudor treasures, let me indicate briefly what the so-called *Murenger House* holds for us. Behind a genuine facade raised in the early years of Henry VIII's reign, sufficient remains for us to recapture the dignity, the taste and the loyalty of these Herberts — these 16th-century Welsh squires.

A three-storeyed building, it must have dwarfed its neighbours. Within the spacious rooms, the fireplaces and especially the wall and ceiling decorations, bear testimony to the demand for beauty in the homes of Tudor gentry in those early days.

Everywhere in this decoration we find roses and pineapples — the Tudor roses and the Aragon pineapples. Now we have to face a further problem. Henry VIII (of whom a portrait in plaster remains on one of the walls) divorced Catherine in 1533. The intertwining of Tudor roses and Aragon pineapples is obviously a pretty tribute from Squire Herbert to Their Majesties. How then can the house be dated 1541? I must leave this problem to the erudite reader.

Here, then, in the busy main thoroughfare of our town we have a magnificent house over four centuries old. The front of the building has been recently repaired, with skill and taste, but structural weaknesses are suspected and some of these may prove to need immediate and costly attention. There is also a threat to its survival from another quarter.

The Murenger House, Newport.

"Why bother about these old places?" I am asked. "Look at the Castle! What purpose does it serve? Knock it down and replace it with something useful. And if the *Murenger House* is decaying, let that go, too. We are concerned with the future."

My answer is two-fold. First, these historic places do not belong to us; they belong to posterity. They have enriched Newport life throughout the centuries. Let not our generation be stained by their removal. And second, as in nature roots are more important than leaves and flowers and fruits, so in a town the buildings and the beliefs and the laws and the way of life which have stood the storms and stresses of the centuries are of greater account than the passing fancies of today; their disappearance will be at our peril. I shall believe that the people of Newport are worthy citizens of no mean city when I find them not merely conscious of their heritage, but determined to preserve it.

St. Woolos Cathedral, Newport.   *Chris Barber*

ST. WOOLOS CATHEDRAL

Stow Hill, over the Usk from Christchurch Hill, marks the continuation of the great ridge pierced by the river and is crowned by the remarkable cathedral church of St. Woolos. The site of the church is remarkable, too, for it is in direct line with four neolithic camps (three within the borough of Newport), so it is possible that the church was built within an ancient circular *llan* (enclosure) which may have been a Celtic homestead.

The view southward from the church tower extends from Avonmouth over the Somerset and Devon coasts, the Steep and Flat Holms and the coast lands of Gwent and Glamorgan. The cathedral is 165 feet long and presents a variety of styles and elevations, but the first question the visitors ask is, "What is that little building between the tower and the main body of the church?"

Around this small sanctuary hang the mists of antiquity, but we know that the first church was built on this spot in the 6th century and that it was made of *boards and rods*.

The story of this *wattle* building takes several forms but I will tell it as it was told to me when I was a boy.

Gwynllw, the Prince, was married to the beautiful and saintly Princess Gwladys, and among their many children the favourite was Cadoc, who as a young man was already revered for his holy life. Mother and son prayed often that Gwynllw might turn from his evil ways, but the fierce Welshman revelled in his adventures and scorned the prayers of his gentle wife and son.

Near the mouth of the Usk, in a creek called Pill Gwynllw, he kept a long fast boat and it was his custom to sally out with his men into the Channel and attack passing ships, killing the crews, commandeering the cargoes. One night, in his home at Caerleon,

141

Gwynllw dreamt that he and his men climbed a hill and saw on the summit a white ox with a black spot on its forehead. On the next morning, as they surmounted the hill which is now Stow Hill, they encountered such an ox. Gwynllw, shocked into sanctity, remained on that hilltop, marked out a burying-place and built a church on the site of the little chapel of St. Mary, which now nestles between the tower and the nave of St. Woolos.

Gwynllw has been corrupted into Woolos but the district of Newport near to the docks is still *Pillgwenlly*.

The 6th-century chapel was replaced by a stone building, part of which probably survives as the walls of St. Mary's. From this ancient chapel, the view of the Norman nave is magnificent, seen through the semi-circular arch. This arch was never an exterior doorway and is itself unique in that its detached pillars have a Roman character and may have been brought from Caerleon.

The Norman arch, St. Woolos   *Bill Barber*

Two steps lead down to the nave. St. Gwynllw's has since the days of Rufus held a close association with Gloucester Cathedral and it may be that monks from Gloucester raised the very beautiful arcades at St. Gwynllw's. Of one thing I am certain; no man who has attended a morning service in summer under those grand old arches will ever forget them. Later Gothic work has more grace, more of aspiration; the nave of St. Woolos is like an avenue of oak-trees, strong, secure, English, bathed in English light.

Rising from the floor of the chancel is an ancient window, about three feet square, still called the *Leper Window*. The name implies that through the opened window lepers might see and take part in the ceremonies conducted at the altar. To describe this window by such a name is to ignore the restrictions placed on lepers, for the leper was forbidden to enter a churchyard. This was a *sacring window,* and the sanctus bell was rung there during the Mass; at the sound, the peasants working in the fields would pause and turn in prayer towards their church.

> *Thy little world can show thee wonders great:*
> *The greater may have more, but not more neat*
> *And curious pieces.*

Extract from George Herbert's *Travels at Home* (1633).

Doorway at St. Woolos Cathedral.

BROWSING AROUND THE CATHEDRAL

In the warm sunshine I spent a pleasant hour, accompanied by the Dean of Monmouth and Mr. Charles Jenkins, strolling around the purlieus of St. Woolos cathedral. Mr. Jenkins was born 74 years ago near the top of Clifton Road and enlivened our talk with his memories.

We visited first the tithe barn opposite the south porch of the cathedral. Used for the last thirty years by Mr. Jenkins as a builder's storehouse, it was previously a tithe barn, a theatre for *strolling players,* a hospital, and a laundry used by the Clewer sisters (who kept a children's home in the adjoining houses).

Strategically placed in Stow village, the old barn was the ideal site for rounding off a day at Stow fair. When the joys of the fair had palled, the visitor had a choice of several taverns, including the *White Horse,* just over the boundary in Newport; the *Bull,* on the site of St. Woolos hospital and the *Lamb,* across the way from the *Bull.*

Mellow and fortified, he could then stroll in the springtime evening (for the fair was always held on the Thursday of Whitsun week) for a couple of hours of melodrama in the dimly-lit tithe barn. There is a legend, by the way, that Sarah Siddons or her company from Hereford once acted at St. Woolos tithe barn and I shall welcome any information about such a visit, or regret any denial.

One of the teething troubles of the famous Newport Playgoers' Society was the search for a suitable repertory theatre. Among the buildings considered was the tithe barn, which was in those days just ripe enough, just musty enough to appeal to our urgent, histrionic souls and I was one of many who regretted that the idea was dropped.

Little of interest survives in the barn. Two old doorways blocked in; two windows with wooden frames cut in imitation, probably, of the original stone mullions and tracery; roof timbers hidden above modern casing; and a chimney-breast in the east wall which contains some interesting and massive mouldings and one corbel — that is all.

Yet when I remember how little places like Wolvesnewton and Trellech have cherished their tithe barns, I wonder if we, the people of Newport, realise our duties to posterity.

From the barn we crossed the road and climbed the steps to see the old boundary stone in the parapet wall. In the charter of Humphrey, Earl of Stafford, dated 1427, and confirming an earlier charter of 1385, the borough boundaries are laid down, and no change in these boundaries took place until 1830.

The dividing line crossed the Stow road and then took the line of the old churchyard wall for some yards, proceeding up Clifton Road and down Clifton Place, and I imagine that in the changes which took place in 1862 the old boundary stone was safely incorporated in the present parapet wall.

I am grateful to Mr. John Collett, our borough librarian, for permitting me to inspect copies of the charters, a tithe map and various other maps and documents. Before me as I write are two maps, one of 1750 and the Thorpe survey map of 1752. It is pleasant to imagine a journey through Newport in those days when there was only one way in — the London road down Christchurch Hill — and one way out — the Cardiff road up Stow Hill.

After crossing the rickety wooden bridge and passing through the bridge gateway, we should dip into the Castle Green and climb to Market Lane (now High Street).

On both maps the market house is shown in the middle of the roadway and close at hand we should see the handsome facade of the Herbert's house, now known wrongly as the Murenger's House. Down the cobbled road we should wend our way, passing the ornate front of the Murenger's House (where now stands the National Provincial Bank).

The great west gate at the foot of Stow Hill, with its attendant toll booth, would admit us to the hilly road for Stow. On the right a path to Payne's (or Bayne's) Well, and

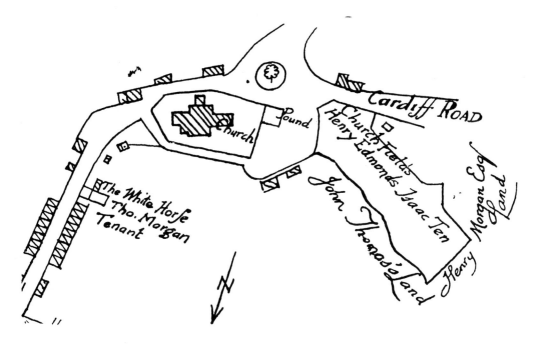

Drawn from a map of 1752.

higher up the road the remains of the Wayside Cross would attract our notice and soon we should cross the borough boundary near the old "White Horse" inn (see the map) and enter Stow.

Passing between the church and the tithe barn we should come to an open space, with a pound adjoining the churchyard wall, fields on the right belonging to Messrs Thomas and Isaac and Sir Henry Morgan and the Cardiff road stretching ahead.

But what is this circular object in the open space? Is it an early attempt at a traffic island? Or is it, as heavy reading of *Westerns* prompts me to suggest, *Lone Tree Tump?* James Hodge and Phillip Smith, churchwardens, could have enlightened us.

Before we parted, Mr. Jenkins told me of his adventure on the day following the death of Queen Victoria in 1901. Preparing to fly the flag at half-mast on the church tower, a young fellow pulled the cord through the pulley. "Somebody had to rethread it," said Mr. Jenkins, "so we tossed and I lost and I had the pleasure of climbing the flag-staff on a cold January morning with the cord between my teeth!"

NEWPORT WAYSIDE CROSS

Snowclad and spiky with icicles, 1961 slunk away. Similarly bedight, the young 1962 tripped in, to the rhythm of our Monmouthshire church bells.

Our hills became Cresta runs, our hospitals filled with toboggan casualties, our water engineers and plumbers tore their hair as pipes burst from Uskmouth to Talybont, and the Watsonians, back home in their Scottish warmth, told fearsome tales of the iron-clad rugby grounds in South Wales.

Immured in my hometown — *motorists are advised to keep off the road* — I took the opportunity of replying to requests. Much interest had arisen in my article on Croes-lwyd and other crosses and young Newport friends made it clear that a generation had grown up with no memories of an ancient wayside cross at Newport.

So I went to our borough museum, where Mr. Cefni Barnett showed me the head of the cross. Measuring 16 inches by 12 inches and some six inches thick, this impressive grey slab was discovered in 1926 by engineers sinking the caissons for the new river bridge at Newport. The stone was buried 21 feet in the mud and 130 feet from the town bank.

Cromwell's Ironsides, of course, were blamed for this vandalism. *Not satisfied with decapitating Jasper Tudor in St. Woollos tower,* people cried, *they must knock off the head of our cross and fling it contemptuously in the Usk.* Not the army, but parliament was to blame, for the law passed in 1643 was responsible for the destruction of our crosses.

Pleasant it is to imagine the ancient cross in its setting. We think that by-path from the old road which is now Fields Road crossed the Stow Hill at the Havelock Street junction and continued down to the river. At that junction stood the cross; at that junction still stands Crosshouse; the field to the north was named Cae-crouch, possibly a corruption of Cae-croes.

It was an evocative site! Mid-way between the Westgate of Newport and Stow hamlet, on the prehistoric arterial road from England to west Wales, the cross stood for much in the life of town and county. By tradition, Baldwin, Archbishop of Canterbury, had preached on that spot the Third Crusade in 1188. For six and more centuries before that time people had toiled up Allt-Gwynllyw (the Welsh name for Stow Hill) to worship at the shrine of the hilltop saint.

Garlanded on festival days, the goal of many a procession, the cross hallowed engagements, rendered contracts binding. News was proclaimed from its steps and, to save the payment of tolls, countryfolk would sell their goods at the cross, causing many a feud with the town merchants.

Stow-fairs, two days in duration, with their *lord-mayors* in charge, were held within sight of the cross. Peripatetic players produced their dramas in the tithe-barn further up the hill and within a stone's throw of the cross stood the *House of Refuge,* erected by the Earl of Pembroke in 1410 for the education and support of the poor children of Newport. Though badly weathered, the Pembroke coat of arms may still be seen above the entrance gateway.

The base of the Newport cross.

The head of the Newport wayside cross.

On the corner of Havelock Street and Stow Hill is *Cross House.* In front of this house, on stone steps, stood a granite wayside cross. Here, in 1187, it is assumed that Baldwin, Archbishop of Canterbury, accompanied by Giraldus Cambrensis and many bishops, clergy and nobles, preached the First Crusade.

The head of the cross, discovered in the Usk during the building of the new bridge, is in the Borough Museum; the steps of the cross are in the churchyard of St. Woolos. It would give many of us great satisfaction to see the whole monument re-erected outside Cross House.

SHIPWRECK AT NEWPORT BRIDGE

In a remote cave of his vast archives my friend the Bookman unearthed a treasure which, as is his wont, he passed to me. Dated May 11, 1844, it was a cutting from the *Illustrated London News* of such interest that I spent a morning in another of his caves reading the *Monmouthshire Merlin* of that year. Pretty denizens of the cave flitted through at intervals while I soaked myself in the juicy prose of 1844.

Shipwreck at Newport Bridge 1844.

Above the newsprint is an excellent sketch showing a wrecked steampacket, Newport bridge, the Bridge Inn, the slipway leading to the Beaufort wharf, the castle (then a brewery), the stacks of the Dos Works and, faintly, the new barracks on the hilltop.

Sloops lie moored on the town bank, while the bank on the east side is crowded with spectators, the men in frockcoats and top hats, the women graceful in their long dresses, capes and poke bonnets. Bridge, wharf and boats are also crowded.

The wrecked ship was the Severn. Built originally for the Chepstow-Bristol service, she was transferred, it seems, to the Newport-Bristol route in competition with the Usk and Glamorgan, steampackets owned by a Newport firm. As one result of this competition, fares from Newport to Bristol, which had been 4s. for an after-cabin and 2s. for a forecabin, fell to 2s. and 1s., with children at half-price, and in 1844 the local packets had reduced the prices to 1s. and 6d.

On May 4, 1844, in the late afternoon, "excitement and alarm unprecedented if we except 1939" swept through the town. The powerful, iron-built, packet-boat, Severn, driven by an Archimedean screw and fitted with four watertight compartments and high-pressure engines, was about to leave the Beaufort wharf with sixty passengers (including twenty females). Her bow pointed towards the bridge, for after her previous trip the captain had neglected to swing her with her bow pointing downstream, and this was the main cause of the disaster.

148

When all was ready, the *south-west quarter fast* was let go *and the engines started so as to warp her around the south-east quarter fast.* A chain suddenly fouled the screw, the mooring chain snapped and on *the five-knot torrent* the vessel swept upstream, crashing her starboard bow on to the cutwater of a bridge buttress, which made a breach in her iron plates several feet long. Immediately afterwards, she struck again, swinging on to the first buttress on the east side.

Fearfully the vessel rolled. Mr. Edward Slaughter (of the Avonside Iron Works, Bristol) entreated the passengers to keep to the centre of the ship. Some were with difficulty prevented from jumping overboard in hopeless terror, *whilst frantic shrieks of wild despair came rolling on the burdened air.*

Amid loud outcries from friends and spectators on the bridge and beside the river, masters of vessels lying at the wharves manned their boats and rescued the passengers, including one female who had bounded into the river.

The luggage was discharged, the pumps fixed but, with the breach extending to two compartments, the gallant Severn sank, taking into her maelstrom two boats, the occupants of which were carried by the impetus of the current through the arches.

On the Sunday attempts were made by steam tug, *horse-power* and other means to raise the foundered vessel. All failed; on the ebb she lay on her larboard side, but with the flood she turned over and lay with her deck against the bridge.

On Monday, May 13, *a dock was dug, the vessel was righted, chained to the pier of the bridge, plugged and caulked, parbuckles and tackles carried out in all directions, resisting the pressures of the tide against the wreck, while fenders and well-greased timbers protected her from the cutwater.*

A single pump was set to work. Then, with all set, hundreds of willing workers, masters, mechanics, apprentices, manned the ropes on the bridge and, to the accompaniment of mighty cheers, the good ship rose, was safely moored on the graving bank and on the Thursday was towed to Pattison's Dock, Bristol.

Her place was taken temporarily by the Dragon, late of the London-Ostend station. The *Merlin* of May 26 records quite laconically that on Monday, May 20, she broke her hawser and was carried away from her moorings under the bridge with her mast broken, but no other injury.

The year 1844 seems remote, yet only three years later Captain William Howe began his long career as commander of the Newport and Bristol steamers, the most famous of which was the Welsh Prince.

My father as a young man knew Captain Howe and made scores of trips in the Prince. One evening, after a boisterous cross-channel trip in this little cockleshell, the captain invited my father to stay to supper, but the meal was not a success. Just as the cook had filled the plates with an appetising concoction of *meat and veg* the mooring ropes slipped, and the plates followed suit.

Captain William Howe.

149

Captain Howe's memorial stone.

It was a grief to me when Captain Howe's memorial stone at Christchurch was irreparably damaged by frost, but I reproduce here a sketch which I made of it in 1922. The portrait of Captain Howe is from an old photograph owned by Mrs. Edgar Twist, of Malpas.

My reference to the tombstone at Christchurch which displayed a sculpture of the Welsh Prince and her master, Captain William Howe, aroused much interest. This has resulted, inter alia, in the decision to re-name an old Newport tavern after the Bristol steam-packet boat. Some young student seeking a title for his thesis should choose *The Newport and Bristol Cross-Channel Service.* A fascinating story begins in very early days and by 1587 Thomas Churchyard wrote of Newport:

> *So downeward loe, is many a Marchants shop.*
> *And many, sayle to Bristowe from that Port.*

The slipways at Newport and *Karlyon* and the wharves and *Backs* and basins at Bristol were kept busy with a shuttle service of passengers and freight.

Councillor Jack Williams of Caerleon tells with glee how the ladies of *the ancient city* — his grandmother among them — used to set aside two days each week in the summer months for the "shopping boat" to Bristol, which left the Hanbury slip one morning or afternoon according to the tide and returned the following morning or afternoon. That boat was a sailing-cutter, with no auxiliary engine!

First steamship to ply between Newport and Bristol was the Cambria, Bristol owned in 1822. In the next year an interesting newcomer, owned by Newport and Pontypool merchants, was the Lady Rodney. Captain William Young and his crew of eight took this 58-ton vessel daily to Bristol, the channel trip usually lasting four hours. She sailed from the Rodney bank near the bridge, with Packet slip on the Maindee, the Rodney office at hand. It is probable that Rodney Parade, dear to the heart of every son of Newport, owes its name to the little packet which steamed between the two ports between 1822 and 1854.

In 1871 a fine new steam packet boat, the Welsh Prince, was launched. Built and engined by Messrs. Hill, she was designed to bear passengers and freight and her owners, Messrs. Ring and Co., appointed Captain William Howe as her master.

This jovial and skilful seadog had already twenty years of service as the skipper of the Avon; he quickly made his new craft popular among the merchants of the ports, and his trips and excursions even more popular among those who loved *a whiff of the briny.* A stewardess and refreshments were provided.

I am amazed to hear from Mr. Giles (of Cashmore Ltd) that the Prince measured 100 feet long, had a beam of 19 feet and gross tonage of 154. In my memory, she seemed to be shorter than a cricket pitch.

From the *Evening Telegram* of May 22, 1871, I extract the notice of sailings by the Welsh Prince during that week:

Newport	Bathurst Basin, Bristol
7.00am	7.30pm
7.15am	8.15pm
8.30am	8.30pm
9.15am	9.30pm
4.00pm	1.00pm

Whit Monday: Excursion down channel 4pm to 10.30pm.

The fares were, for cabin, 2s. 6d., deck, 1s. 6d., with corresponding return fares of 3s. 6d. and 2s. 0d. For fifteen years this pleasant amenity, like the Campbell steamers in later years, enriched and enlivened Newport.

Then in September, 1886, the sad news was published that, with the opening of the Severn Tunnel, the passenger service of the Welsh Prince would cease. She continued as a cargo ferry for five years, was sold in 1904 — "port of entry, Bridgwater" — to Messrs. Sully.

In 1930 a message came: *If you wish to see the last of the Welsh Prince go to Cashmore's wharf.* There I found her; there I sketched her from the opposite bank; sad, dismantled, robbed of her glamour, she seemed to point an accusing funnel up stream. So much pleasure she had given to so many.

Her master, Captain William Howe, had died in 1891, aged 78. There are still plenty of men and women who remember him, plenty also who remember how the Prince used to wallow lengthwise in the hollows of the Atlantic combers blown up by the south-west winds of the Channel. *Get it up, m'dear,* was the skipper's advice, *you'll be all the better for it.*

THE HOMELAND OF W. H. DAVIES

I asked an old Newport lady if she remembered Captain Davies of Church House, the grandfather of W. H. Davies the poet.

"Captain Davies was a sturdy old man," she replied, "but I remember his wife more clearly. She wore pretty little clips, with bebe ribbon, tiny roses and puce trimmings. Their grandson is a poet, you say? Does that keep him?"

Church House, Portland Street, Newport.

Church House, the tavern in Portland Street, Newport, where W. H. Davies was born some seventy years ago, was built like a ship. Ship's timbers once decorated the exterior and the corner of the inn protrudes over the entrance like a ship's bluff prow.

In *A Poet's Pilgrimage*, Davies writes, *No sooner would my grandfather see us all preparing for bed than he would stand in the middle of the kitchen — a big, red-faced, bearded old man — and roar, at no one in particular, "Is everything made fast?" The maidservant would always answer for the back door . . . but my grandfather was always the last to go to bed and he was to be heard trying all the locks, bolts and latches for some time after we had all gone upstairs.*

A long description of Church House occurs in *The Child and the Mariner*, but I turn to *The Richest Stones* for the characteristic picture.

> *The little house where I was born*
> *And where my early childhood lies*
> *Was built with solid blocks of gold*
> *And all its walls had diamond eyes.*

Yet Portland Street, Pillgwenlly, Newport, seems scarcely a *fit nurse for a poetic child.* We must seek elsewhere for the moulding forces which gave his poetry its intense individual qualities.

A clever girl said to me, "Any child could write like W. H. Davies." Truer to say, "Any child could see like W. H. Davies." While yet a boy he stored his mind with memories of the countryside round his native town. In later life he expressed these memories in lyrics which have given the sweet singer of Gwent an immortal place alongside Herrick and Burns.

Living and working far away, Davies called forth with ease the magic of his homeland in Gwent. He meets "a lovely maiden with a jaunty air —"

> *The red carnations flamed in both her cheeks.*
> *Her teeth were white and shown; while either eye*
> *Shone like a pool on Christchurch hill*
> *When it has stolen half the sky.*

The pool still remains. You may find it opposite the school at Christchurch, to the east of Newport, and at the same time see

> *. . . from the hills of Gwent the earth*
> *Burned into two by Severn's silver flood.*

Moonlight on Newport Castle. "The moonlight like a big white butterfly, dreaming on that old castle near Caerleon, while at its side the Usk went softly by" — W. H. Davies.

The tumbledown castle at Newport left a deep impression on him —

> *When I would go alone at night to see*
> *The moonlight, like a big white butterfly,*
> *Dreaming on that old castle near Caerleon,*
> *While at its side the Usk went softly by*

and the smile is seen to be perfect when the moon shines on the central keep, with its walls and end towers stretched out on either side.

In *Days That Have Been* he teaches us to listen not only to bird song and river music, but also to the melody of our beautiful village names.

> *Can I forget the sweet days that have been,*
> *The villages so green I have been in;*
> *Llantarnam, Magor, Malpas, and Llanwern,*
> *Lliswerry, old Caerleon, and Alteryn.*

153

All these places, except Magor, are within easy walking distance of Newport and, while the greenness of some of the villages has been lost, much of beauty and interest remains.

Visit the Abbey and church at Llantarnam, and call for refreshment at the "Green House," with its quaint sign:

Y Ty Gwyrdd
1719
Cwrw da
A Seidir i chwi
Dewch y mewn
Chwi gewch y brofi
The Green House
1719
Good beer
And cider to you
Come in
And you shall taste it

Archdeacon Coxe tasted *cwrw da* here in 1799 and wrote, *Cwrw is new ale in a turbid state before it is clarified by fermentation. To persons accustomed to clear and old malt liquor, this beverage is extremely forbidding to the sight and nauseous to the taste.*

Malpas is near at hand and is the gateway to grand walking country, either over the hill towards Caerleon or through the Henllys fields to Twyn Barlwm.

Llanwern is a typical Gwent village, on the moors to the east of Newport. The ancient church sleeps amidst rich meadows and, with the inn, and the neat cottages, the wooded slopes and the barns, remains as Davies knew it.

Caerleon would demand a book to itself. Yet, when all the world-famous sights have been viewed, you will find in the back streets the Caerleon which Davies loved.

Alteryn, last on his list of *villages so green,* was his best-loved memory. From Fields Road the Alteryn Road bears you to the brow of the hill overlooking the wonderful green valley. The tide of industry has swept from Newport in two main directions, leaving this land sweet and smokeless. No railway encroaches here; no factory belches forth its fumes; but the landscape, crowned by the great range of the Mynydd Maen, swells and dips in rhythmic undulations.

Always lovely, Alteryn is exquisite at twilight. The pale moon sails in a silver-blue sky; a warm glow lingers in the west. The canal slumbers, its shadows streaked with silver bars. Bridge and cottages are bathed in a ghostly half-light, while the chestnut trees, solemn and massive, tower above in majesty.

Returning to Alteryn after many years of absence, Davies was deeply affected by the unchanging beauty, and wrote

Thy water, Alteryn,
Shines brighter through my tears,
With childhood in my mind;
So will it shine when age
Has made me almost blind.

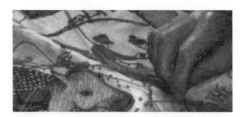

THE LAST INVASION TAPESTRY

DESIGNED BY ELIZABETH CRAMP R.W.S.

The embroidered Tapestry was made as a community project initiated by **Fishguard Arts Society** as their chief contribution to the 1997 Bicentenary Commemorations. Seventy eight people were involved in making the 30.4 metres (100 foot) long tapestry which is estimated to have taken around 40,000 hours to complete. Its format is similar to the Bayeux Tapestry which describes the 1066 Invasion. Like its famous predecessor, the Fishguard Tapestry depicts actual events but it also includes many of the local legends which have grown around the historical facts of 1797.

The invasion lasted for two days and this is reflected in the colours of the tapestry which flow from day into night and night into day. Artistic licence was needed to depict events which happened at night in the dark and to allow for an excitement in the colours - for example purple horses and green-faced frightened soldiers. The main incidents are briefly described in Welsh and English lettering in the top and bottom borders and a wealth of detail both factual and mythical is included in the embroidery.

A full-colour 36 page book - "THE LAST INVASION TAPESTRY, the story behind a community project" - has been produced by Fishguard Arts Society and is available at the exhibition and in local bookshops. Four books about the Invasion are in print in 1997 as well as accounts of the Invasion in several general histories of Pembrokeshire. These are available in local bookshops and libraries.

As a legacy of the Bicentenary Commemorations an Invasion Centre is planned for Fishguard which will incorporate the tapestry as a major feature. Meanwhile the tapestry will be held and safeguarded by Fishguard Arts Society. A Lottery Award has facilitated the design and construction of a display case in readiness for that centre.

Support for the tapestry project has come from many individuals, businesses and organisations. A book of names of all who contribute is included in the archives of the project.

Main supporters: STENA LINE, THE ARTS COUNCIL OF WALES, THE CALOUSTE GULBENKIAN FOUNDATION, THE WELSH DEVELOPMENT AGENCY, THE LAST INVASION BICENTENARY COMMITTEE, MR PAT SMITH, MR & MRS C. BETTY.

TAPESTRY EXHIBITION: St Mary's Church Hall, Fishguard, Pembrokeshire
Feb - 31 Oct: Tues-Sat: 10am - 5pm, Sun: 2pm - 5pm, ~~CLOSED~~ MONDAYS
November - Easter: Telephone: 01348 - ~~811892~~ 874997 for information on opening times

open every day

Looking along the Tapestry a number of people and events stand out. The first character shown is Nelly Phillips, aged nine, who was said to have sighted the approaching ships. Retired sailor, Thomas Williams, realised they were French ships and the alarm was raised. Lieutenant-Colonel Knox left a party at Tregwynt Mansion and galloped to Goodwick where a volunteer force was gathering. A maidservant was said to be so terrified that she raced to a nearby farm but without spilling a drop of the beer she was carrying. A blank shot was fired from Fishguard Fort across the bows of a reconnoitering sloop forcing it to sail away. The French then landed at Carreg Wastad in the late afternoon in perfect weather. As darkness fell they lit their way up the cliffs by burning gorse and hanging torches in the trees. They pillaged local farms and were soon drunk and ill through eating half-cooked food. Alarmed by a ticking noise they fired a shot into a grandfather clock (the clock with its bullet hole still exists). Some soldiers played with a small child and others tiptoed away when they came upon a mother and her new born baby.

Local people began to attack the French with an assortment of home-made weapons but a frightened maid and youth hid in Llanwnda Church where they witnessed it being ransacked. At Trefgarne, Knox and his volunteers met Lord Cawdor who took command of their combined forces and led them back towards Fishguard. At Manorowen some French soldiers tried to escape into a walled garden (the small summer-house can still be seen there). Meanwhile the French ships obeyed their orders and sailed away, further demoralising the soldiers.

Many Fishguard residents had fled in panic, but hundreds poured in ready to fight. Only the cavalry and some local people spent the night in the Square.

A local woman complained that a French soldier had stolen her silver watch. Orders were given to shoot him, but fellow soldiers refused to do this and turned their guns on their own officers. Next day the same soldier stole from another French soldier and his punishment is shown in the tapestry border - his throat was cut and he was thrown into the sea.

The local heroine, Jemima Nicholas, is surrounded by so many stories that it is difficult to tell fact from fiction. In the tapestry she is shown as a formidable woman with a very frightened French soldier in her grip.

The next scenes depict the delivery and discussion of a conditional surrender note prepared by Colonel Tate, and the British troops gathering in readiness for battle in case their demand for an unconditional surrender was rejected. At this stage it is alleged that local women marching around a hill (The Bigney) in their red cloaks and black hats were mistaken by the enemy for a large force of red-coated regular soldiers. An unconditional surrender was declared and Lord Cawdor galloped to Trehowel Farm where he received Colonel Tate's sword.

In the final scenes British officers, holding the Old Jack Flag, watch the French troops march down hill to Goodwick. They were lined up on Goodwick Sands before being taken to prisons in Haverfordwest, Pembroke and Carmarthen.

TAPESTRI'R YMOSODIAD OLAF
CYNLLUNIWYD GAN ELIZABETH CRAMP R.W.S.

Fel eu prif gyfraniad i Ddathliadau'r Daucanmlwydddiant roedd **Cymdeithas Gelfyddydau Abergwaun** wedi cychwyn prosiect cymundeol i greu Tapestri Broadwaith yn adrodd hanes y Glaniad yn 1797. Roedd 78 o bobl leol wedi bod yn cydweithio i wneud y tapestri sy'n mesur 30.4 metr (tua 100 troedfedd) o hyd ac mae wedi cymryd tua 40,000 awr i'w gwblhau. Mae'r cynllun yn debyg i'r Bayeux Tapestry enwog sy'n adrodd hanes Ymosodiad 1066. Yn debyg i'w ragflaenydd enwog mae'n adrodd yr hanes ynhyd â nifer o storïau lleol sydd wedi datblygu o gwmpas ffeithiau hanesyddol 1797.

Parhaodd yr ymosodiad am ddau ddiwrnod ac fe welir hyn yn lliwiau'r tapestri sy'n dangos y dydd yn troi'n nos a'r nos yn troi'n ddydd eto. Roedd angen gwaith dychymyg i ddarlunio gweithgareddau'r nos er mwyn creu cynnwrf mewn lliwiau fel y ceffylau porffor a gwynebau gwyrdd y milwyr ofnus. Mae'r prif ddigwyddiadau wedi'u disgrifio mewn ysgrifen dwy-ieithog ar ymylon y gwaith ac mae cyfoeth o fanylion ffeithiau hanesyddol a chwedlonol i'w gweld yn y brodwaith.

Mae llyfr lliwgar, 36 tudalen, "Tapestri Y Goresgyniad Olaf", wedi ei gynhyrchu gan Gymdeithas Celfyddydau Abergwaun ac mae e ar gael yn yr Arddangosfa a gan llyfr-werthwyr lleol. Mae pedwar llyfr am y Glaniad ar gael yn 1997 ynghyd â nifer o hanesion a geir mewn llyfrau hanes Sir Benfro. Mae rhian ar gael gan llyfrwerthwyr lleol hefyd ac mewn llyfrgelloedd.

Er mwyn cael coffadwriaeth barhaol o'r Dathliadau Daucanmlwyddiant bwriedir sefydlu Canolfan y Glanio yn Abergwaun lle bydd y tapestri yn ganolbwynt. Tan hynny bydd y tapestri yng ngofal Cymdeithas Gelfyddydau Abergwaun Cafwyd cefnogaeth i gynllunio a chreu câs gwydr i'w arddangos a'i ddiogelu yn barod i'r Ganolfan. Hefyd cafwyd cefnogaeth gan nifer o unigolion, busnesau a mudiadau. Cyhoeddir llyfr yn cynnwys enwau pawb sydd wedi cyfrannu at y prosiect.

Prif gefnogwyr: STENA LINE, THE ARTS COUNCIL OF WALES, THE CALOUSTE GULBENKIAN FOUNDATION, THE WELSH DEVELOPMENT AGENCY, THE LAST INVASION BICENTENARY COMMITTEE, MR PAT SMITH, MR & MRS C. BETTY.

ARDDANGOSFA'R TAPESTRI: Neuadd yr Eglwys Santes Fair, Abergwaun, Sir Befro
Chwefror hyd Hydref 31: Dydd Mawrth - Dydd Sadwrn10am - 5pm,
Dydd Sul: 2pm - 5pm, AR GAU DYDD LLUN.
I gael gwybodaeth ychwanegol ffoniwch 01348 - 811392

Wrth edrych ar hyd y tapestri mae nifer o gymeriadau a digwyddiadau yn amlwg. Y cymeriad cyntaf a welir yw Nelly Phillips, naw oed; dywedir mai hi oedd y cyntaf i weld y llongau'n dod. Y nesaf yw Thomas Williams, morwr wedi ymddeol. Deallodd ef mai llongau o Ffrainc oeddynt ac aeth i rhybuddio'r dref. Gadawodd Cyrnol Knox barti ym Maenor Tregwynt ar unwaith a charlamodd i Wdig lle roedd llu o wirfoddolwyr wedi ymgynnull. Dywedir bod morwyn fach wedi dychryn ac fe rhedodd nerth ei thraed i ffermdy cyfagos ond heb ollwng un diferyn o'r cwrw roedd yn ei gario. Taniwyd ergyd wag at un o'r llongau, o Gaer Abergwaun, a'i gorfodi i ffoi i'r môr. Glaniodd yn Ffrancwyr ar Garreg Wastad yn hwyr y prynhawn mewn tywydd perffaith. Pan oedd hi'n nosi goleuasant y ffordd i fyny'r graig gan gynnau'r eithin a chlymu ffaglau yn y coed. Buont yn ysbeilio ffermdai'r ardal gan ddwyn bwyd a chwrw-cartref a chyn hir roeddynt yn feddw gaib ac yn sâl ar ôl bwyta'r bwyd oedd heb ei goginio'n iawn. Clywsant y cloc yn tician mewn un ffermdy ac fe saethodd un o'r milwyr ato. Mae'r twll i'w weld ynddo hyd heddiw. Dywedir bod rhai o'r milwyr wedi bod yn chwarae gyda plentyn bach ac eraill wedi mynd i ffwrdd ar flaenau'u traed pan ddaethant ar draws mam a'i baban newydd-ei-eni.

Ymosodwyd ar y Ffrancwyr gan nifer o bobl yr ardal gan ddefnyddio casgliad o arfau amrywiol. Roedd bachgen ifanc a morwyn fach wedi dychryn a rhedeg i guddio yn Eglwys Llanwnda lle y gwelsant y Ffrancwyr yn difrodi'r adeilad. Roedd Knox a'i wirfoddolwyr wedi cyfarfod â'r Arglwydd Cawdor a'i fyddin yn Nhreffgarn a daeth y ddau lu yn ôl gyda'i gilydd tuag at Abergwaun. Ym Manorowen gellir gweld hyd heddiw y lle bu rhai o'r milwyr yn cuddio mewn gardd ar ôl ceisio dianc. Yn y cyfamser roedd y llongau wedi hwylio i ffwrdd gan adael y milwyr yn ddiymadferth.

Ciliodd llawer o drigolion Abergwaun mewn dychryn ond daeth rhai cannoedd ymlaen yn barod i ymladd. Dim ond y Marchogion ac ychydig o drigolion a fu ar Sgwar Abergwaun dros nos. Roedd un gwraig leol wedi achwyn bod un o'r Ffrancwyr wedi dwyn ei wats arian ond gwrthododd y milwyr Ffrengig ei saethu ac fe droisant eu gynnau ar swyddogion eu hunain. Trannoeth roedd yr un milwr wedi dwyn wrth filwr Ffrengig arall ac fe welir ei gosb yn y tapestri - taflwyd ei gorff i'r môr ar ôl torri ei wddf â chyllell.

Ceir llawer o hanesion am yr arwres Jemima Nicholas ond ni ellir profi a ydynt i gyd yn gywir. Fe'i gwelir hi yn y tapestri fel gwraig nerthol yn gafael mewn milwr ofnus iawn.

Mae'r golygfeydd nesaf yn darlunio'r drafodaeth am gytundeb amodol a baratowyd gan Cyrnol Tate â'r milwyr Prydeinig yn ymgasglu yn barod i frwydr rhag ofn y byddai'r gelyn yn gwrthod ildio'n ddiamod. Dywedir bod nifer fawr o wragedd y dref wedi cerdded oddiamgylch y Bigni gan wisgo hetiau duon uchel a sioliau coch gan dwyllo'r gelyn bod llawer o filwyr yn gwisgo cotiau coch yn barod i ymosod arnynt. Cafwyd cytundeb ildio'n ddiamod ac fe garlamodd yr Arglwydd Cawdor i Ffem Trehowel lle y trosglwyddwyd cleddyf Cyrnol Tate iddo.

Yn y golygfeydd olaf gwelir y swyddogion Prydeinig, yn dal hen faner Jack, yn gwylio'r Ffrancwyr yn martsio i lawr i Wdig. Safasant mewn rhesi ar draeth Wdig ac yna fe'u carcharwyd yn Hwlffordd, Penfro a Chaerfyrddin.

BOYHOOD MEMORIES OF MAINDEE AT THE
TURN OF THE CENTURY

Early life in a happy home colours and brightens the memories of childhood. So it is that when I think of my boyhood in Maindee I see long sunny summer days with no rain and short, sparkling frosty winter days frequently white with hard, not slushy, snow.

We bathed, surely from March to September in warm seas or streams and as surely we spent the remainder of our months tobogganing or skating.

Very little rain. Weren't the water supplies turned off on many summer days? By the same token, why was Wentwood reservoir constructed? Maybe Newport was expanding; maybe my memory of endless sunshine is true.

Hard winters. Before October was over we took our superfatted pal up to the pools on Christchurch road and when the ice supported him we knew that we had months of skating ahead.

When I meet men now who were boys of Maindee with me, I recognise the effect of all that sunshine and frost. The true son of Maindee is compounded of sunbeams and frost crystals. When he awakes of a morning he feels always that birthday call — "What gorgeous thing will happen to me today?" That is due to the sunshine but, in the presence of vice or cruelty, he becomes cold and hard. That is the effect of the long frosts.

Our lives centred around our homes, our schools and our churches or chapels. My home, like the homes of all my friends, was a place of warmth and happiness, symbolised best by early visions of the family seated around the two-burner paraffin lamp on the table.

Gas, with its wall-burners, incandescent burners, and inverted incandescent burners and electricity ("how cold this light is, after the gas!") came later and were less cosy.

My father was a *clerical worker* and, like all his tribe, dressed the part. His bowler hat, swallow-tailed coat, with handkerchief in tail, his gloves and his pink immaculateness and dignified walk conveyed to an observer an impression of English assurance and well-founded pride. We, too, were proud of him; our mother adored him.

He was typical of his time. When chapel service was over on a Sunday morning, a dozen such men walked slowly along Duckpool Road discussing the points of the sermon. These were the Baptists. From St. John's and St. Matthew's, from Summerhill and Victoria Avenue, similar little coteries emerged, long after the crowded congregations had left. These men were the salt of Maindee earth. Their influence lives on to this day.

Vivid in my memory shine our religious leaders. Our own Reverend A. T. Jones, whose long hair and Quaker hat were the outward sign of a burning zeal for righteousness; the quiet, retiring Reverend G. H. Cook, whose deacons discovered that his threadbare clothes were the result of quite indiscriminating charity on his part; and the saintly Vicar Swinnerton, who was later to devote his life to the service of the blind — these three seen, perhaps invidiously, to have been the torchbearers of Christ in an impoverished, restless and sometimes riotous little township.

Then came the Midland invasion, when the men of Wolverhampton, tough, full of *drive,* descended on us. Colonies of decent brick houses were built for them, but our Mr. Cook saw that environment was not all. A mission-chapel, temporary in fabric, was erected and soon afterwards a young and handsome minister was placed in charge. Our boyish hearts burned within us as we saw him and his Lysaghts men, laying the foundations and raising the walls of a fine new church. I have often wondered whether the Rev. C. E. Pugh owed his later triumphs on the Congo to his faith in the men of Corporation Road.

Most vivid is my crystal-clear memory of a short, thick-set, bearded, pink-cheeked headmaster — Philip Gregory Gale. He knew me as a pupil and later as a member of his staff. His influence on my generation and several others was profound and whenever old Maindee pupils forgather the central topic is always Mr. Gale.

Mr. P. G. Gale, first headmaster of Maindee School.

Let me add that I knew many of the teachers who served under Mr. Gale. Among them were strong, forthright characters and some of brilliant academic achievement, but never did I see his authority challenged.

On the other hand, a very prominent Newport citizen who had called to ask for special treatment for a young teacher was met by the command, as the Head opened his door, "Sir, I will bid you good morning!"

Our mothers took us to Maindee School on our fourth birthdays. After spending three years in the infants' school with Mrs. Atkins, Miss Good and Miss Pool, we were transferred to the upper floor of the main building where, shivering with apprehension, we were ushered into the Presence. Over and above us along the frieze was the banner headline, *Order is the First Law of Heaven,* but we did not see that. All our eyes were inescapably focused on the great man.

For seven years or more, in spite of our growing knowledge and confidence, he held with ease his dominance over us. We admired and respected him; sometimes we dreaded him; in later years respect warmed into affection. I see him now, seated majestically before a hundred-and-twenty boys. They repeat the books of the Old and New Testaments; he questions them closely on Paul's missionary journeys — and heaven help the clot who knows not what happened at Antioch in Pisidia.

I see him on a snowy morning. He has been up since dawn preparing two "slides", the length of the playground. As the boys arrive, he places an orange half-way along each slide, and shows them how to collect the orange at full speed. School opens when the sack of oranges is empty.

The original Maindee School, built in 1866 (from an old drawing).

Maindee was a church school, administered by the Christchurch School Board. The headmaster lived on the premises and his garden, filling the space between the school building and the road, was always of exhibition standard. My illustration, copied by permission of the present headmaster, from a washdrawing done many years ago by Mr. W. J. Bush, Jun., shows the school, erected in 1866, as it was before the garden was made, and before the shops opposite were erected.

By the time when we reached the upper standards, our classrooms in the new building abutted on the main road, and we knew the intense pleasure of seeing our teachers relapse into silence when the town band or the barrel-organ performed outside.

"THE BACON-BOX."

MAESGLAS CASTLE

South of the Cardiff Road we have Pillgwenlly, Cwrt-y-Bella, Mendalgief, Maesglas and many other Welsh puzzles. *Pillgwenlly* is the tidal ditch of Gwynllyw, where our pirate prince kept his long fast boat before he became a convert to Christianity. "Cwrt-y-Bella" was the court of the wolf. *Mendalgief* has floored every Welsh authority to whom I have submitted it.

"Maesglas" is just greenfield, but should not be pronounced "maze glace;" make it rhyme with "buys glass."

The mound of Castell Maesglas, Newport.

In a children's playfield, not far from the school, I came across a rectangular mound which recalls the famous Castell Maesglas or Greenfield castle.

Four centuries ago, Churchyard described it thus:

> *A goodly seate, a tower, a princely pyle,*
> *Built as a watch, or safety for the soyle,*
> *By river stands, from Newport not three myle . . .*
> *The name thereof, the nature shewes alright,*
> *Greenfield it is, full gay and goodly sure.*

Coxe visited the site in 1800 and found *a square tower with a spiral staircase, a stone edifice with several apartments in one of which is a large fireplace with a fine Gothic entrance and some detached ruins. At a small distance is a circular mound, probably the site of the ancient keep or citadel.*

Greenfield castle was one of the seats of Henry, Duke of Lancaster, whose daughter Blanche married John of Gaunt. Strange it is that these Lancastrians held interests in the south as well as the north of Gwent and a pretty fancy to associate the red rose with Maesglas as with Grosmont.

THE GOLDEN MILE IN TREDEGAR PARK

"Everyone in Newport knows a small house at the bottom of Lover's Lane (rightly named), Cardiff Road. Samuel Fairfax lives there. His gross rental is £6, ratable value £4 10s. He pays rates £1 0s. 3d. annually, being 62½ per cent in excess of what is received from the Park Mile with its £10,000 or £12,000 income."

James Brown in *The Park Mile*, published 1883.

Among the letters sent to me following my article on the big railway bridge at Ebbw Vale was one from an old Newport boy, now in Cheshire, who has devoted many leisure hours to the study of railways.

In it he referred to the three pillars of the Park Mile railway in Tredegar Park as *historic monuments in their own right as interesting as the Pyramids or London Wall or the doorway of the Westgate.*

Boundary stone of the "Park Mile", near Park Junction, Newport.

These stone boundary pillars are indeed of historic interest. My drawing shows one of the two near Park Junction signal box, reached by way of Park Crescent. The pillar at the Bassaleg Junction end of the Park Mile stands against the upper stonework of the bridge at Pye Corner.

Seven feet in height, the pillars bear at the top a baronial crown, then a capital T (Tredegar) and *Park Mile Railway;* the pillar at Bassaleg Junction shows signs of colouring. I could find no trace or memory of the fourth pillar.

I am indebted to William J. Skillern, of Stockport, for drawing my attention to the pillars. I am equally indebted to my good friend the Bookman for two documents which he excavated from his labyrinthine archives.

Like all sons of Newport, I had regarded the *Golden Mile* as a quaint commentary on equality of opportunity — "Unto him that hath shall be given." *The Park Mile,* by James Brown (1883), and the 1927 report on the Park Mile Railway drawn up by the Monmouthshire county council supplied the essential facts of a fantastic story.

In 1792 the act was passed for constructing and maintaining two canals, one from Pontnewynydd to the Usk at Newport, the other from Crindau to Crumlin bridge, and the making of railways therefrom to several *Iron Works and Mines in the counties of Monmouth and Brecknock.* A marginal note read, *Tolls not to be liable to Parliamentary or Parochial Taxes.*

This immunity from rates and taxes seems to have been granted to encourage new ideas in transport.

Ten years later the *Sirhowy Act* empowered Samuel Homfray and others to make the Sirhowy railroad. In it comes the passage, *And Sir Charles Morgan of Tredegar, Baronet, hath proposed to the said Company to undertake, at his own expense, one mile of the said Railway or Tramway through and adjoining to Tredegar Park, now belonging to him, upon having the benefit of the Tolls to arise thereon.*

Thus originated the golden mile. Some three years after the act of 1802 was passed, the railway through the park was opened and the stonepillars were raised later as boundary stones. The acts of 1792, 1797 and 1802 authorised conveyance of iron, coal, limestone and other commodities, with no mention of mails or passengers.

In 1848 an act repealed the provisions of the 1792 act, and thus the property of the Monmouthshire Company was liable to rating. In 1860 a similar act directed that the property of the Sirhowy Railway Company should be rated. Yet in 1880 it was alleged that the Park Mile was realising a net profit of £5,000 per annum without paying the normal rates.

In 1883 the widening of the Park Mile to take the Pontypridd and Caerphilly railway was authorised, and in that year it was recorded that four million tons passed annually along its lines. The lowest charge was ½d. a ton for coal; iron paid 1d. and these, with mails, etc., it was reported produced £10,000.

In 1889 the Monmouthshire county council pressed for an assessment of the Park Mile and Lord Tredegar undertook to pay £200 annually as county and police rate.

Thirty years later, in 1919, in his evidence before the Sankey Commission, Lord Tredegar stated that the Park Mile cost £40,000 and that he received income therefrom at £19,000 per annum.

On January 1, 1923, the Park Mile was transferred to the Great Western Railway Company. And in 1927 it was estimated that the continued exemption from rating of the Park Mile had cost the ratepayers of Monmouthshire throughout the years well over £50,000.

From an old railway servant at Bassaleg I learn that a pipeline running alongside the Park Mile railway conveys water from a reservoir in the fields above Bassaleg to Tredegar House.

Painting of 1821, showing horses and coal trams and Mr. Samuel Homfray passing Court-y-Bella farmhouse on the Cardiff road.

Footnote: The Bookman informs me that James Brown, who wrote the pamphlet *The Park Mile,* was mayor of Newport in 1853, 1861 and 1862, that he established the *Star of Gwent* newspaper, that he and his brother were the first to utilise waste gases from the blast furnaces of Ebbw Vale and that he strove for uniformity of gauge on the railways. Pugnacious, sturdy, far-seeing, he revelled in controversy and on one of his bright days he advised an alderman opponent, *When you have fleas in your bed, burn the bed!*

Christchurch. *Old Engraving*

CHRISTCHURCH

Until the 19th century, there was only one road into Newport from the east and this was continued by a single way out westwards. Both these roads were ancient ridgeways; both, in my opinion, were pre-Roman tracks.

The eastern ridgeway comes down from Wentwood through Catsash to Christchurch. Along this road the Romans travelled. Above the Usk Valley they must have halted and, looking down, seen a setting which reminded them of Rome. "Cupped in the calyx of the hills," the British settlement at Caerleon became the precursor of the capital Roman city of Isca Silurum — Caer Lleon, the camp of the legions.

The Romans built a road southward from Caerleon, over the hill and across *Netherwent* to the sea, where they erected a great sea-wall. Where this road cut the ridgeway was already a mound, holy land to the Britons, for their road looped around it to the south. About ten centuries afterwards, the Norman invaders chose this holy land at the cross-roads as the site of a church, built partly for worship, partly for residence and partly for defence.

In Tudor times the priests, seeking better quarters than the dreary monastic chamber in the church tower, built the *Priests' House,* adjoining the churchyard. This, though much restored, retains some original windows, very thick walls, the old bar-room of its unregenerate days as the first inn out of Newport on the coach-road to London, stone stairs, huge fireplace and, as you would expect, a legend of a secret passage to the Priory at Caerleon. When the restoration took place, a hollow-sounding part of the inner wall was laid open and five "churchwarden" pipes were found in a recess.

All my life Christchurch has been "my church", although I am not a Churchman. My father took me there on our earliest walks and showed me a hilltop gate, overlooking Caerleon. "Years ago," he said, "I used to see a tall, bearded gentleman leaning on this gate, smoking a pipe and watching the sunset. He used to stay at the Hanbury Arms, near Caerleon Bridge. His name was Alfred Tennyson."

When very young, I heard also the story of the Healing Stone of Christchurch. All through the ages, on the eve of Corpus Christi, sick children were brought to Christchurch and kept in contact with the Healing Stone throughout the night. "The records of the church," the old vicar used to say, "contain not a single instance of its failure . . ." As time passed, the annual pilgrimage became an occasion for revelling, a system of bribes was set up and the profiteers reaped a rich harvest from the friends of the little sufferers. Squire Van of Llanwern thereupon decided to end the scandal.

It was the eve of Corpus Christi about a hundred and thirty years ago. The usual influx of visitors and sick children had taken place. Business was brisk in the inn; the sexton was reaping his annual harvest of bribes. Suddenly the Squire rode up and demanded the key, cleared the visitors out of the church, locked the door and rode off with the key. Night fell and a great storm arose, the thunder reverberating among the hills.

At the height of the storm the bells of Christchurch rang an unearthly peal. Startled beyond measure, the villagers and visitors ran out to listen. Soon the bells clanged again, and now two of the younger men rode on their ponies to Llanwern. They roused the Squire and the three galloped up to Christchurch, where by the lightning flashes they saw a white and shaking mob listening to the appalling clangour of the bells.

The Healing Stone, Christchurch.

162

With the crowd trailing after him, the Squire opened the church door. The lightning threw sudden shafts of light through the stained glass across the nave. Summoning their courage, some bold spirits crept forward to see the angelic bell-ringers . . .

Tugging frantically at the ropes was a poor idiot boy, who had hidden himself when the others had left and who now chose this method of announcing his imprisonment. Thus ended, in ridicule, the long story of the Healing Stone of Christchurch.

Christchurch has two dedications, for it is also known as the Church of the Holy Trinity. The church has the usual southern porch, on whose stones, if you look closely, you will see masons' marks by which the ancient masons claimed their payment; one mark — a trowel — is very clear.

The Norman doorway has columns five feet high. Its builders learnt the art of the semi-circular archway from the Roman churches which they found in Normandy, but they left the Christchurch arch less ornate than the arch in the cathedral church of St. Woolos.

Standing in the centre of the nave at its western end you will see that the chancel axis is set in a more southerly direction than the nave alignment. One theory suggests that the nave represented the body of Christ on the Cross, the transepts His arms and that the chancel out of alignment symbolized His head, fallen on one side. Modern writers scorn this explanation and argue that the builders were at fault. This view, however, is hardly tenable when we consider the accuracy of the builders' work in every other particular.

'The Beauty of Christchurch'.

In the north aisle, near the door, is a tombstone carved with a woman's head, known as *The Beauty of Christchurch*. Dated 1712, the head is circular, supported by a neck which must have snapped under its weight and the details are so primitive that if it were exhibited now it would be acclaimed as the work of a master.

In the plaster of the south aisle is the imprint of a man's hand. You should note that the imprint is not of angels' fingers but of the hand of a 20th-century plasterer.

No trace of the screen remains. Cromwell's men removed that and smashed all the window-glass except one tiny orange-coloured pane still remaining in the east window.

Under the carpet, on the floor of the chancel, is the famed Healing Stone. It is a long narrow sepulchral stone, of 1376, to the memory of Johannes Colmer and his wife, Isabella. Nothing is known of John or Isabella, although the portrait of Isabella makes it clear that the *halo hats* worn quite recently by our ladies were the mode in Gwent in 1376.

Evening — Twyn Barllwm.

THE ASCENT OF TWYN BARLWM

How many Newport boys of 12 years or less have climbed Twyn Barlwm? Such an ascent bestowed merit in the old days, but I believe that the 1,374 feet climb is not essential now to the membership of any gang.

Part of the fascination of the mountain is the big Tump, surrounded by the elliptical trench of a prehistoric camp 200 yards long and 80 yards wide. The climb to the trench is easy, but the final scramble "up the Tump" tests the wind of most adults.

Take your 1in. map of South Monmouthshire and prick pins into the centres of the Gaer, Twyn Barlwm and Lodge Camp encampments. The Gaer and Lodge Camps stand three miles apart, and each of them is five miles from Twyn Barlwm. Our forefathers laid down tracks from camp to camp which are still in use today.

The Western Valley bus will drop you at the Cefn *Forge,* whence a short walk will lead you over the canal bridge into open meadows. Twyn Barlwm lies ahead, but look backwards; the field track which you are treading — an immemorial right of way — certainly directs from the Gaer to the Tump.

When you have to leave the fields in order to cross a road, diverge slightly to the left and, with a little trouble, you will find a vestige of the ancient track itself — a stone-lined hollow-way.

Get back then on to the right of way through the golf links and sense the nobility and grandeur of Twyn Barlwm as you approach him. If it is a still evening in summer or autumn, you may see the slopes change from green to blue and, with after-glow of gold above, take that magical transformation into royal purple.

If you have time, turn aside for Nightingale Hollow — Pant-yr-Eos. Later, at your destination, you will see the great pool nestled into its hollow, but few people take the prospect of Twyn Barlwm from Pant-yr-Eos, that prospect which seems to intensify and emphasise the rhythm of those mighty mountain shoulders. And so to the top!

The second route is of equal interest. Climbing from Caerleon, the track cuts through Lodge Camp and continues past Park Farm through the fields as a green road 22ft. wide leading straight through the Llantarnam Abbey grounds. Our course, however, is to the left when we reach the road and soon we cross the main Pontypool road at Croes-y-Mwyalch *(The Cross-roads of the Blackbirds).*

Now we are in Henllys Vale, where the spirit of W. H. Davies broods among the brooklands. We pass the 15th-century homestead of Pentrebach ("the little village") and climb the steep ascent to Castell-y-Bwch *(Buck's Castle),* where we take rest and refreshment. Then comes the drop into the warm valley, the crossing of Nant-y-Pandy and the good climb to the summit.

Those were two routes used in ancient times to reach the Tump. Pontypool boys love the ridgeway walk through Cwmyniscoy and Cwm Lickey; sons of Cwmcarn sing the praises of the heavenly climb along the banks of the Nant Carn; but, if you live in Abercarn, you will know that all other approaches to Twyn Barlwm are mean and monotonous when compared with their Gwyddon Valley, where in springtime you may see acres and acres of larches bursting into that indescribable fresh green which no other tree can show.

Let us rest now on the summit and contemplate. Buried underneath us is a mighty British chieftain; so we were taught; so we believe. The modern student laughs at our gullibility and teaches his children that the Normans built the great mount in order to give them control over the Western Valley!

Sons and daughters of Gwent, can you imagine our ancestors at Risca being cowed by a battalion of cloud-cuckoos a mile away? And such a mile!

Normans forsooth! Look at the view. You gaze to the south over Uskmouth, the Severn and Somerset. Return, and pick out the sapphire jewel which is Pant-yr-Eos. Can you make out the Holms and the Monkstone, and Penarth Head? See how many of the heights of Glamorgan and Gwent, swimming in a golden sea of light, are known to you. Rest your eyes now among the silver mists of the Carn Valley. Then explore the great hills of Brecknockshire and Herefordshire and Gloucestershire, to come to rest again on our own Wentwood and the Vale of Usk. And can you arrange for your shadow to fall on Christchurch tower?

When you have taken your fill of views, slip down the Tump and walk along the green ridgeway northwards. Soon you will see below to the east a rectangular reservoir. Turn left and descend past a farmhouse towards the Carn Valley, and soon you will reach a wild boggy hollow formed by a landslip. In winter this becomes a mere, known as the *Pool of Avarice.*

An old legend tells of a great house which stood on this spot. The mistress was basting a fowl with bacon. Outside, the air was heavy and thunderous. Suddenly there was a knock on the big door and a gentle, tired voice — the voice of a poor cousin — implored, "Spare us food, please, please spare us food. We starve." The door was banged contemptuously and the hungry woman retreated. But she looked back later and saw the hill lift, sway left and right, and crash. The house and all its occupants were swallowed in the maw of the landslide. Even now, so the older shepherds aver, when you stand on the bank of the pool you may hear the groans of the lost souls below, doomed by their avarice.

The Twyn Barlwm *organ* has always eluded me. During dry summers, fortunate people on the Tump have heard the rolling harmony of a church organ. It may be that the wind passing over the mouths of the dried water-runnels produces musical notes. Finally, seek the peace of Llanderfel. The foundations of the ancient church may still be traced, recalling many similar sites in the Black Mountains.

Chapter Ten

A JOURNEY FROM NEWPORT TO CHEPSTOW

Visiting the churches of Llanmartin, Magor, Caerwent, Caldicot and St. Pierre.

LLANMARTIN

Nowadays when we visit Llanmartin, we turn south-east from the Newport-Chepstow road at the New Inn. There is, however, another route — the walker's route — which follows a right-of-way as long as any in Gwent.

It starts at the *Garden City,* leads over the fields to the southern edge of Llanwern golf links, crosses Monksditch near Great Barn, enters Llanwern Park at the old forge and continues under the wooded heights to the Llanmartin lane. This route does not end at Llanmartin but proceeds on to Pencoed Castle and beyond.

A view of St. Martin's Church, Llanmartin.

There are three Martins in the Saints' Calendar, but we do not know which of the three is commemorated at Llanmartin. The first rector, Roger de Mesyndon, was there in 1352 and the church which he directed was possibly the one mentioned in Domesday Book which received annually two hogs, a hundred loaves of bread and beer *(ij porcos et c panes cum cerevisia)* for the good of the King's soul. Inclusion in Domesday is fair evidence for a pre-Norman foundation.

The whole of the church except the tower was rebuilt in 1858 and consists now of nave, chancel and vestry. This vestry replaced the Morgan chapel, which contained several tombs and memorials of the Knights of Pencoed Castle. With a destructive passion unusual even with Victorian *restorers* the rebuilders of Llanmartin demolished all the Morgan memorials except one, to Sir Thomas Morgan, the first Knight of Pencoed, who died in 1510.

One of the monuments inside the church.

Many years ago I drew this monument for Sir Joseph Bradney's *History of Monmouthshire*. More recently I took great pleasure in making a new and detailed drawing and I trust that reproduction by our skilful process-men (for whom I have high admiration) will enable my readers to perceive not only variations in costume but also the careful and individual portraiture of this, one of our most precious relics.

The central panel shows an angel (note his wings) supporting (note his fingers, one on each side) a shield of arms the impalement of which (three lions passant in pale) represent the second wife of Sir Thomas.

Of the seven males on the right, the first and last have bared knees, the first also baring his breast, maybe to display a chain and jewel, while the fourth also bares his breast; and all, except the first, are hooded. The sixth figure is kneeling sideways and the second and fifth are heads only.

The five female figures nearest the centre wear similar and becoming hats, three of them display beads, the next a rose-shaped ornament and the next a pendant jewel. Notice, however, that the two figures on the left have neither headwear nor ornament, and bear in mind that Sir Thomas Morgan had but five daughters.

He had also eight sons, but only seven male figures are shown and the last figure on the right is a lone mourner, for all the other figures are in groups of two or three.

I am forced to the conclusion, therefore, that when the *Morgan tomb* was being reassembled in 1858 the five daughters and six sons were placed to the left and right of the shield-of-arms and the end spaces filled with odd figures.

But that any of these splendidly rendered portraits fall into the category of "weepers" — stylised mourners — I cannot agree. As I wrote long ago, "Doleful melancholy kneels cheek by jowl with half-restrained hilarity: retiring shyness next to the sophistication of a Hollywood star."

Nor are they, as one writer declares, portraits of children. They portray grown men and women with strongly developed facial characteristics which *sing out* after 444 years.

See them for yourselves, dear readers and imagine the Morgan family arriving at Llanmartin Church in 1500 AD.

On my way to the church I had passed an interesting old house with a three-storeyed porch and Elizabethan chimneys. I called there later, to discover that it was Ford Farm, named after the ford over the brook which later becomes Monksditch.

Mrs. Duthie and her highly intelligent young son showed me the slit windows in the porch, a chimney wall ten feet thick and two spiral staircases, one of stone with oak treads, the other of solid baulks of oak.

At a corner of the room to the left of the porch my hostess opened a door leading into a very small room, so small that my interest was at once aroused. "Is there a similar room," I asked, "on the floor above?" She nodded. "And on the top floor?"

"Yes, indeed," she exclaimed and young Douglas asked excitedly, "But what were these little rooms used for?"

There is no doubt that here, as at Cillwch, Trevella, Treowen and dozens of other old houses in Gwent a vertical drainage shaft saved much running up and down those spiral stairs.

Twelve pigeon-holes, a house-leek on the roof above, a baking oven and a door and doorway of the 16th century leading into the dairy lent character and interest to an ancient home. And with what interest would its builders view a television aerial affixed to one of their Elizabethan chimneys!

Ford Farm, Llanmartin.

MAGOR

Long ago, during evensong in York minster, I looked up and was startled to see a stone face grinning at me. It was surrounded by oak leaves, two of which were growing from the mouth. This was my introduction to the strange being who appears so often in our cathedrals and churches — that figure who has been so well cherished by Lady Raglan, *The Green Man.*

Before leaving Magor church, I examined the heads and figures carved on the corbels which once supported the roof groins. During this inspection, I was delighted to discover in the south wall of the nave a splendid Green Man, carved on an isolated corbel.

Full in the face, with a shapely moustache and with oak foliage growing from his mouth, he stares nonchalantly downwards at the passing show of his village. For I have no doubt that Lady Raglan is correct in her view that the Green Man of our churches were portraits of figures which played a great part in the fairs and village ceremonies.

In the May day shows there was frequently a figure known variously as Jack in the Green, the Green Man, the King of May, etc., bearing a wicker-work structure entwined with greenery, through which his eyes peered out. Sometimes his face was blackened to imitate a chimney sweep. After the fires of winter, the sweep was a busy and important functionary and his significance became recognised on May day.

These May day customs are as widespread as they are ancient. They are still practised not only by the settled races but also by the gipsies, who have in Rumania and elsewhere a boy decked with leaves who is called Green George.

How many children in our county, I wonder, will be making this evening a calennig. Let them take three twigs, silver them and use the twigs as a stand for the reddest apple in the house. Then let them insert a sprig of box or holly into the apple and impale on the spines of the leaves, currants or raisins, nuts or grapes.

They should then take the calennig around to their neighbours who will meet good fortune in 1955 if they are generous to the children. Then the pretty gift must stand in the house until the apple has withered, whereupon everyone will have a happy new year.

It would be pleasant if the many women's institutes and guilds in these sadly materialistic days could stage a revival in our homes of happy old customs.

All these ruminations of mine were aroused by the stone faces in Magor church. But what is this weird rumour which has come to be about the bewitching of the church clock? Have any of my older readers any exact evidence? Who, for instance, was the witch? When did she cast her spell on the clock? How long did the spell operate?

The Green Man.

Figure in south aisle.

A Calennig.

CAERWENT

Stephen we know as the first martyr, but who was St. Tathan? In that strange period of the Dark Ages when we in Gwent were sending missionaries to Brittany — for was not St. Malo a native of Caerwent? — the Irish, filled with the same zeal, were posting missionaries to us. Was not Bridget the pure virgin saint from Kildare? Tathan was the son of an Irish king.

With eight disciples, so we read in a delightful old record, he sailed from Ireland and landed at a port *called by the addition of the name of the country*. At Caerwent they were welcomed by a Christian and left their ship, unmoored at the quay. Later, when a servant went to fasten the ship, he found the loose mooring rope held by a stag. In or near this walled city of Venta Silurium, by tradition the Irish saint built a church and a monastery, and presided over an academy.

Caerwent Church.

Where was the site of Tathan's monastery? The land given to Tathan by King Caradog lay *to the east of the city, and between the walls and the river*.

Was that the earliest church at Caerwent? That fascinating little structure raised by the Romans over the foundations of their baths tempts one, especially by its apse and plan, to see there a Christian temple. Pending further investigation, that remains a conjecture and, until the Normans came, Tathan's church of the Holy Trinity and the monastery must be marked as the centre of Christian religion and culture in Netherwent.

It must have been a thrilling day for the visitors from Normandy when they captured the ruined Roman city. There, as at Caerleon, they found relics which must have reminded them of their own land. The conquest over, they settled on a central site for their new church and built it parallel to the old road which bisected the city, dedicating it to St. Stephen.

The oldest fabric visible now is Early English. Lancets in the east wall of the chancel, and the interesting segmental arches in the south wall — piers and arches chamfered — are of that period. It is of interest, however, to read in Freeman's Survey (1851) that when the early English chancel arch was taken down for repair a Norman impost was discovered.

The chancel, he notes, had two aisles and the nave one, *all of which have gone.* The north wall of the chancel had been rebuilt, with three lancet windows similar to the genuine windows in the east wall. I found the north porch of absorbing interest. The vicar showed me first the sun-dial stone to the right, then the six members of the external arch, the outer member of which had once held projecting ornament and the inner member retaining its crockets.

Within the porch were relics and, of equal interest, a handsome little doorway with stone steps leading to an upper floor. This upper room has a window which gives a clear view of the main road and was possibly used originally by a semi-chorus when the procession *made a station.* In later years such rooms became libraries, stores for armour, etc. While the floor has gone, the sockets in the wall for the beams are visible.

The beautiful niche over the inner door probably held an image of Stephen and it was of interest to note the damaged stoup in the porch, so near to the stoup within the church. Chancel and nave appeared to be equal in size. The tower, battlemented and battered, seemed designed for defence, until one examined the windows. I liked especially the octagonal stair-turret with its entrance doorway at the base.

In the floor of the nave was a sepulchral stone carved with a floriated cross and an inscription which I could not decipher. Incorporated into the walls of the south aisle were the "bishop's stone" from Dinham, a couple of primitive consecration crosses, some ornamented stones of varying age and an impressive Roman cinerary urn.

The interesting list of abbots and vicars ranges from St. Malo and St. Tathan to the present vicar, the Rev. J. Barrie Evans, MA, to whom I owe deep debt for his courtesy and generosity in displaying the treasures of his church.

During my talk with the vicar of Caerwent, I was surprised — for I thought that I knew his church — to hear him ask, "Of course you have noticed our little head with the tongue poked out? No? Well, see if you can find him."

On my second visit, I searched that church in vain. When Mr. Barrie Evans arrived, he was pleased at my discomfiture and led me to the stone head, with the tongue out and the derisive grin, shown in my sketch. I leave it to my readers to discover it for themselves. It is not a *green man.*

The Grotesque.

Meanwhile, I had examined and sketched one face of a head of a cross resting on a window-sill in the south nave.

"Undoubtedly the head of the village cross," commented the vicar. "It was dug up in a cottage garden and brought and preserved for us by the father of Tom Till.

"This face is a crucifixion with St. Mary and St. John. The reverse shows the Holy Child and his Virgin Mother, she apparently holding the stem of a lily. One end shows a mitred bishop (or an abbot — why not St. Tathan?) holding a crozier."

In the north porch are priceless relics of the Roman occupation. The massive *Silures stone* bears a tribute in this outpost of their empire, to the wisdom of the Romans in granting the Silures a measure of autonomy. It reads:
". . . PAULINO LEG LEG I (I) AUG PROCONSUL PROVINC NARBONENSIS LEG AUG PR PR PROVI LUGUDUNEN EX DECRETO ORDINIS RES PUBL CIVIT SILURUM."
(To Claudius Paulinus Legate of the II Augustan Legion. Proconsul of the province of Narbonensis, Imperial propaetorian Legate of the province of Lugdunensis, set up by decree of the tribal senate by the Commonwealth of the tribe of the Silures).

I agree with the vicar that this stone is too precious to remain in the porch, where at times — now for instance — conditions are arctic. It should be removed into the church.

With it also I would remove the smaller *altar* brought down from Dinham and inscribed, "DEO MARTI OCELO AEL AGUSTINUS OP V.S.L.M."
(To the god Mars Ocelus Aelius Agustinus optio paid his vow willingly and duly).

Due for removal also, to a site where it will be visible to all, is Ben Prichard's memorial stone. Ben was a farmer who collected the parish tithes:

> *Here rests for ever old good-natured Ben,*
> *Who rested when alive but now and then,*
> *And lived by gathering only one in ten.*
> *Born to no title, heir to no estate,*
> *Yet drove no hungry belly from his gate.*
> *That he was kind and just, no churl or knave,*
> *The poor have proved by weeping o'er his grave.*
> *Let many a rich man blush, if blush he can,*
> *And learn his duty from this poor old man.*

The handsome oak pulpit was a gift from Sir Charles Williams of Llangibby in 1632. In addition to inscriptions, it bears a carved representation of Llandaff Cathedral (Ecclesia Landaven).

Roman coins.

From his treasury the vicar brought me scores of Roman coins. "Others are found quite frequently," he remarked. "A roadman sweeping recently heard a tinkle and discovered quite a good specimen." Of even greater interest is the silver penny of Hardicanute found *within the city walls*, probably in the churchyard, some forty years ago. The size of a sixpenny piece, it has been examined by the greatest authority on coins of that period.

"The legends," he writes, are as follows:
Observe + CNVT REC + Reverse + FARGRIMON-LEGECE +.

The coin was struck at Chester by a moneyer of the name of Fargrim . . . who was striking coins before 1042 and the same mint in 1050. Only five other coins by him are known. We may date this coin, I gather, as of 1042, two years after the Witan had offered the crown to Hardicanute. "Coins of this issue are inscribed with the names Cnut or Harthacnut quite promiscuously."

Like a practised showman, the vicar now proceeded to withdraw dramatically from a secret receptacle "perhaps my greatest treasure." "One of my predecessors digging in the churchyards found in a stone coffin the skeleton of a priest. This priest had been buried in his cope as the clasp indicated. On the breastbone stood this 13th-century pewter sepulchral chalice."

Seven centuries had petalled the pewter yet the beauty of the cup and its broad base were still clear, still inexpressibly poignant. And finally the registers, early entries in Latin, date back to 1568.

Head of the village cross.

CALDICOT

Like Rumney in Wentloog, Caldicot is expanding rapidly and, with its new houses, its playing field and its projected community centre, should soon recapture the importance which caused the whole of the eastern sea moors to be named *Caldicot Level*. The castle must remain always the chief historic attraction in the village, but I reserve that for a later series of articles. Meanwhile, let us glance at the other treasures of Caldicot.

An ancient map, now in the Bodleian Library, shows a road leading from the prehistoric landing camp at Sudbrook, passing through Caldicot, Magor, Bishton and Llanwern to Christchurch and Newport. This was crossed at Caldicot by a Roman track from Caerwent to the mouth of the Nedern brook; hence the significance of the village.

The porch, St. Mary's Church, Caldicot.

Caldicot church, dedicated to St. Mary, has an interesting and beautiful porch. As my drawing shows, it is embattled and buttressed, and the doorway is enriched with crocketed pinnacles and a lovely ogee canopy.

Inside the porch are two niches, one on the outer wall containing an ancient figure, the other on the inner wall a modern Virgin and child. The recess in the outer wall holds a headless and mutilated stone effigy which may be of the founder, but which is known locally as *Old George*.

Crosses cut into the stones simply indicate the level of the upper floor, which was reached by stone steps from the door on the right. In this upper room, with its stone faces of ancient Caldicot worthies — more solemn and sedate than the Magor faces — the village school may have met, or it may have been a store for books or armour. On the inner porch archway, a consecration cross survives.

Caldicot Church from Court House garden.

The central tower seems to be of two periods, the window on the lower south side being the oldest in the church. There is no south aisle and the modern vestry built against the north wall of the chancel has preserved an original window and buttress of that wall.

Elegant capitals surmount the clustered columns of the arcade, the stonework here, on the porch canopy, and the cinquefoiled ogee tracery of the windows being far in advance of the masonry in most of our simple Monmouthshire churches.

I found that the legend of the *haunted pew* persists in the village, but I do not propose to give the details. Much more to my taste is the practice at Caldicot of muffling the bells at the passing of the old year and freeing them to ring in the new.

One of the bells, made in the old Bristol foundry in 1450, is inscribed, *In Honore Sancta Marine* (Mariae), and full details of all the eight bells are recorded in Arthur Wright's *Church Bells of Monmouthshire.*

At Caldicot, we met the vicar — a perfect reincarnation of the jovial monk. He was walking in his beautiful garden, surely "contented with his lot," but, when he introduced his wife — a charming lady — we tried to forget the monkish similitude. The vicar showed us some entries in his ancient register. One referred to a *Thomas Shone Cattery,* another to a parishioner who was a *monster of iniquity* and a third to a village worthy known as *Thomas stop-and-drink.* This last-named seemed peculiarly appropriate in a village possessing a tavern called *The Tippling Philosopher.*

Caldicot, we agreed, implied a sheltering place alongside an ancient road. Very ancient is this road, for it leads from the prehistoric landing-camp at Sudbrook and is joined at Caldicot by the Roman track from the mouth of the Nedern Brook. *Coldharbour* has the same implication as *Caldicot.*

175

Caldicot Church, like the churches at Magor and Undy, has no aisle to the nave, but the north wall of the chancel was an external wall. So it is that in the vestry, a later addition, is a good buttress and one of the original windows. The capitals of the nave arcade are decorated with exquisitely-wrought stone foliage.

There is rumoured to be a haunted pew in Caldicot Church — a pew in which prayer cannot be made — but this may be the product of the aforementioned village gossip. More to our taste was the vicar's description of *watch-night* at Caldicot. "We muffle our bells to ring the old year out, but set them pealing free to ring the new year in!"

Cross Inn, Caldicot.

THE CROSS INN

When our finest small Tudor house, Church House, Magor, was demolished this year the architect of the brewery firm promised that great care would be taken of the priceless screen, the stone stairs and light, the fireplace, beams and representative windows.

At the entrance to the car park on the site of Church House the fireplace, stairs and tiny light are now preserved. The windows are in safe keeping, but what of the screen and beams? During the last war an American officer offered a blank cheque for the screen. I can imagine the furore it would cause if installed in a modern mansion in Massachusetts. For the present, however, it is fixed with a number of Church House beams and joists, in old Cross Inn, Caldicot.

As the name implies, this ancient tavern stands at a road junction. Chepstow Road meets Church Road, and Sandy Lane meets Newport Road *at the Cross*. I cannot be sure but I suspect that it was hereabouts that John Wesley preached, for in his diary he notes: *Thursday, October 21, 1741: About one I came to Callicut and preached to a small attentive company of people. Between seven and eight we reached Bristol* —obviously by the New Passage. The pulpit which Wesley used survived for some years, but was removed, I was informed, because it had become *a gossiping place for women.*

So our Church House screen is found now in the Caldicot Inn. Why do we go to such lengths to preserve an oaken relic 14ft. by 7t. 6in.?

During the Elizabethan and Early Stuart eras the ground plan of a house always included a passage from front to rear. To the right, generally, of this passage were the service rooms; to the left lay the hall — the principal room. Entrance to the hall from the passage was by way of one or two doorways in an oaken screen, and as the years passed this screen and its doorways became the object of decoration by the craftsmen.

During the reconstruction this year of the Cross Inn a teapot yielded a paper napkin decorated with dog-roses and tributes to King Edward and Queen Alexandra in July, 1908, together with a copy of the *Evening Express* of November 11, 1918, displaying a portrait of Lloyd George and his speech on the declaration of peace.

During the last few years, I have seen the transfer of beams, staircases, windows and fireplaces from a number of old houses during demolition to more modern houses. I fear that historians of future years may be misled by such changes. Would it not be wise to fix plaques on or near these transferred treasures indicating their places of original use?

The White Hart Inn, Caldicot.

Ightfield House and tumulus, Deepweir, Caldicot.

IGHTFIELD HOUSE AND TUMULUS — DEEPWEIR

That tumulus has been a lifelong challenge to me. Like a big inverted green bowl, it stands at a three-lane junction, with the mysterious Nedern flowing near. One is tempted to connect it with the landing camp at Sudbrook, and indeed the N.W.S.E. track which has come from Five Lanes over Highmoor, passing Brockwells, seems to direct towards the camp.

Readers who have fallen into the fascination of the old, the very old tracks, will see that this particular track continues N.W. from Five Lanes into the mystic camp and circle and tumulus areas of Wentwood. Let them also note that this is but one of a series of N.W.S.E. tracks across Caldicot Level, and many more in the Forest of Dean. Friends of mine in Lydney, attacked by the same problem, agreed with me that sailors living in the hills were cheered when they set out at dawn in mid-winter to know that their shadows lay behind them!

What is the other lane, from Chepstow and St. Pierre, seeking? It ends at Caldicot Pill, but was certainly not constructed to take the produce of the old tinworks there . . .

At all events, our green tump stands, as it has stood throughout the centuries, on duty at this lane-junction. What has saved it from demolition?

Many years ago I put the same question to Mr. Roger Keene, of the Cayo, in connection with the tumulus in his ten-acre field at Five Lanes: "Once again I notice that your ploughmen are steering clear of that tumulus. Why?" His answer came pat: "They daren't touch it. Fathers and grandfathers have warned them. It's an ancient landmark!" And was not the menhir near Llanfihangel-Roggiet (the "maen-gobaith," stone of hope, the guiding stone) preserved by a similar built-in belief?

You may be sure that the survival of the Deepweir tumulus (as indeed the fact that it is scheduled as an ancient monument) is due to the same belief. Let no man, therefore, and no authority, interfere with this venerable relic.

At hand is Ightfield House, historic in its own right. Mr. and Mrs. G. L. Wakelam — he a civil engineer, she a bonnie housewife from Clitheroe — and their daughters live there. With enterprise and good taste they are converting a combined Stuart and Victorian house into two modern homes. The results are already admirable. Modern windows and doorways disguise the age of the older house, seen on the right of my sketch. Clues within enabled me to place it as early 17th century. Delightfully, Mrs. Wakelam kept her tour de force to the last, when she remarked, "Come and see where my daughter holds her parties."

Hewn out of the living rock (as Rider Haggard used to say), a vast cellar has been divided into three rooms, the temperature of which is assured by a modern boiler. Strange it was to stand surrounded by walls of old red sandstone which, if a certain young lady has her way, will be decorated with Red Indian murals.

Roughly 7ft. by 10ft. by 20ft., this chamber must have yielded some 1,400 cubic feet of rock. Where was this dumped? That tumulus will yield its secret only to excavation. It may be a burial mound; it is not an ice-house, as at Piercefield or Tidenham or the Grondra; it may be a guiding mound, useful when snow has hidden the track surfaces; but suppose that the 17th-century excavators of the Ightfield cellars took the easy way and dumped their rock on the spot. I do not know and I have no desire to interfere with age-old traditions. It is an ancient monument and must be preserved as such.

ST. PIERRE

My correspondence has for many years proved that the *Argus* finds its way to the *uttermost ends of the earth*. With this in mind, I interpolate at the little church at St. Pierre, where the timbers of the church roof have been severely damaged by the death-watch beetle.

The rector tells me that £650 is needed to repair the roof and that he will gladly acknowledge any gifts sent to him at the Rectory, Portskewett, Mon. An inexpert inspection convinced me that immediate replacement is advisable.

I was glad to hear scientists on the "Brains Trust" — including one clear-thinking Scot — aver that a house may assume personality. It has seemed to me that our ancient churches reveal something approaching personality and, strangely, as I write, the warm welcoming images of six Monmouthshire churches — all small — come to my mind. I jot them down as they appear — Itton, Llanwern, Cwmyoy, Penterry, St. Pierre, Llandegfedd.

Because my heart is small, I feel engulfed in a massive church. These little sanctuaries of ours seem built to my scale and so, when I arrived at St. Pierre, the simple line and warm stone of the building, St. Peter with his keys and the cock alongside the east window, the turret with the one bell, and the bottle-glass in the windows — is there bottle-glass in any other church in Gwent? — called to me, welcomed me.

This church is 800 years old. Conquest over, the invaders from Normandy set up their houses of prayer near their new homes. Here, at St. Pierre, the church shelters under the cliff-like walls of the gatehouse — that vast grey edifice where on the first floor the tiny room survives in the thickness of the wall where for twenty years Harry of Monmouth's crown jewels were stored as surety for a loan made to him by Sir David ap Philip of St. Pierre, governor of Calais.

179

St. Pierre, the church of St. Peter.

To read the pedigree of the family of Lewis of St. Pierre (Bradney — *The Hundredth of Caldicot*) is to create a cavalcade of picturesque figures from all Britain — and Ireland — many of whom must have worshipped in St. Peter's.

Gamage and Jenkins, Morgan, Herbert, Vaughan, Kemeys and Van of Gwent rub shoulders with Stoughton of Ballyhorgan in Kerry and Bucknall of Hampton Court; Thomas ap Lewis, of St. Pierre, who had married Elizabeth Morgan of Langstone, is killed at Bannockburn; in 1715 we find Thomas Lewis, MP for the county, while in later years we have the Lewises appointed rectors of Portskewett and St. Pierre.

Difficult it was on that sunny afternoon to visualise the great days of the mansion. Yet, from the church I could imagine across the meadows in 1711 the *ancient pill or landing for shipps, barkes, barges, boats and water-vessells near unto the river of Seaverne and the Seaverne sea,* and hear the baying of the hounds as they raced across Colt's Hay, the Wharf, Cow Lease, Baker's Close, Maes Fawr, the Sturges, Tump Ground and the rest.

I explored the interior of the church. Under the rotting timbers I saw the well-remembered treasures, the Norman windows in the north and west walls, the Norman doorway (now blocked) in the west wall, the font and the two stone slabs near the south entrance.

The first of these slabs shows a hand holding a floriated cross, with doves beautifully disposed around the base and is a tribute to 13th-century craftsmanship. The other displays a cross and sword and has the rhyming inscription, Norman-French, in Lombardic lettering:

ICI GIT LE CORS V DE SENE PERE
PREEZE PUR LI EN BONE MANERE
QE IHV PVR SA PASIVN
DE PHECEZ LI DONC PARDVN
AMEN RP

This may be translated, *Here lies the body of Urien de St. Pierre. Pray "in good manner" for his soul that Jesus for His Passion sake would forgive his sins. Amen. RIP.* It may commemorate Urien de St. Pierre, who in 1257 was given power *to admit to the King's peace all the Welsh who would come in.*

St. Peter with his keys.

Cock near the east window.

St. Pierre Mansion.

Chepstow — the town gate.

Chapter Eleven

GLIMPSES OF CHEPSTOW

Chepstow is a walled town where a substantial length of the walls remains and the old town arch has survived not only the storms of centuries but the profanity of the drivers of heavy motor vehicles.

Chepe-stow is market-place. A fine, friendly little place it is, with a strong civic sense, a pride in its history and a go-ahead spirit.

Life at Chepstow centres around Beaufort Square, where there were as many inns as houses. The most famous inn was *The Three Cranes* — where Nelson used to stay — a famous coaching inn, now a private dwelling. Close at hand was the Moot Hall, now the Food Office, but still retaining its groined roof and secret passage leading, it seems, to the Castle. Near also is *The Five-Alls* inn:

Ecclesiastic	(I pray for All)
Lawyer	(I plead for All)
Farmer	(I feed All)
Soldier	(I fight All)
Devil	(I take All)

The old cobbled road of Hawker's Hill Street gives an idea of ancient Chepstow. To the left of the Town Gateway (the Gatehouse is entered by a doorway known as the eye of the needle) is an oak doorway leading into the Council Offices and carved with the inscription: "AN . D . 1609 . M.C."

"M.C." was Margaret Cleyton. She lived at the Town Gate from 1609 to 1631, and her picturesque monument — children and two husbands all present — is in the south transept of the church.

On the archway, which was presented to the town by the Duke of Beaufort in 1899, is the watch-bell of H.M.S. Chepstow.

Outside the Town Gate is Welch Street, leading to the right towards Monmouth. The end house here in 1800 (according to Archdeacon Coxe) was named *World's End.* The town wall has a battlement path four feet wide, with bastions and embrasures and was built on the earthwork of the first castle.

Chepstow, in the early years of last century, was the most prosperous port in South Wales, its trade exceeding that of all the other ports combined. Over 3,000 men worked in the ships and wharves loading the Dean timber, oak-bark, pig-iron and nails from the wire-works in the Angidy valley above Tintern. There was a bobbin factory in Lower Nelson Street which became the Bob Inn; there was a glass-house and furnace in the Castle; Chepstow bell-makers were busy and thriving from 1680 onwards. Imports included vast quantities of wine from Portugal, iron bars, bell-metal, deals, hemp, pitch and tar and as late as 1850 Chepstow was still a port-in-chief for South Wales.

The first notice of a bridge at Chepstow was in 1228. Repairs to this bridge were paid for out of legacies left by Bristol burgesses, who recognised even in those early fourteenth century days that the prosperity of Bristol was linked with that of Chepstow, Caerleon and Newport. In 1399 Richard II allowed tolls on cattle, sheep and pigs for bridge repairs, but by 1537 the bridge was a ruin. Two further bridges were built and destroyed by 1645, but two years later Cromwell's men took charge and repaired the new bridge. A great storm in 1703 swept away the standards — the wooden trestles supporting the bridge platform. The next bridge was constructed by the two counties of Gloucestershire, which used timber and Monmouthshire, which used stone supports, the county boundary being half-way across the Wye. The present bridge was built in 1814.

Soon after the Norman Conquest, William Fitz Osbern built a Castle Keep on a steep cliff between the Wye and what is now the *Dell.* The legend that a previous castle had been erected by Longinus, father of the soldier whose spear pierced the side of Christ, is due to Leland. As the first base conquered in Wales, Chepstow was regarded by the Normans as of great importance and the strength of their building, united to the advantages of its site, made Chepstow Castle for centuries almost impregnable.

Norman and Early English periods of architecture are easily recognisable and the *Banqueting Hall,* known to Archdeacon Coxe as the *Chapel,* is full of interest. So is Henry Marten's Tower.

Henry Marten was a member of the High Court of Justice and, with others, signed the death warrant of Charles I. He received vast wealth for his zeal, but when he opposed the dissolution of the Long Parliament, Cromwell rounded on him and instead of enjoying the liberty of his *perfect commonwealth,* the republican bias of which had had no appeal for Cromwell, he fell into debt and was imprisoned.

At the Restoration Marten was tried as a regicide and found guilty, but, in view of his quarrel with Cromwell, was sentenced to perpetual imprisonment, first in the Tower, thereafter at Chepstow. That he ever lived in the basement of "Henry Marten's Tower" is improbable, for he enjoyed almost complete freedom, his wife lived with him and he received visitors and made frequent visits to the great houses of the countryside. He died in 1680, aged 78, and was buried in Chepstow Church.

Soon after the Conquest, a Benedictine priory was founded at Chepstow as a cell to the Abbey of Cormeilles in Normandy, which had itself been founded by William Fitz Osbern in 1060. The ancient priory has disappeared, but parts of its minster remain in the present building, notably the western front and the nave arcade. The effigies of the second Earl of Worcester and his wife, the epitaph of Henry Marten (composed by himself) and the pretty stone portraits of Margaret Cleyton and her family are worthy of inspection.

Chepstow is the gateway to the enchanted land of Gwent. My best advice to those who think of Monmouthshire in terms of collieries and Rugby football is to spare a week for Chepstow and another week for Abergavenny and to lose themselves in the magical beauty of an unknown paradise.

Inscription of doorway — head of council offices at Chepstow.

Against the Port Wall and near the Town Arch stand the Council Offices, entered by an oaken doorway. There, sure enough, carved in the doorway-head, I saw the inscription, A.N. D. 1609. MC. The carving of letters, figures and border decorations was in relief and the unfortunate sculptor who had cut his N mirror-fashion was unable to correct it.

Pleasant it is to stroll around the back lanes of Chepstow. With my pipe activating sweetly I drifted down Upper Nelson Street, Benson's Court and Nelson Street, enjoying the view of the church tower stereoscoped in the sunshine against the cliffs beyond the river. "Try the church," suggested my subconscious.

The Battle of Hastings was a ten-year-old memory when the builder of St. Mary's nave died. Massive, satisfying, it owes almost as much to the colour of our Old Red as to its arches. I glanced at Henry Marten's tomb with its acrostic, I paused to admire the painted pomp of the tomb of Henry, Earl of Worcester and his wife Elizabeth and then, as I turned into the south transept, I saw "M.C."

Above the huge monument leers a skull with crossbones, to the left is Father Time with his scythe, to the right a skeleton. Ionic columns support the lintel. The panel inscription reads.

IN MEMORY OF
Thos. Shipman and Margaret his wife (Daughter of John Maddock of Woollaston Gent) and their 12 Children. Also Richard Cleyton Esq., who was married to Margaret the Relict of the above-mentioned Thos. Shipman.
1620

Students of Stuart costume will be rewarded by a close inspection of Mrs. Cleyton, her two husbands and twelve children. Like the Marten tombstone this vast memorial stood originally in the chancel and its removal, half a century ago, left it undamaged. Fortunately also it was not affected by the Civil War, in which Chepstow was dramatically concerned.

Mistress Cleyton is a worthy addition to our list of Monmouthshire ladies. As her recumbent effigy seems to indicate, she was of considerable personal charm and would hold with ease a prominent place in Chepstow society in those years of affluence.

Like poverty, but more insidious, affluence is a test of character. During the years following the Golden Age of Elizabeth I, the good folk of Chepstow passed that test with distinction. Heart-warming it is to read of their beneficence. I select Hugh Watkins who in 1606 left £30 for maintaining three lights in lanthorns on posts 1 November to 1 March from 6pm to 9pm and £100 towards maintaining four poor scholars. Of the others I note Richard Cleyton, husband of Margaret who "most charitablie and lyberally gave to the erecting of a school to the maintenance there of for ever, to the poore of the towne, the bridges and many, other godly uses." That schoolhouse was built next to the Bellhouse. Margaret Cleyton's munificence included gifts annually to the poor on St. Thomas' day, two decent carpets for the church, 8d. annually to the clerk for keeping the carpets in order and annuity of £6 13s. 4d. and one noble for the teaching of one more scholar, and four scholars from her native village of Woollaston.

In 1626 she drew up her will. In it she left to her son-in-law James Flower *one musket, a blacke bill, a glave, my harness, my twiggen chaine, my cloack which I did weare unto the church, my warming pan, my pestell and morter.*

She died, a widow, in 1627, seven years after the year named on her monument!

PYE CORNER

In an article describing Pike Corner at the turnpike — Llanfaches — I permitted myself a flash of myopic insight. "Maybe," I suggested, "the Pye Corners in our land owe their names to the turnpike."

A yellow flash of discretion impelled me to add later, "But it will not surprise me if one of my readers discovers a Pye Corner older than 1756, the date of the Turnpike Act."

Pye Corner remains unexplained. A tactful note from Mr. Ivor Waters, historian of Chepstow and my good friend, atomised my pretty theory. In the oldest parish record of Chepstow he had lighted on this entry:

Elizabeth her father unknown borne in the house of Hughe Masone called Pye Corner was buryed the 3rd of September, 1644. "Now," added the note, "the White Lion."

In his invaluable book on the inns of Chepstow district, Mr. Waters tells us that in the 17th century the House at Pye Corner was first the White Lion and later the Magpie; in 1798 it was the Red Lion and soon afterwards reverted to the White Lion. There is a tradition, as with other Chepstow houses, of underground communication with the castle.

Now the only entrance to Chepstow other than the Wye bridge is by way of the arch in the Port Wall. Threading that arch, with the *eye of the needle* on my near side, I turned left and there, glowing in midsummer September sunshine, basked the White Lion.

I parked my car, I cogitated. Like the Westgate at Newport, the Chepstow archway had of old a tollgate. On third thoughts, had the House at Pye Corner any association with a turnpike, long before the passing of the Turnpike Act? Oh, forget it!

The innkeeper of the White Lion, Mr. Mervyn Thomas, is proud of his handsome house. He showed me how this L-shaped inn has one arm of the L built against the port wall and how this arm is extended by stables. Parallel to these was another range of stables and all had troughs and cobbled floors — sufficient accommodation for 14 horses. It was evident that horses for the coaches were changed here after their stiff climb.

The White Lion Inn, Chepstow, 'The House at Pye Corner'.

Noting and admiring the oaken frames and doors of the gabled front, the decorations (ivy and pineapple) and mouldings on the Bank Street facade and the attractive old stone tiles on the roof, I decided to record it in line. A well-built young fellow stepped down from his van, watched me and commented, "I'd love to do that, boss, but I can't draw a straight line." I advised him to put down two dots and take the shortest route from one to the other, but he commented sadly, "Not for me, boss."

An examination of the ceiling beams confirmed my impression that this house was raised in the early 17th century. Chepstow folk will know that there was other building activity at the arch in those days and I hope to recount in another article how a Chepstow lady added to her town's grace and charm.

I sojourned with the landlord for half an hour in his pleasant bar. Displayed in a place of honour was the coach-horn from the last mail-coach to pass through Chepstow. Behind the bar, I peered down the steps leading to the beer-cellar. Hanging near the coach-horn was a harvester's cider-barrel, "filled every Christmas as a gift to our clients."

And then I saw the two big pictures. "This one on the left," said Mr. Thomas, "is Jem Ward's splendid portrayal of the 42-round fight at Farnborough in 1860 between Tom Sayers and J. C. Heenan.

"Every face in this big crowd is reputed to be a portrait and here, prominent in his cap, is the Dreadnought — our own Bill Benjamin of Shirenewton."

On the opposite wall and of equal interest, especially to students of Victorian costume, hangs a picture of *The Meet at Badminton, 1847.* Amid the concourse of the great, a winsome little lady drew my careful scrutiny. I cannot be certain, but hazard the guess that this sweet, well-poised lassie, so reminiscent of our Queen and her sister, is Victoria herself.

As I left, Mr. Thomas remarked, "In the old days when the Chepstow shipyards were booming, the bar of the White Lion was opened at 5.30am when the workers could buy coffee at 1½d. or coffee and rum at 3d. a cup."

The Bush Hotel, Chepstow.

THE BUSH HOTEL

The Bush at Chepstow will soon be but a memory. Its beams and roof-timbers were heavily infested with woodworm and, in the opinion of one judge, there was not sufficient of interest in the old building to justify its retention. So Chepstow will be relieved of some of its woodworm. Is that all?

When I called at the Bush I felt like a visitor to a convict in his condemned cell. Bright morning light shone through the hundred-and-forty panes of the windows; the handsome roof tiles looked good for three more centuries; a couple of beam-ends protruded through the thick walls in protest against their impending downfall. Yet not one of the toiling and moiling crowds, not one of the lorry drivers poisoning the crowds with diesel fumes, not one of the motorists driving down to the Wye spared a glance towards the doomed inn.

Of the two inns in Chepstow with the same name, the Bush, in High Street, was the more famous. There is no reason to connect it with stage-coach transport, but my friend, Ivor Waters, to whom Chepstow is an open book, assures us in his *Inns and Taverns of the Chepstow District* that the Bush was an inn as early as 1850. After careful examination, I am sure that the house was then two-and-a-half centuries old.

Around 1600 AD there was a fashion in Gwent of building houses *around a mast.* A great tree-trunk was fixed upright in solid masonry, stairs were keyed spirally into the trunk and the house was built around the stairs.

That happened at Trevella in 1599, at Allt-y-Bela in 1600, at Treworgan, in Llandenny, in 1605, and at the Pwll, in Llangwm, in the same period. The Bush, at Chepstow, was raised in similar fashion and, although its trunk was slighter, it was obviously early 17th century work. At Llangwm, long years ago, I was advised to visit Trevella. "There's a house for you," I was advised. "It's built around a mast from one of Drake's ships."

Mr. Waters was informed by its old landlord that the Bush was converted to an inn by a retired sea captain, who built a staircase round the mast of his vessel. Essential fixtures on the mast of a sailing vessel leave marks on the ship's mast. No such marks were visible on any of the tree-trunks in our five houses.

The trunk at the Bush arose from the cellar floor. Twelve stone steps spiralled it to the ground floor, 15 oak steps were keyed in it to the upper floor, whence further steps led to the trunk-top in the attic. The whole system was housed in the delightful stair-turret shown in my smaller drawing.

Throughout the house the craftsmanship of the artificer in oak was evident and, with the forest at hand, there was no need to stint the timber.

The dimensions of the beams and roof-timbers wee accompanied by a pretty pattern of half-timber in the bedroom walls. The beam surmounting one wall was ten feet by one foot by one foot three inches; in that wall was a doorway five feet high, and the original door, one of several, swung sweetly and silently on its ancient hinges. In the bedroom near the top of the stairs was a remarkable fireplace, topped by a massive lintel and a moulded mantelpiece.

Amid some reconstructions in the bar I noted several genuine survivals. Among these was a grand beam resting on a carved corbel at one end and supported at the at the other by an iron post. There were, I am told, traces of patterns painted at the rear of the bar. I opened the back door and stood on the green. Here, records Mr. Waters, was a quoit ground, in 1859 (we had quoits at the George, in Maindee); here, he continues, on November 5, 1881, a blazing tar-barrel was brought through the inn and extinguished. With all that oak in the huse it might have been a *burning Bush.*

Tears of regret have no place in this age of destruction. It behoves all owners of historic buildings — grants are available — to end the ravages of timber-pests. Sound timber is, in general, a good argument against the *developers,* who seek justification for their misdeeds.

Chapter Twelve

A JOURNEY FROM CHEPSTOW TO MONMOUTH

Visiting the churches of Penterry, Trellech Grange, Llanishen and Penallt.

PENTERRY CHURCH

Climbing gently from St. Arvans, the Tintern road soon forks right at a beautiful pool. This is the motorist's way to the Abbey, but we who have walked this district know that if we keep straight on for a time we come to a path into the woods which leads down to the Wyndcliff platform and thence down the steps to the road.

If, again, we ignore the Wyndcliff path, the track leads to a farmstead named Porth-y-Caseg — the Mare's Gate. The land here was granted to Llandaff in the time of Bishop Oudoceus by King Meurig and there may have been, so Bradney tells us, a church on the site.

Continuing between the farm buildings, the lane descends, passes a pool, and climbs to meet the lane to Penterry. That I remembered from the days when William Stanford ("Bill") and I tramped this heavenly corner of Gwent. Yet, when Colonel Hill stopped his car near the beautiful pool above St. Arvans, I was surprised to hear him say to his son Michael, "Take them up the Roman road and I will join you later."

The Bookman and I took our bearings. South of us stretched the racecourse, the lost glories of Piercefield, the Chepstow golf links, and the prehistoric camps of Pierce Wood. This "Roman" road, then, must have led from these camps to the pool, and continued across the road into the colonel's fields. Michael showed us the ancient trackway. It was a typical hollow way, like many that we had explored in Gwent and in the Forest of Dean and, when I asked what crowned the hill which we were climbing, we were not surprised to get the answer, *The Gaer,* for we were obviously tracing the relics of a pre-Roman track, joining pre-Roman encampments.

The Gaer, at the hill-top, is an elliptical camp 800 feet above sea level, overlooking St. Arvans just as Lodge Camp towers above Caerleon, Llanmelin above Caerwent, and many another hilltop settlement above its successor on the plain.

We found the colonel awaiting us near Piccadilly. Draw no wrong conclusions, Eros was not in sight. *Piccadilly* is the name of a house, a field, and part of a lane. Our indefatigable Welsh place-name specialists need waste no time over this name, for like *Pennsylvania* and *Sebastopol* — both in Gwent — it had no Silurian origin.

With the hedge greenery brushing the car on both sides, we threaded the narrow lane, stopping now and then to take a noble view. Halting at a gate held in position by a Y-shaped twig, we saw the grey walls, bell turret and porch of Penterry church.

Saved from loneliness by its bevy of trees, Penterry smiled in the afternoon sunshine, yet it is *miles from anywhere.*

Our guide showed us this little lost church with the same pride as the Dean of Canterbury displayed when he took us around his immense cathedral, and the Bookman and I shared his delight for, while St. Mary's, Penterry, has been wholly rebuilt, it retains, in a built-up lancet window, in the bell ("The Gift of Thos. Hacket," recast by William Evans, of Chepstow, in 1734) and in its atmosphere, the beauty of holiness which we associate with an ancient country church.

"Surely," I remarked to Colonel Hill, "this is the cleanest, the most spotless little church in the county! Who is responsible?"

The little lost church of Penterry.

"Ah!" he replied, "Here you have a good example of hereditary service. Miss Bryant, of St. Arvans, cares for it now, following her father, Hezekian Bryant, now aged ninety, and 'Gran'cha' Owen. She walks over the fields in summer and up the lane in winter."

And "up the lane" is your best route, if you wish to see Penterry. Find St. Arvans post office, with its pretty garden full of petunias, and take the lane alongside.

Our journey beyond Penterry, uphill and down dale, past unexpected pools, through dark woods with names like "Fedw" and "Ravens' Nest," enlivened all the way by our guide's comments, came to its climax when we looked down almost vertically on to the brookside cottages sleeping, hundreds of feet below, in the valley above Tintern.

TRELLECH GRANGE

Old inhabitants of Trellech believe that the first settlement of that name was in the district known as Trellech Grange. I do not accept that theory, for the name is always associated with the prehistoric stones of Trellech.

But without doubt a church existed in the Grange area in the 7th century, for King Ffernwael is noted in the *Book of Llandaff* as the donor to Llandaff of the church of "Trylec Llan Mainuon" and three modii of land.

In the 12th century this and the surrounding district became a grange of Tintern Abbey. With its far-flung acres of rich farmland, its streams and mills, it must have proved for four centuries one of the most productive properties of the abbey, and it is easy to imagine the pride of fat, jovial bailiff Laurence as he surveyed his paradise in the early 1530s, little guessing how short his tenure was to be.

Standing full-face to the southern sun midway between Trellech and Tintern, the Grange is still truly rural. In 1869 it comprised an area of 1,774 acres, with 24 houses and 137 inhabitants and I doubt if there has been any development since.

My journey to the Grange was made in company with my old friend Will o' the Hills, now recovered after a sojourn in hospital. Petrol restriction lay still a week ahead and we travelled in a mood of "condemned, but not yet executed," light-heartedness.

A thin mist veiled the landscape as we drifted down into Tintern and up the Angidy valley, where the ochre of the beeches glowed in a kind of ember splendour and a grey squirrel sitting on a wall apparently manicuring his nails took little notice of our intrusion.

The morning was still young when we passed the Fountain Inn, that sequestered little hostelry which has survived the blizzards and the floods of three centuries, none worse than the two which attacked it in recent years. We turned left and picked up our guide, Mr. Moore, of the Orchards, who kindly shepherded us around the Grange.

We chose a viewpoint which gave on to the surrounding country. To the west we could descry Crumbland and the ridge running from Cobbler's Plain to Llanishen; in the dip northward lay Lan-y-Nant and beyond it Hygga with its dovecote and the Gaer; and to the east, we knew, the long straight road ran from the *Fountain* to Parkhouse and Trellech Cross; but let me confess that, although I had walked this district on many a halcyon day, I had not previously lighted on the little church of Trellech Grange.

Trellech Grange — the church.

Very simple, almost pathetic, it seemed to me. Obviously of great age, it had suffered from restorations, as was the fate of so many of our churches in Victorian days. But I was glad to learn that the turret with its bell and wheel — the only one I know — is now safe under a preservation order. I wish that I could report in similar confidence about the fabric of the church. My two companions agreed with me that the ominous cracks in the walls indicated the need for immediate attention and I am quite sure that our authorities will do all in their power to repair this beloved little sanctuary.

In the north wall is a beautiful modern window inserted *in loving memory of the two Grange boys who gave their lives in the Great War, 1914-1918 — Private John Edward Davies of the South Wales Borderers and Lieutenant Ralph Wrigley of the Mon. Royal Engineers.* Around the feet of the figures are lilies-of-the-valley, which still grow wild in these parts. And the road to the church — Jubilee Road — will be seventy years old this year, commemorating Queen Victoria's jubilee.

I asked one of the Grange ladies to compile a list of their field-names for me. Already the list shows that here, in the east of Gwent, the spoken *tongue* was Welsh and these field-names, as spoken still, are, you must agree, picturesque.

How would you translate Cascaborum, Cattycachus, Cakeffil, Calans, Dyers and Saeffron? I am reminded that my gifted friend Canon E. T. Davies found a field in Llangibby named *Cape of Scotland,* which he deciphered as *Cae-psygodlyn* — the fish-pond field. It may be that in the Grange field-names we shall find equally interesting derivations; I think that a barn and a nag will appear among them.

Our first stop was at Great House. Square, solid, prosaic, this ancient structure seemed externally to hold little of interest, but three or more centuries slipped backwards when we entered the spacious hall, with its stone floor, Elizabethan doorway, stairs, beams and screen.

Our host plied us with good sherry and possibly blamed that for our interest in these relics, whereas in reality his screen, although papered on one side, contained moulding and decoration of unusual value.

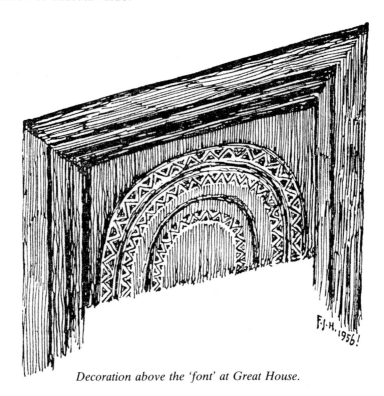

Decoration above the 'font' at Great House.

The main portion of the screen to the right of the door has been known through living memory as *the altar,* while the recess to the left of the door, surmounted by the semi-circular hatchwork carving, is named *the font.*

We could find no other traces of ecclesiastical association, but long experience has taught me to respect names handed down through the ages and, although the church is not distant, this ancient Ty Mawr may have known a priestly occupant. My sketch indicates that the "shrine," whatever its function, was a place of significance.

Down in the valley, powered by the Angidy — how many mill-wheels were turned by this lovely stream! — we came across Trellech Grange mill. The smithy up the lane, the mill here and the inn at hand are sure signs of a self-contained community, and this mill, or an earlier mill on the same site, was doubtless one of the Trellech mills mentioned in Tintern records. Strange, but attractive, it was to hear our guide refer to the mill-race as the "flume."

On the brow of the hill beyond we came to a cottage which I should have passed without a second glance. Mr. Moore knew better and, when we entered *the Tump*, we found it to be of *cruck-truss* construction, with the trunks and boughs still evident.

Mr. and Mrs. Prewitt showed us around this delightful little house, which they have restored with much respect to the old place and with skill in adapting it to modern needs.

I find no disharmony when television and good modern furniture are in the same surroundings as the stone lintel and uprights of a 16th-century fireplace.

Mr. Prewitt spoke of the slag found in some of the fields. One area to the west of the Tump is known as Cinder Patch, reminding us of the days when the Angidy valley above Tintern was the centre of the wire-working industry.

Much more we saw on that busy morning. As a postlude, Mr. Moore took us to his own pretty house, where we drank coffee under an incredible number of ceiling beams, where we heard how the ceiling of that room was *insulated* from the floor above by a thick layer of hazel nuts and where we saw the threshold stone of an outbuilding under which a Bristol farthing and a farthing of Charles II were discovered.

Old Mill at Tintern (19th-century engraving).

193

St. Mary's Church, Penallt.

PENALLT

Readers who complain that they cannot find some of the remote places which I describe may reach Penallt from Trellech, from near Mitchel Troy, or up the Whitebrook valley. Arrived at the village they will see finger-posts marked *Penallt Old Church,* and at the only unmarked junction they should turn right, where a lovely leafy lane — now goldleaf, with majestic views — will lead them direct to a mounting-stone at the top of a steep hill, a lych-gate, a canopied church path and the wonderfully beautiful church *at the summit of a declivity* — for that is the meaning of *Penallt.*

And what a declivity! Walk down the churchyard. Look over the wall. Many hundreds of feet below you is the Redbrook-Monmouth reach of the Wye, beyond are the cars, bumper to bumper. Above the road, scarlet, gold and russet, is Lord's Grove and away to the right Bunjups Wood stretches towards Knockalls Inclosure, south of Staunton.

Fill your lungs with Penallt air, the air that makes children dance and old men sing. Then inspect the mighty yew, the base and stump of the churchyard cross, the sundial on the porch and the saddle-back tower.

Within that tower are four bells, three made at Chepstow in 1740 and 1751, the fourth, when Sir George Probert was a churchwarden, in 1662. They are inscribed with the initials of the churchwardens and bell-founders (Evans of Chepstow and Palmer of Gloucester).

The date, 1539, on the church door is the date when the door was fixed, but the church is at least three centuries older. Of the three-decker pulpit with its reading desk and clerk's seat only the pulpit remains; the oak communion rails are dated 1743; steps to the rood loft, an oak coffer five feet nine inches long, the wagon-roof, Queen Anne's coat of arms over the chancel and the extraordinary passage from the south aisle into the chancel will engage your attention, and, although pews replace the old box seating, you will agree that St. Mary's, Penallt, wears the loveliness of a serene old age.

The altar was carved by the chief wood-carver of Malines cathedral, who was a Belgian refugee during the 1914-18 war. It is a copy of a stone altar at Ravenna.

Among the tomb inscriptions you may see:

Here resteth the body of Dorety the wif of Lewis ye vance of Readbrooke, 1643.
Mourn not dear parence nor Lament for me
children with god canot unhappy bee.
William Evanes died June ye 4th, 1754, aged 6 years.
Mourn not for me my parencs dear,
I am not ded but sliping here.

I prize a letter from Mrs. E. M. Evans, of Llanfihangel Crucorney. She wrote to me in 1952:

I am eighty years old, and lived in the parish of Penallt for 34 years. My forefathers had lived there since 1644. The round stone where the coffin rested whilst a hymn was sung was the base of a cross which was thrown down by men crying, 'No Popery in England.' The stocks stood underneath the old chestnut tree not far from the lych-gate and the cottage above was the old public house. These things were told me by my grandparents and no doubt were handed down. It seems a pity for all the old things to be forgotten.

Close to the rectory is *Anne's Cottage*. It was near this cottage that one of the octogenarians of Penallt said to me, "So you are Mr. Handel, the man who wrote all that music."

I am told that *Anne* is a lady who is devoting her life to the education of children whose minds are not so well-equipped as the minds of normal children, and that she and her helpers come out to the cottage for contemplation and refreshment. God bless them all!

Anne's Cottage, Penallt.

The walker gets to know his countryside intimately because the villages — aye, the cottages — mark stages on his sensibly slow journey, but the motorist notes the beginning and end of his run and has but a sketchy idea of the places en route. Believe me, in an idyllic county like Gwent, the journey is at least as fascinating as journey's end.

INDEX

ACKNOWLEDGEMENTS

I am grateful to Mrs. Susan Hando for allowing me to purchase the copyright of Fred Hando's work. My thanks are also due to Derek Lawton for his assistance with the design of the cover; my father, Bill Barber, for helpful suggestions and my brother, Steve Barber, for preparing the index. Steve Lawless and David Tilton of Able TypeSetters are thanked for their quick and efficient service and South Western Printers for their high quality printing. To Mrs. Bramley of Caerleon I am particularly grateful for allowing me to borrow her collection of Fred Hando articles which helped to make this publication possible.

Chris Barber 1989

THE MYNDE.
CAERLEON.

BOOKS BY FRED HANDO

Rambles in Gwent.
The Pleasant Land of Gwent.
Journeys in Gwent.
Monmouthshire Sketchbook.
Here and There in Monmouthshire.
Monmouth Town Sketchbook.
Out and About in Monmouthshire.

OTHER TITLES BY CHRIS BARBER

Walks in the Brecon Beacons.
Exploring the Waterfall Country.
Ghosts of Wales.
Exploring the Brecon Beacons National Park.
Exploring Gwent.
Mysterious Wales.
More Mysterious Wales.
Cordell Country.
The Romance of the Welsh Mountains.
Hando's Gwent (Volume One).
The Ancient Stones of Wales (jointly with John G. Williams).